TOURISM
AND
CULTURE

SUNY Series in Advances in Applied Anthropology
Erve Chambers, Editor

TOURISM AND CULTURE

AN APPLIED PERSPECTIVE

EDITED BY

ERVE CHAMBERS

State University of New York Press

Published by
State University of New York Press, Albany

© 1997 State University of New York

For information, address State University of New York
Press, State University Plaza, Albany, N.Y., 12246

Production by Diane Ganeles
Marketing by Nancy Farrell

Library of Congress Cataloging-in-Publication Data

Tourism and culture : an applied perspective / Erve Chambers, editor.
    p.   cm. — (SUNY series in advances in applied anthropology)
Includes bibliographical references and index.
ISBN 0-7914-3427-3 (hc : alk. paper). — ISBN 0-7914-3428-1 (pb :
alk. paper)
    1. Applied anthropology.   2. Tourist trade—Research.   I. Series.
GN397.5.T68   1997
301—dc20   96-41497
                                                                  CIP

10 9 8 7 6 5 4 3 2

To
Ratchadawan

Contents

1

Introduction: Tourism's Mediators

ERVE CHAMBERS

Jamaica Kincaid's *A Small Place* is an angry and unrelenting portrayal of tourism on the Caribbean island of Antigua. In her account, Kincaid suggests that the Antiguans who annually play host to thousands of international visitors might not be as pleased with their roles as their welcoming smiles and presumed passivity seem to suggest. Rather, for most Antiguans, tourism is an ever present reminder of their own relative poverty. Given the means they would prefer touring to being toured, and they cannot help but resent the disparities that consign them largely to the service sector of a vast and pernicious industry. Kincaid reminds us of the unique but often unacknowledged intimacies that are occasioned by modern travel and its concomitant touring. Few large industries evoke such close, face-to-face contact between people of different means, class, ethnicity, religious, and cultural backgrounds. Few human activities have such a great potential for exposing on a personal level the considerable inequalities that do exist between people, particularly between people of different countries and different color. Kincaid's account decries the extent to which many international tourists are able to avoid the consequences of this exposure, and thereby to remain ignorant of the extent to which they, as members of a privileged class that has acquired the opportunity to routinely tour, actively participate in maintaining the disparities of wealth and cultural expression they encounter in their travels.

For Jamaica Kincaid, contemporary tourism is an extension of colonial opportunity and authority. It is inextricably linked to economic exploitation and racist sentiment. Her account is unforgiving and she

1

offers no alternative in terms of a more appropriate standard of tourist behavior. "Stay home," is the best advice she can give to the tourist who might ask for a better or more responsible way to tour.

A Small Place is a book I use in a course I teach on the social and cultural consequences of tourism. It is the first of several texts required for the class, and it leaves most students feeling understandably confused and not a little guilty. The dilemma they face at this juncture is, I believe, at the core of our attempts to understand the consequences of modern tourism. The students tend to take the book personally, as they should. Voluntary travel has for the more privileged of the world, including most of these students, become an integral but poorly understood part of our culture (while, ironically, the involuntary travels of displacement, seeking refuge, and forced emigration have become such a great part of the lives of the less privileged). Invariably several students ask, "Does this mean I can't go *anywhere*?"

Of course, few if any of the students will actually decide to curb their own ambitions for travel, and it is not clear that they should. As compelling as is the case made by Jamaica Kincaid, we are left wondering whether her answer is a practical solution to the human problems that are associated with tourism, as well as whether it is the best informed. Part of the clue to our wondering lies beneath the surface of Kincaid's account, in her absolute indictment of her fellow Antiguans, who seem to so easily and uncritically accept the indignities she associates with tourism. There is something missing here. We are left with little understanding of those other Antiguans' motivations or intentions (or, to put it another way, of their "agency"), or of the standards by which they actually do engage visitors to their island. There is a lack of the native's point of view, an absence of *ethnography*. In the end, there is a failure to represent the surely complex experiences of those Antiguans who have become involved in the enterprises of tourism.

It is in these delicate spaces—between a complete condemnation of some of the consequences of modern tourism and a further recognition of the pervasive and complex nature of the industry—that anthropology has the most to contribute to our study of the subject. Although the anthropology of tourism is still a relatively new area of concern within the discipline, its contributions over the past two decades are notable. Two recent reviews of anthropological contributions are worthy of mention in this regard. Malcolm Crick (1989) has offered a critical review of the contributions of ethnographic research. He concludes that useful gains have been made, but that the complex, culturally diffuse nature of tourism suggests the need for more imaginative approaches to ethno-

graphic inquiry. In an article directed to the interests of industry researchers and professionals, Nelson Graburn and Roland Moore (1994)
have pointed out that anthropological research devoted to tourism has
matured considerably over the past couple of decades. Although earlier
studies tended to dwell almost exclusively on the negative aspects of
tourism, more recent inquiries have considered the variable nature of
both negative and positive consequences of tourism on local communities. Although there are conclusions to be drawn from recent anthropological research on tourism that seem to confirm Jamaica Kincaid's view,
there are other conclusions that do not. In its totality, recent research indicates that the social and cultural dimensions of tourism are extremely
diffuse and remain difficult to judge.

Anthropological research on tourism has begun, though barely, to
challenge some of the assumptions maintained in other approaches to
the subject. For example, the tourism industry, and most of the social science research that has followed the growth of the industry, has been both
practically and theoretically focused upon the motivations of the tourist.
Relatively less attention has been paid to the communities that receive
tourists. The assumption here is that travel is the activity that best informs our understanding of tourism. It is in this regard that anthropologists, with their increased interest in the way communities engage with
touristic activities, have the potential to contribute uniquely to our
understanding of tourism. Here the *cultural* perspective that anthropologists bring to our understanding of human institutions and behaviors seems particularly useful. Culture is expressed by the ways in which
members of a group determine and symbolize the meaningfulness of
their lives. While anthropologists have in the past used this concept
largely to describe the unique meaning systems of particular groups of
people, there has been a growing interest in thinking of the cultural as a
process that originates in occasions in which different groups are led to
confront and then attempt to reconcile each others' standards of meaning and significance. Tourism, with its multiple realms of human interaction, provides ample opportunity for the play of cultural processes
and for the invention of new forms of cultural expression.

The intent of this volume is to express some of the complexity that
accompanies recent anthropological interest in the subject of tourism.
A part of this complexity is represented in the diverse subject matter
and perspectives of the authors contributing to the volume. The unify-
ing focus in this regard is that each author deals in some manner with
the idea that *tourism is a mediated activity*. This mediation intervenes
between and helps shape the relationships of the parties we usually

think of as tourism's "hosts" and "guests" (cf., Smith, 1989). Recognition of tourism as a mediated activity, subject to a wide variety of interventions and an equally diverse array of interpretations as to the meaning of those interventions, encourages us to pay more systematic attention to those actors and institutions that stand outside the host/guest relationship but that so greatly influence the consequences of tourism. This perspective also opens the door to considering, as several of the articles in this volume do suggest, that there are a number of ways in which anthropologists might themselves become involved in the mediation of touristic activities.

A second common problem in tourism research and development, addressed in different ways by the anthropologists contributing to this volume, has to do with the interpretation of the impacts of tourism on the communities that are, accurately or not, cast in the role of "host." This has clearly been the most significant problem addressed by the anthropology of tourism, and is also perhaps the most difficult from which to draw clear conclusions or guidelines. Starting with Jamaica Kincaid's lead, we can readily observe that tourism does in its intimate associations expose stark differences in economic and cultural opportunity. But where do we go from this recognition? The articles in this volume do not offer a single view in this regard. Together they suggest that contemporary tourism has both contributed to and helped expose the inequities that do exist, and that it is at least still possible to attempt to direct tourism development to these issues with the aim of encouraging greater equity. In a world that simply will not stay home, in which the ideas of "home" and "away from home" are themselves increasingly scrambled and contestable (cf., Clifford, 1992), such possibilities certainly seem worth pursuing.

Revisiting the Host/Guest Relationship

We can at least imagine a past in which relations between travelers and their hosts were considerably more direct than they generally are in our time. In this past the conditions of travel were determined to a greater extent by the conventions of hospitality in a given region than they were by the norms and expectations of the traveler. The advent of mass tourism has altered all this, to the extent that in many instances of travel the distinction between guest and host has become blurred if not irrelevant. Western tourists are increasingly the guests of their own airlines, their own hotel chains and resort complexes, buying their own goods (or close imitations), and engaging in familiar recreations on terrains that seems only vaguely "foreign" or different. The local communities that are in closest contact with popular tourist destinations are often distanced from participating in any meaningful respect in the relationship. In some cases, even their labor is not required; it is more easily imported along with the foodstuffs and amenities required by the visitors. Where indigenous representation is desired, it is often presented in only the most superficial of ways, limited to those cultural distinctions and elements of "local color" that are compatible with the tourists' home grown expectations.

This dimunition of the host/guest relationship is not inevitable. It is largely the consequence of an approach to tourism that has become almost entirely guest-centered. The bias is apparent whether we are considering the development of tourist facilities, the marketing of travel opportunities, or the pursuit of a theory of tourism (cf., MacCannell, 1989; Urry, 1990). Whether our assessment of particular instances of tourism development is positive or negative or somewhere in between, the focus of most of our observations and inquiries has been upon the tourist. As noted above, anthropologists have made recent gains in describing in greater detail the ways in which local communities have responded to tourism. In some cases, as several of the articles in this volume illustrate, this research has led to greater awareness of the diversity that exists within most such communities, indicating that community members and groups within communities do not participate or benefit equally in tourism initiatives. Neither do they share equally in bearing the costs of such activities. As in other areas of social inquiry, these results challenge earlier, more homogeneous notions of community. In this respect. tourism research has also begun to contribute to a broader concern with how communities are actually constructed, and with the manner in which group identities and traditions are invented and authenticated, in part as a result of deliberate attempts to engage the interest of tourists or otherwise appeal to the imaginations of outsiders (cf., Handler, 1988; Norkunas, 1993).

The idea that communities are largely invented is not new (cf., Benedict, 1983), but the extent to which modern tourism has come to play a major role in the reconstruction of community has only recently been recognized. Just as Robert Van Kemper (1978) has suggested that some popular tourist sites might now be thought of as "tourist cultures" because of the prevalent cultural influences of visitors, so is it possible to consider the inventions of *tourist communities* that have little relationship to either the local populations among which they arise or to the normal life experiences of the tourist. Such communities might be based on recreational life-styles, as is the case with beach and ski resorts, and more recently with some "ecotourism" sites. Major theme parks (with the Disney parks being just the most notorious of the type) are designed quite deliberately as fantasy communities. Sex tourism has contributed to the invention of brothel communities in many parts of the world. Historic preservation efforts and tourism development are often linked in the invention of ghost communities that are built of fragments and idealized images of the past. In many cases, these various tourist communities have become powerful cultural images in their own right. Rarely are they constructed in a vacuum—they develop alongside, and often in clear contrast to, preexisting communities.

Thinking of tourism as being predominantly a relationship between "real" (i.e., residential) hosts and their guests has become problematic in several respects. Not the least of these is the extent to which most tourism has become a thoroughly mediated activity, dependent on the intervention of others who serve as neither hosts nor guests in any conventional manner. This is rather obvious when we consider large-scale tourism developments, such as theme parks, resort areas, and inner-city revitalizations designed to attract visitors to urban areas. It is equally true of recent attempts to fashion more sustainable, environmentally sound and culturally appropriate avenues of tourism development. In this respect, even tourism research might be seen as a form of mediation, capable of altering the shape of tourism development.

It is the increased scale and variety of tourism throughout the world that has added layers of mediation to the fading host/guest relationship. The motivations for mediating tourism vary greatly, as do the ideas and values mediators convey in attempting to assess the interests of tourists and the nature of local communities that are likely to be impacted by tourism. Yet, with some exceptions, it seems most mediators share a tendency toward invisibility. This tendency is encouraged in part by a desire to maintain at least the appearance of more traditional host/guest relationships (because that, it is felt, is what travellers seek and what their "hosts" expect). Unfortunately, the invisibility of the mediator is also often encouraged by a desire to conceal the unequal benefits to be enjoyed from many tourism endeavors. It has become almost axiomatic of the tourism industry that those who benefit the most from its development are those who are the most insulated from its impacts.

The exploitation of tourism resources, often exemplified in the commoditization and delocalization of place and culture, might be deliberate or might as well be quite unintentional. In the case of the latter, unequal exploitation might be based simply on the inability of developers and other mediators to recognize the extent to which the expressions and images of tourism have come to represent ideologies that permeate the structures of social life. In our time tourism can be considered not only as an activity but also as an orientation to the modern world. It is an orientation that privileges acts of travel, sightseeing, and recreation as distinct expressions of modernity. New expectations and protocols of visitation, promulgated to define social relationships in tourist communities, have begun to interact with and contribute to a much broader redefinition of relations between people.

Anthropological research has tended to focus on international aspects of tourism, often as another kind or expression of the host/guest relationship. This is a relationship in which the industrially developed, principally Western countries assume the role of guest and the developing nations, eager for foreign exchange, become the hosts. The assumption of this relationship does describe one important aspect of modern tourism. Its development has often followed the path of earlier imperialistic ambitions of the Western nations, in which travel is expressed as one of several colonial privileges. But again the imagery of a host/guest relationship can be distracting. In this instance we ignore, for example, the continuing and in many cases increasing dependence of developed countries and Western nations on tourism (a phenomenon which, as R. Timothy Sieber suggests in his chapter in this volume, often serves to make even more ambiguous the ideas of either "host" or "guest"). The assumption of a multinational context for tourism, while correct in its own right, often serves to obscure the intensity of more localized and nationalistic mediations.

Most of the articles in this volume describe national and regional patterns of mediation and dominance as they have emerged in locales where tourism has been encouraged. In this respect there has been a deliberate attempt to visit as great a variety of locales as possible. It is important to recognize that these mediations do not invariably imply negative consequences for the communities associated with tourism. Neither are the ideologies associated with modern tourism of a single kind—the imposition of tourist resorts and theme parks, urban revitalization efforts, ecotourism, and even attempts to counter the effects of mass tourism with "sustainable," community-based tourism initiatives—all of these represent varieties of dominance to the extent that they seek their particular ends by attempting to control the terms by which the tourism experience is defined.

What this leads us to is recognition of the increasing prominence of tourism-related activities in altering a host of social and cultural (and, of course, economic) relationships. These alterations do not occur simply as a result of the development of tourism facilities, or as a reflection of the ambitions and desires of tourists, but can also be attributed to efforts to mitigate tourism's effects and to the varied ways in which communities respond to tourism initiatives and to the presence of tourists in their midst.

An Applied Perspective

The articles brought together in this volume represent a comparative and applied anthropological perspective on some of the social and cultural consequences of modern tourism development. Most of the articles have their origin in papers originally presented at two meetings of the Society for Applied Anthropology. They are evenly divided between those that focus principally on international tourism and others that describe varieties of domestic tourism in the United States. Although applied anthropology enjoys a unique and well-established position within the discipline, applied anthropologists have only recently turned their attention to problems associated with tourism. Considering the rich potential for research and practice in the field, it is surprising that there is so little precedence for this volume (cf., Johnston, 1990; Smith, 1992).

Elvi Whittaker's case study of tourism in Broome, Australia, offers a historic perspective on several important aspects of tourism development, showing not only how the effects of tourism can vary over time, often in association with cycles of economic boom and bust, but also providing insight into how difficult it is to generalize community reaction to tourism. In this case, tourism has become a major focus for a community's debate over the shape of its future. In her discussion of the development of a crafts cooperative among the Eastern Cherokee, Betty Duggan also takes a historical view. One of the important features of this chapter is that it points out the extent to which beneficial tourism development is associated with a group's ability to find an appropriate economic and cultural base for their activities. This case is all the more significant in that it describes how a community has maintained a distinct and rewarding relationship to tourism within a larger tourism environment that is marked by the exploitation and misrepresentation of Native American imagery.

The next two chapters demonstrate the value of exploring relatively neglected (for anthropologists) areas of tourism inquiry. R. Timothy Sieber's portrayal of ways in which tourism has become a vital part of efforts to revitalize downtown Boston offers a valuable contrast to the tendency of anthropologists to focus on relatively distant subjects. His article offers a clear challenge to a more traditional focus on host/guest relations. Here commonly accepted notions of both "host" and "guest" become problematic. In her contribution, A. Lynn Bolles encourages us to consider the importance of gender relations in tourism development. Her discussion of the experiences of Jamaican women who have gained employment in that country's tourism industry points again to how difficult it is sort out the true costs and benefits of tourism. While recognizing that the types of tourism employment available to most Jamaican women reflect and to some extent serve to legitimize gender inequalities, Bolles also finds that a number of her informants report that their employment in the tourism sector has all the same enabled them to improve their lives.

All the chapters in this volume deal in one way or another with cultural or ethnic tourism. These are activities in which the distinction of a people becomes a part of the appeal of a tour. Robert Hitchcock's case study of tourism among the Kalahari Bushmen describes an instance in which much of this appeal has been generated by Western representations that serve to make the Bushmen an "interesting" people. He discusses how the Bushmen have fared in this environment, both with tourists and in their relationships with neighboring communities and national elites.

These first chapters offer challenges to tourism development policies that assume little or no negative consequences to the communities and people visited by tourists. The next four articles describe the attempts of anthropologists to become directly involved in aspects of tourism development. George Logan and Mark Leone's description of their experiences in furthering public archaeology in Annapolis, Maryland, illustrates a case in which anthropologists have attempted to have a direct impact on the way in which a city's past is represented to a visiting public. They have been especially concerned with the manner in which local elites have represented African-American contributions to the city's development. This article is representative of a growing interest among anthropologically-trained archaeologists in the ways in which their activities lend themselves to tourism-related intitiatives.

Stanley Hyland's chapter devoted to tourism development in the Lower Mississippi Delta reflects his direct involvement in the attempts of a regional development commission to envision new strategies for economic and cultural development in this part of the country. His discussion is especially interesting, and not a little disconcerting, in light of the contrast he makes between the lengthy and painstaking efforts of commission members to encourage the development of tourism initiatives founded on the region's cultural heritage, and the relative ease with which promoters of casino gaming managed to move their own initiatives forward.

Anthropologists who approach tourism development primarily from a research perspective sometimes find that their involvement leads to opportunities to become more directly involved with the communities they have studied. In discussing her own "crossover" from researcher to consultant and decision-maker in matters pertaining to tourism development in Bethlehem, Pennsylvania, Catherine Cameron describes both the benefits and perils of working in one's own community. In his contribution to the volume, Erve Chambers points to the need for institutions of higher education to play a greater role in preparing future tourism professionals, and especially in promoting greater understanding of the social and cultural consequences of tourism development. The chapter is based on Chambers' professional experience with several university-based tourism programs in Thailand.

A useful way to look at the varied contrbutions to this volume is to note the extent to which they reflect the discipline's breadth while adhering to the common purpose of offering useful insight into salient patterns of tourism development. In this vein, M. Estellie Smith offers a critical overview of the participation of local elites in tourism development. Her chapter helps expand our sense of the variety of relationships that shape contemporary tourism and that provide some of the rationale and ideology for its development. In keeping with the observations provided by many of the other chapters, Smith argues that attempts on the part of national and local elites to control the course of tourism are not based solely on a desire for economic gain, but are also invested in expressions of political and cultural dominance.

References

Benedict, Anderson. (1983). *Imagined Communities*. New York: Verso.

Clifford, James. (1992). Traveling Cultures. In L. Grossberg, C. Nelson, & P. Treichler (Eds.), *Cultural Studies*. New York: Routledge.

Crick, Malcolm. (1989). Representation of International Tourism in the Social Sciences. In *Annual Review of Anthropology*, Vol. 18. Palo Alto: Annual Reviews.

Graburn, Nelson H. and Roland S. Moore. (1994). Anthropological Research on Tourism. In J. R. Brent Richies and C. R. Goeldner (Eds.), *Travel, Tourism, and Hospitality Research*. New York: John Wiley & Sons.

Handler, Richard. (1988). *Nationalism and the Politics of Culture in Quebec.* Madison: University of Wisconsin Press.

Johnston, Barbara R. (Ed.). 1990. Breaking Out of the Tourist Trap. Special Issue of *Cultural Survival Quarterly,* Vol. 14, Nos. 1 & 2.

MacCannell, Dean. (1989). *The Tourist.* New York: Schocken.

Norkunas, Martha K. (1993). *The Politics of Public Memory.* Albany: State University of New York Press.

Smith, Valene L. (Ed.). (1989). *Hosts and Guests.* University of Pennsylvania Press: Philadelphia.

Smith, Valene L. (Ed.). (1992). Anthropology and Tourism. Special Issue of *Practicing Anthropology,* Vol. 14, No. 2.

Van Kemper, Robert. (1978). Tourism and Regional Development in Taos, New Mexico. In V. Smith (Ed.), *Tourism and Economic Change,* Studies in Third World Societies, No. 6. Williamsburg: William and Mary Press.

Urry, John. (1990). *The Tourist Gaze.* London: Sage.

2

The Town that Debates Tourism: Community and Tourism in Broome, Australia

ELVI WHITTAKER

For nearly a century, the town of Broome, Australia, remained relatively isolated from the rest of the world. Then, through the singular efforts of a wealthy British entrepreneur, coupled with the development of a highway in 1986, Broome found itself being carried swiftly into the mainstream of tourism development. This article by Elvi Whittaker demonstrates how quickly tourism can transform a region's sense of its own destiny and contribute to local factionalism. This seems to be especially true in cases in which the impetus for tourism development is seen to have originated from outside the community, and where planners emphasize the economic benefits of tourism and tend to discount local concerns related to quality of life issues and opportunities for self-determination. Although initiatives to attract tourists to Broome were focussed on the distinct cultural and natural resources of the area, including the presence of a large Aboriginal community, Whittaker suggests that many local stakeholders felt powerless to influence decisions concerning future development. One conclusion to be drawn from this contribution is that there is often a very thin line between the mutually beneficial celebration of regional heritage or culture and the appropriation of cultural resources in ways that bear little relationship to local knowledge or vitality.

Recognizing the fallacy of misplaced concreteness is particularly important to establishing economics for community, because community is precisely the feature of reality that has been most consistently abstracted from modern economics. (Daly & Cobb, 1989:43)

In 1980 Lord Alistair McAlpine saw the town of Broome for the first time. He fell in love with it, or so the story goes. This Englishman, peer of the realm, Treasurer in Margaret Thatcher's conservative government, chief holder in Australian City Properties, great grandson of the McAlpine building dynasty, and a man of considerable means was destined to have an unprecedented effect on the town. Broome is a small tropical town in the Western Kimberleys, located in the most remote northwest area of the continent, in the state of Western Australia. Tourist pamphlets conventionally describe the town in the following manner: The town settles in a semi-arid landscape on deep red pindan soil on the shores of an azure sea, the Indian Ocean. It is situated amidst picturesque mangrove swamps, fragile sand dunes, ribbons of white sand beaches, heath, cliffs, red dust and dinosaur footprints. The surrounding areas are comprised of large tracts of pastoral land. Over the years Broome has developed an international reputation as a pearling capital, which has not only defined the industrial base of the town but also created the diversity of the population found there.

What conventional tourist texts do not say is that Broome is also home to six Aboriginal communities and is positioned in the midst of about twelve others. Thirty-nine different Aboriginal languages and dialects are spoken in the Kimberley region as a whole (Hudson and Yu, 1988:3–7). Within the town limits are the communities of Burrgugun (also known as Morgan's Camp), Janyjagurdiny, Mallingbar (also called Kennedy Hill), Meat Work Camp, Nillir Irbanjin (also called One Mile Reserve) and Billgungurr (also called Airport Reserve). They function as part of the town. The languages spoken in these areas are Bardi, Yawuru, Karajarri, Nyulnyul, Mangala and Nyikina.[1] The Aboriginal population of Broome Shire was recorded at 3,168, and that of the urban center of Broome at 1,887 in the 1991 census (Australian Bureau of Statistics, 1991a).

The Aboriginal population of the Kimberley area is a large one and it is estimated that one of every four persons of Aboriginal descent in Western Australia lives in the region. This population constitutes 36 percent of the total population of the area (Australian Bureau of Statistics, 1991b). The Aboriginal population of Broome is 21 percent of the total town population of 8,905. What the tourist texts also do not explore is that the Aboriginal community in Broome is assuming leadership in a renaissance of Aboriginal culture. Broome has become the urban center for promoting, disseminating and providing the context for the work of some of Australia's most renowned Aboriginal artists, musicians and writers.

The tourist texts evoke romanticized images of an "exotic past," of the existence of "many races and cultures," and promise tours through

Chinatown and the Japanese Pearl Divers' Cemetery and frequently refer to Broome as the "Town of the Pearl." They do not, however, elaborate on the cultural diversity and ethnic history of the town. In addition to the large Aboriginal population, the pearling history of the town and the pastoral history of the region have attracted entrepreneurs from Europe and the rest of the Australian continent and a labor force mainly from Asia. Broome shares a stereotypical nineteenth century history with that of other emerging industrial towns in the colonized world. When Broome was instituted as a townsite in 1883, it was given the name of the West Australian Governor, Sir Frederick Napier Broome. At that time it was a small pearlers' camp of transient lugger crews and not yet ready for the formal status placed upon it.[2] Yet within fifteen years it developed rapidly: a British company established a pearling base there, a cable was laid to Banji Wanji, Indonesia, a telegraph line was connected and many of the amenities and services of a small town were put in place. Consequently, in the first part of the new century, Broome was to produce eighty percent of the world's pearl shell. The diving and other laboring was undertaken by Aboriginals workers, and by Malaysian, Ceylonese, Timorese, Indonesian, Indian, Japanese, Chinese and Filipino migrant laborers.[3] It was almost entirely a male labor force, with the exception of some Aboriginal women who worked as divers. To round out the colonial portrait, the pearling masters and overseers were European—English, Irish, Scottish, German, Dutch and New Zealanders.

Prior to 1986, the town was accessible only by sea, by the sturdiest of four-wheel drives over rough hewn roads, by camel, and by air (since 1934) from the capital Perth, from Darwin, the largest city in the Northern Territory, and from Singapore and Indonesia. The paving of the Great Northern Highway, completed by 1986, was the final link which made Broome and many towns in the Kimberleys accessible to motor traffic. At least initially, the residents became the somewhat surprised hosts of adventurers circumnavigating the whole continent by road, and also of Australians on bus, car and caravan tours. The theatricality of the unknown, the exotic promise of wilderness and the Australian version of The Last Frontier are usually cited as the inducements that brought tourists to this remote part of the continent.

The town had always had a certain pride in its romantic isolation, so that when television made a very late appearance and arrived in town on September 28, 1980, not everyone welcomed the inevitable intrusion. The comments which greeted this arrival reflected pride in pioneering and in withstanding the seductions of big city life and the evils of unnecessary communication. "I think it's shocking," "It's a total social disaster" and "Who needs television, we've got the Roe-buck" (a popular local pub). This Australian commitment to a rural existence, the distrust of urbanism and of the imposed changes synonymous with it was to serve as a backdrop to the development debate to come (Aitkin, 1985; Whittaker, 1994).

The "Lord of the Bush" and the Lure of the Road

Alistair McAlpine was to have a profound effect on Broome's isolation. He was destined, almost single-handedly, to inspire the chain of events which was to culminate in an unprecedented spurt of growth and prosperity. His interest sent a message about the unique worth of Broome in the international marketplace, and his influence set a course to be realized in a plethora of revitalization and development activities. Added to the emergence of a new vision of Broome, was the completion of the Great Northern Highway giving both the promise and the threat of even more accessibility. The stage was set for what was to become a classic debate. Deeply felt convictions congealed: pride of place and its inaccessible splendor, an Australian respect for the nobility of the bush, the sacredness of the rural lifestyle, an inherent fear of pollution by the vulgarities of cities, a sense of ownership of the status quo, and a distrust of those who wield monetary and political power. These traditional values fueled opposition to plans to develop the town into a major tourist destination.

Voices from many sectors of the community proclaimed wrongful appropriation, asserted the rights of citizens and questioned the morality and feasibility of unmediated development. The story became one about a familiar confrontation—the voices raised in defence of tradition and suspicious of change against those eagerly planning and propelling these changes. The discourse, which developed to argue the ideational complexities of these debates, was similar on both sides. Words of caution and constraint—controlled growth, planning, environmental priorities, sustainability—were evoked by ideological opponents to further quite different vested interests and to rally support.

Having fallen in love with Broome, McAlpine began to purchase various parcels of real estate. His appreciation and energetic refurbishing of the original architecture of Broome gave birth to the notion of the "Broome house", a single-storied, tropical, residential structure with a corrugated roof and a long cool veranda. These structures came to be viewed as "heritage" and to be prized and protected. He was to direct equal attention to recreating the original splendors of some commercial properties, preserving the Chinese and colonial influences, as well as the original architectural and design intentions of buildings constructed at a later period. One of these later buildings was the delapidated movie house built in 1916 to accommodate an early twentieth century audience and respect the tropical climate. Thus the refurbished Sun Pictures permitted Broome to lay claim to having the oldest operating open-air movie theater in the world. Further, he purchased the mansions of various pearling masters, sometimes transporting them from one location to another, and furnished them with genuine Australian colonial furniture and original works by Australian artists like Sidney Nolan. His real estate holdings and resulting preservations were large-scale by any standards and, some eight or nine years later, he was believed to have purchased over eighty different pieces of property.

In 1984, on property directly adjacent to what was later to become the Cable Beach Resort, McAlpine constructed a licensed twenty-six hectare zoological garden, the Pearl Coast Zoo. Established with zoological consultation and expertise, the zoo offered a comprehensive selection of endangered species from the tropical zones of the world, an impressive collection of exotic and rare Australian parrots, and a 13,000 square meter lake which provided a rest area for migratory birds. All of this was made accessible to visitors by a one kilometer walkway which permitted the visitor to walk over and above the animals in their natural niches. The zoo was envisioned as an Ark, an institution scientifically devoted to species survival, with an emphasis on breeding colonies and with the ultimate aim of returning birds to their original habitats.

Among his other large purchases was a caravan park at Cable Beach, the most desirable of beach locations. Beginning in 1987, he developed a resort complex on the site—the Cable Beach Club—which dwarfed anything previously constructed in Broome, or anywhere in the Kimberleys. It not only offered the luxury of two swimming pools and four or five restaurants, but added a flair that was unique and came to be known as his style. The resort was furnished in colonial wicker, genuine antiques and decorated with Asian art, as well as original oils and watercolors by prominent Australian artists. To this he added quality service. The many attributes of the Cable Beach Resort were added to McAlpine's visible accomplishments in Broome itself to inspire a litany of approval of his "good taste."

He also turned his attention to Aboriginal artists and promoted a new art style of sculpted heads for which he arranged a museum exhibit. Inspiring further innovations in Aboriginal art styles, he arranged exhibitions for Aboriginal works in paper, stone and tin. In addition he is credited with directing public attention to the existence of colonial furniture, and yet another museum exhibition established its unique value. Most of these exhibitions relied on artifacts from his own large collection.[4]

To round out his conservational and promotional zeal, McAlpine was a major force in founding the Broome Preservation Society. For some years, McAlpine's involvement with Broome was intense. He was known to spend some months of each year there. All of this commitment earned him the media titles of "the unofficial Baron of Broom," "the Lord of the Bush" and "Lord of Parrots" and his engagement with Broome and with Australia, came to be called a "genuine love affair." The *Broome News* described the relationship thus:

> His love of Broome was genuine and infectious. Columnists throughout Australia were writing about it and Broome was becoming nationally recognized.
>
> "Broome has the most beautiful landscape in the world," he was often quoted as saying ... on the 13th August 1984 ... the Member for North Province, Peter Dowding ... said that Lord McAlpine, the man who had financed the venture [the Zoo], had made a unique philanthropic gesture to the people of Broome. "Lord McAlpine has already spent a fortune ... I cannot remember anyone previously making a financial commitment like this one with no thoughts of profit or return on their investment." The people of Broome were beginning to get to know this rather odd, eccentric property developer from England and were beginning to approve of him (1991a : 22–23).

Parenthetically he also bought property in neighboring areas such as Derby, Kununurra, Walcott Inlet, Exmouth, as well as in Darwin, Perth and Sydney. Some wondered whether McAlpine and his Australian City Properties were intending to develop the whole of northern Australia. On the surface and in the beginning, a commendable relationship seemed to be emerging between large scale development and the conservation of the ecological system as well as the cultural one.

While the McAlpine developments were ongoing, Broome seemed to provide a nurturing urban milieu for a renaissance of Aboriginal culture. The Kimberley Aboriginal Law and Culture Centre, the Goolarabooloo Aboriginal Arts and Crafts Centre, and the Mambulanjin Resource Centre fostered Aboriginal culture, law and heritage. Magabala Books, the first Aboriginal controlled publishing house in Australia, was established in 1987. Several artistic, musical and dance organizations arose. The Aboriginal musical, *Bran Nue Dae*, locally written by Jimmy Chi, with Stephen Pigram and Michael Manolis as co-writers, has toured the continent and Britain, and received a prestigious theater award. The author and cast have established a production company to promote future Aboriginal theatrical creations. The town also claims several Aboriginal bands: the rock band Scrap Metal, which has reaped several honors, produced several albums and has toured the Australian continent with great success; Kuckles, an original culture band; Bingurr, an electric band with a distinctive Broome guitar style; Gunada, a multicultural band; and Johnny and the Ballas which plays electric reggae. In 1991, an Aboriginal Radio Station, Goolarri, a Broome Media Association station, began broadcasting via the Australian Broadcasting Commission. All this activity created a revival of Aboriginal culture in the modern idiom. Yet, with the exception of the Lurujarri Heritage Trail, a guided walk following part of a traditional Aboriginal song cycle, the Aboriginal population has not officially ventured into tourist management.

The activities of McAlpine's Australian City Properties had immediate effects on the region. In the first few years of his involvement, the population of Broome increased by 57.6 percent in five years to number 5,778 in 1986 (Australian Bureau of Statistics, 1986). Although tourism had always been present in a more modest form, officials now began to boast of Broome being the fastest growing town in Western Australia, and of the Kimberleys being the fastest growing region on the continent. The population growth between 1986 and 1991 was 41 percent, to the present estimated total of 8,905 (Australian Bureau of Statistics, 1991a ; see also Hudson, in press). The arrival of tourists has matched the growth in local population, increasing by 48 percent in five years. In 1981–82 there were 141,600 arrivals, by 1983–84 this had increased to 166,700, by 1985–86 to 192,900 and by 1989–90 to 248,800 (Western Australian Tourist Commission, 1990). This signifies an increase of 76 percent since 1980 and 29 percent since 1986. During this time three new major tourist complexes were being developed in Broome. One of these was an attempt to accommodate a different kind of tourist, the backpacker. New restaurants and businesses were opened. In the retail industry the number of establishments increased 100 percent between 1980 and 1986, and 57 percent between 1986 and 1991. Similarly retail turnover increased 160.8 percent, wages and salaries increased 158.8 percent and the number of people employed increased 76.6 percent (Australian Bureau of Statistics, 1986, 1992). The growth was unprecedented.

Tourists had become so common a sight around town that local people in Broome began to adopt the familiar vernacular by which tourists are denigrated in places where they appear in abundance—

"put the caravan park in the middle of the ocean so all the tourists can float away," "have an open tourist hunt each year and exterminate," "keep it low-key, we don't want another Queensland." An article in the *Broome News* points out that:

> Well it's hard being a tourist . . . the responsibility of showing city, street-wise slickness to local yokels is high pressure stuff . . . where do they [tourists] find those Khaki safari hats? . . . It's obviously a joke someone thought of at one of those slick promotion agencies down south—"and let's give them all funny little hats so we can count them." What these southerners do have to answer for is their downright patronizing attitude. What's so quaint about us . . . that requires monosyllabic questions asked through clamped, dentured smiles? "Do you live HERE?—How extraordinary!" (Chang, 1985 : 35).

The cautions evoked by townspeople about the dangers of becoming like Queensland refer to that state's two major tourist meccas—Surfers Paradise and Cairns. Neighboring Kimberley communities, developing at a slower pace than Broome, are known to caution against the horrors of becoming "like Broome." Meanwhile, McAlpine and the Shire Council were discussing plans for enlarging the golf course to twenty-six holes. Most importantly McAlpine and Ansett Airlines discussed the construction of a larger airport, privately owned, with a runway long enough to accommodate 737s and consequently international flights connecting Broome to Singapore, Bali and London.

"Knocked at Every Turn": Locals Speak Back

This state of affairs was not destined to last. Between 1988 and 1991 a series of economic reversals befell Broome. Firstly, the fall of the stock market in 1987, the recession and high interest rates were felt in the town as they were elsewhere in the world. Secondly, a disastrous pilots' strike in 1989 affected tourism, especially international tourism, in most of the northern parts of the continent, as these locales were up-market destinations served mainly by the airlines (Norington, 1990). This meant that only travelers making the trip by car, caravan or bus continued to arrive. As they generally occupied caravan parks, backpacker lodgings and, far less frequently, hotels, the latter suffered from a vacancy rate as high as 70 to 80 percent. Within a few years, most hotels were for sale or in receivership. Some were eventually withdrawn in recognition of the sluggishness of the real estate market. One of the resort hotels under construction remained unfinished, went into receivership, and in the early nineties stood as a lifeless shell, a monument to bankruptcy.

As these events occurred, Lord McAlpine also was withdrawing from Broome. Half of the Cable Beach Club was up for sale, attracting prospective buyers like Japanese entrepreneurs and the Club Med. Other McAlpine properties were also on the market. The Pearl Coast Zoo was being dismantled and many of the animals were sold to a private zoo in the Northern Territory. His collection of Australian colonial furniture was sold or auctioned. McAlpine withdrew from his involvement in the airport, and his share was eventually purchased by Airport Engineering Services Pty. Ltd.

The townspeople, with no explanation forthcoming from McAlpine, attempted to account for his withdrawal. Some argued that he had fallen victim to hard times, the recession, high interest rates, and that he needed to retrench. Others pointed out that his father died in 1989 and that his sister now had charge of the family fortunes. Consequently, they argued, he no longer had the luxury of indulging himself in entrepreneurial compulsions or in philanthropic conservation schemes. Others countered this explanation by indicating that Burke's Peerage showed that McAlpine had no sister. Still others reasoned that he recently underwent by-pass surgery and had decided to bow out of the demanding world of high finance. Another account focused on his character, indicating that Broome was for him "an Englishman's eccentric folly" and that he was now "doing something in Italy." Others elaborated on this shift of commitment, centering their argument on the man as an eccentric collector now wearying of Australian artifacts and furniture, and finding a new preoccupation with Venetian furniture and glass and nineteenth century photographs. Those more familiar with the financial record of the Australian City Properties rationalized that in 1988 the company made a profit of $16.1 million, but in 1989 it lost $10.7 million. A liquidation of assets would be sensible under such circumstances. They argued that McAlpine was not a stupid man and that he would not be selling at a loss, but at good market value, indeed at considerable profit. Others did not blame the depressed state of the economy nor personal proclivities for his withdrawal, but placed the responsibility on the growing anti-development lobby in the town. A story of a different stripe suggested that McAlpine came to Broome originally because he was on the hit list of the Irish Republican Army. It was well known in town that his house in England had been bombed. This account proposed, with some pretense of alarm and an indication of the incredulity of the possibility, that the Irish Republican Army was even then closing in on him in Broome.

On the whole, however, the people of Broome treated McAlpine with respectful ambiguity—the sense of resentment reserved for the very wealthy, the genuine appreciation for his carefully considered developments, his "good taste," his attention to ecological matters ("No other developer put the world first and agreed to stop using tropical timber in his buildings"), his respect for Aboriginal culture and his support of Aboriginal art and music. Others noted with nostalgia that the town would not be the same without McAlpine sitting in the pub of a local hotel. Ambiguity and the admiration combined to exempt the entrepreneur from the harshest criticism with regard to the evils of development, reserving resentment for those on the Shire Council or for developers as a generic category. McAlpine's own voice had not been heard on the issues of withdrawal. While he was frequently interviewed by local and national newspapers, and his development plans were closely followed, he remained a mystery and his motivations remained unexplored. The only view of these elusive qualities that emerged was his own single allusion to his "philosophy of hope" (Zubrycki, 1990).

While development issues have always been of concern to the town, the fast-paced development of tourist infrastructures and attractions have brought into focus those agendas which run parallel, or even in opposition to such developments—environmental preservation, the protection of cultural traditions, the developmental needs of the community. The issues in contention are apparent in the platforms of candidates for Shire Council in May 1991. One prospective councilor argues that Shire Councilors should consider community needs and the environment as well as developer needs, that local people have had few opportunities to comment on plans or on the fast-paced changes. Another asserts the view that Council should be composed of a balance of business and community leaders and they should be sensitive to the unique character of Broome. A third advocates long term local and regional planning, proper consultative procedures, accountability and monitoring, support for senior citizens, for small business, for the employment of local people and for the enhancement of the uniqueness of Broome and its environment. A fourth voices support for "Old Broome charm" and enthusiasm for community organizations. Finally, a fifth candidate proclaims well-considered development, taking into account the needs of local people. To this is added a condemnation of councilors who are in public life to help themselves with a total disregard for local people and their opinions (Broome News, 1991b : 2–7).

These issues are also apparent in consultations with the community that emerged in *The Broome Study* distributed in 1989. The study identified "major themes, issues and development opportunities associated with the town" and had a mandate to "collect a range of information on each (and determine priorities)." Ultimately it attempted to suggest "a series of workable, recommended actions" (Shire Council of Broome, 1989).

Even as the rather dramatic economic events continue to occupy center stage, a variety of voices from the community are still raised, demanding to be heard. They define themselves as ideologically different from a category they subsume under the single label of "development." For some years there has been a growing disillusionment based on several unspoken assumptions which appear to have been violated. The assumptions stem from an ideology, widely cited by Broome residents, that development should rest on sustainability. They bolster the unquestioned goal of sustainability with its importance for their common future, for proper equity and for quality in growth. They assert that successful development cannot be measured in touristic and economic terms alone, but must also be measured in terms of consensus and support from the community. Residents describe themselves as being confronted by the power of "development" which has become ordered into priorities over which they have no control. Growth by consensus is their demand. A few activists, prepared with internationally recognized moral tools, point to the World Commission on Environment and Development as a guiding declaration (1987 : 43 ; see also Starke, 1990). This is not a new story, or a new rallying.

A coalition appears to have emerged in the town around issues of proper development, sustainable growth and the democratic process of seeking consensus. The coalition asserts itself publicly and determinedly in packed open meetings with the Shire Council. Voices are raised in support of specific issues and in condemnation of others. On occasion the coalition becomes activated as when it performed as a body in a demonstration of resistance against the removal of sand dunes at Cable Beach to permit the development of a Surf Club. Coalitions such as these are recognizable in many contemporary communities facing changes. Aboriginal people, environmentalists, feminists, social and human rights activists, senior citizens, sometimes the church, government workers in welfare, employment and other services, and "old-timers" find common ground in such resistance movements. For the Broome coalition the debate rests on three major issues which are seen as violating the common good. The first is the need for the recognition of democratic procedures for proper consultation. The second is recognition of the virtue of development at a slower, and presumably at a more manageable rate. The third is that development, at least in moral terms, demands more than partial consensus or an interpretation of silence as consensus, but an involvement and agreement of all the stakeholders.

While the epistemic discourse remains untapped, a series of issues receive, if not undivided attention, at least undivided support. Usually introduced with the words "the community needs . . ." a series of complaints are aired and solutions proposed. The discourse is produced in the Broome newspaper, in bars and stores, at social events and at Council meetings. The absent audience is always either "business" or the Shire council—those institutions deemed in need of instruction and proper management. Some agitate for a Nature Park, a Coastal Park and a Kimberley Environmental Centre. Others loudly proclaim their opposition to any development whatsoever, regardless of its nature. Others position themselves bodily, as in the event of the bulldozing the famed sand-dunes. The case of the controversial curbing installed in town is frequently raised as an example of the misuse of Shire funds, and it is loudly proclaimed that better alternatives for the use of the funds would have been a senior citizen center, or improved transportation facilities to permit young mothers to leave outlying homes during the day. "I don't understand the curbs. They make each street a torrential river in the wet season." Any visible construction in town is immediately proclaimed to be the outcome of the vested interests of specific members of the Shire council, or of unauthored bureaucratic ventures.

> Before Shires make any decisions on roads, etc., Councillors and engineers should put themselves in the users' shoes—not just go by some office Johnny with a few letters after his name sitting in some way-off office (Griersen, 1988 : 2).

Tourist development is seen as the root cause of the escalation of food prices, which is variously reported as increased by 20 percent and even 100 percent. Some indicate that the inflation in real estate prices "at least double or triple" in the wake of developers purchasing property, make home-ownership a luxury most people cannot afford. The monopoly of the single airline which connects the town to the rest of Australia is frequently cited. It is noted that while cheap fares are now available to fly from west to east on the continent, the fare from Broome to Perth is still in the $900 category. These matters are viewed with barely concealed suspicion as "business" makes decisions out of reach of any individuals in town. While some suggest that encouraging backpacking as an alternative to the dreaded "mass tourism" would promote eco-tourism, others complain that this particular group is guilty of just as many ecological sins. Some townspeople cite the absurdities of an uncaring Shire Council and "business interests" attending single-mindedly to large-scale tourist developments that few people supposedly want, while most members of the community wring their hands in horror at there being only a single dentist in town. "Can you see getting a toothache when he is on holiday?"

Activists note that while money readily flows through the major hotels, it quickly goes out of town to the cities. At a time when unemployment is high in the Kimberleys, not only are the hotel managers from the city, but even the service jobs go to transient young people from Perth and the east coast. "I can think of only two or three local people working in the hotels." An underground document circulating in town produced evidence of the low number of local people hired by the hotels. The implications were that "the powers that be" attempt to suppress such evidence from the townspeople. Even while McAlpine's contribution to natural and cultural conservation is widely praised, questions are raised about the wisdom of an overseas absentee owner controlling such large investments and exercising the great power such ownership entails. The size of his holdings are sometimes cited as being more than a third of the town. In particular, opposition is voiced against the proposed new airport and runway, against what new evils it will facilitate, and the nameless tourists who will come either from the vast northern continents and from Japan, or the Australians who will use Broome as a stopping place on their way to a holiday in Southeast Asia. To this is added an anxiety about the unknown fate of the land where the old airport is now located.

Heritage and Ownership: the Aboriginal Presence

The position of the Aboriginal population, the preservation of their culture, their laws and their lands is particularly poignant. In most of the northern areas of the Australian continent, from the York Peninsula to the Western Kimberleys, one of the most marketable tourist items is Aboriginal culture. Broome provides an interesting exception to conventional notions of indigenous cultures as tourist objects on permanent display for tourists. Broome's tourist literature, gives scant recognition to the familiar promises of exposure to "ancient cultures and customs." Instead, reference is made to Aboriginal artistic and musical achievements, to Magabala Books and to Broome as the home of the nationally known *Bran Nue Dae*. Despite this difference, Aboriginal groups are involved in some of the debates on legitimacy and recognition that is the ongoing norm in other Australian locations. Paddy Roe, the custodian of the Aboriginal Heritage Trail, in referring to his interactions with McAlpine, establishes precepts for a non-appropriative relationship:

> I'm sitting in the middle . . . we come together to look after the country . . . Some of the European people, they can't understand . . . Mr. McAlpine, a big man. He listens. That's the way he should be. I work with him very close. He knows who to come to. When I want anything, I ask. When he wants anything, he must ask . . . Black and white we should become one (Zubrycki, 1990).

Although morally in a powerful position, it comes as no surprise that Aboriginal people are underrepresented in the arenas of power.[5] Despite this formal political disadvantage, it is known that at the end of 1991, Aboriginal groups were blocking three major developments, one being the golf course extension. Aboriginal people everywhere in the postcolonial world are inclined to view tourism as another racist activity, catering to non-Aboriginal people, and involving developments in which the Aboriginal populations have no say (Senate, 1991 : 1248). All too frequently, development initiatives do not seek clearance under the Aboriginal Heritage Act, do not adhere to a check list of environmental priorities, and do not observe proper protection of Aboriginal sites, sacred or otherwise. Tourists are generally completely uneducated about Aboriginal culture, ignorant about how to behave on Aboriginal lands, completely lacking in relevant information and frequently guilty of trespassing. Even in parts of the Kimberleys where tours are owned and led by Aboriginal people, the problem persists. Aboriginal tour operators are seen as committing the same violations as their Caucasian counterparts. They bring tourists to Aboriginal communities and sites without seeking permission or informing the hosts. In addition, none of the benefits of tourism are returned to communities. The resentment is deemed to be stronger when the tour operator is Aboriginal (Senior, n.d. : 33).

Consultants suggest that the relationship between Aboriginal communities and tourism could be improved and advise that it is important to protect sites, to educate tourists, to develop an Aboriginal ranger scheme and an honorary warden system and to attend to the Coastal Development Plan (Senior, n.d. : v–x). This Plan calls for a full consultation with Aboriginal people before any management plan is finalized. Of particular importance would be the appointment of an Aboriginal

Liaison Manager to the tourist industry in the Kimberleys. In general, however, consultants express a genuine doubt that tourism can in any way be a solution to underdevelopment and the present dependence on the welfare state, although, undoubtedly, it could provide supplementary income (Senior, n.d. : 97; Altman, 1987).

By way of epilogue, it should be noted that in the year in which this chapter goes to press, four years after the observations reported above, some specifics of development have been decided, if not resolved. The airport runway has been extended and the old airport area is up for possible redevelopment into a large supermarket. The hotel industry has reviewed. The Zoo has been dismantled. McAlpine still visits Broome. In the area of Aboriginal land rights, Broome is being considered as constituting a prospective test case given its location in the midst of considerable rural undeveloped Crown land. The debate itself, however, continues. A development boom is considered imminent, even as it was in 1991. The demands for "sensible development" and for developers "to come to the table" remain unabated.

Even as the debate over tourist development continues, it becomes clear that various levels of government and the law cannot legislate the parameters of the common good. All of the many players ask to have a voice in setting the boundaries and goals of procedure and examining the ends sought. The motivations of host communities, the impacts they experience on the one hand and those they are willing to tolerate on the other, are some of the many issues debated in the seeking of this common good. The debate merely serves to show that Broome adds its name to those examples where the success from promotion has out-stripped both the mechanisms for regulation and the conservation of the cultural traditions that the participants consider a proper part of their identity.

Acknowledgments

An earlier version of this chapter was read at the Annual Meetings of the Society for Applied Anthropology, Memphis, Tennesse, in March 1992. The research discussed is part of an ongoing project on indigenous tourism funded by the Social Sciences and Humanities Research Council of Canada. While most of the work centers in the Northern Territory, my interests in the developments at Broome were peaked by the intensive promotion given that location in the Australian media. I am indebted to Robin Hanigan, Robert Perrin, Ruth Perrin, Judith Wagner, the librarians of the Broome Public Library, the officials at the offices of the Broome Shire, and Bill Syms of the Australian Bureau of Statistics.

In particular I wish to show appreciation to those inhabitants of Broome who shared their thoughts and their hopes with me. Finally, I thank the two anonymous reviewers of the volume, and Erve Chambers for general good-naturedness, useful suggestions and editing.

Notes

1. See Hudson and Yu (1988) for a fuller description of the communities in and around Broome, and for the many languages spoken there. The authors also describe the origins of these communities, e.g., communities on traditional lands, Aboriginal communities running their own cattle stations, communities where members work on nearby cattle stations, Aboriginal Reserve communities, and communities on land once run by missions.

2. Much of this historical material is recorded in Edwards (1983) and in various documents at the Broome Historical Society. It should be noted that these texts constitute an essentially white Australian and a male history. Aboriginal histories, women's histories and ethnic histories have yet to be written. A beginning on writing Aboriginal histories for tourists has been made by Burnum Burnum (1988 : 199–201).

3. The White Australia policy, officially known as the Immigration Restriction Act, instituted in 1901 and significantly changed in 1958, placed a severe threat on the survival of the pearling industry. The pearling community retaliated with a strong and successful appeal, arguing that Asiatic laborers were a necessity as their diving skills could not be replicated by white men. Nevertheless, the exception made for Broome is not reflected in continuing immigration during the century, as the contemporary statistics of Broome reveal that the majority of the present population of the town is Australian-born (84.3 percent), and the largest group of foreign born were from the United Kingdom and Ireland (6 percent), and other Europeans (2 percent) (Australian Bureau of Statistics 1991a). The most frequently spoken language after English, however, is German, followed by Chinese, Italian, Dutch and French.

4. The exhibitions arranged through McAlpine were: *Kimberley Sculpture: A Selection of Carvings by Aboriginal Artists of North Western Australia from the Collection of Australian City Properties Limited* (Dodo, Akerman & McKelson, n.d.), a touring exhibit; *Paper, Stone and Tin in the Collection of the South Australian Museum* (Adelaide: South Australian Museum, n.d.); and *Bush Toys and Furniture* at the Powerhouse Museum, Sydney (Cornall, 1990).

5. For a discussion of Aboriginal and white attitudes, decision-making in the public sector and government policies in a small town in Western Australia, see Edmunds (1989).

References

Aitkin, Don. (1985). "Countrymindedness"—the Spread of an Idea. *Australian Cultural History,* 4:33–40.

Altman, Jon C. (1987). The Economic Impact of Tourism on the Warmun (Turkey Creek) Community, East Kimberley. East Kimberley Working Paper No. 19.

Australian Bureau of Statistics.
(1986). Census. Shire of Broome. Canberra: Queen's Printer.

(1991a). Census. Population and Housing. Canberra: Queen's Printer.

(1991b). Census. Aboriginal and Torres Strait Islander Population of the Kimberley (Statistical Division). Canberra: Queen's Printer.

(1992). Census. Retail Survey. Canberra: Queen's Printer.

The Broome News. (1991a). The Rise and Fall of Australian City Properties. February, pages 22–26.

(1991b). The Election Profile. May, pages 2–7.

Burnum Burnum. (1988). *Burnum Burnum's Aboriginal Australia: A Traveller's Guide.* David Stewart (Ed.), North Ryde, N.S.W.: Angus and Robertson.

Chang, Claire. (1985). Local "Blow-In" Blasts Tourists. *The Broome News.* August, page 35.

Cornall, Graham. (1990). *Memories.* Perth: Australian City Properties.

Daly, Herman E. and John B. Cobb, Jr. (1989). *For the Common Good: Redirecting the Economy toward Community, the Environment and a Sustainable Future.* Boston: Beacon.

Dodo, Big John, Kim Akerman and Fr. Kevin McKelson. (n.d.) *Kimberley Sculpture.* A Touring Exhibition sponsored by Australian City Properties Limited.

Edmunds, Mary. (1989). Opinion Formation as Political Process: The Public Sector, Aborigines, and White Attitudes in a Western Australian Town. *Anthropological Forum,* 6:81–104.

Edwards, Hugh. (1983). *Port of Pearls: A History of Broome.* Adelaide: Rigby Ltd.

Griesen, Sue. (1988). Difficulties of a Tour Driver. *The Broome News.* November, pages 2–3.

Hudson, Joyce and Sarah Yu. compilers. (1988). Kimberley Aboriginal Communities. Broome: Nulungu Catholic College.

Hudson, Philippa. (in press). Population Growth in Northern Australia: Implications for the 1990s. *The Challenge of Northern Regions,* P. Jull and S. Roberts (Eds.).

Norington, Brad. (1990). *Sky Pirates: The Pilots' Strike that Grounded Australia.* Crows Nest, N.S.W.: ABC Book.

Senate Standing Committee on Environment, Recreation and the Arts. (1991). Australian Tourist Industry. Commonwealth of Australia, Canberra: Queen's Printer.

Senior, Clive. (n.d.) Tourism and Aboriginal Heritage with Particular Reference to the Kimberley. Report prepared for the Museum of Western Australia.

The Shire Council of Broome. (1989). The Broome Study. Broome: The Shire.

South Australian Museum. (n.d.) *Paper, Stone, Tin.* Adelaide: South Australian Museum.

Starke, Linda. (1990). *Signs of Hope: Working towards Our Common Future.* Oxford: Oxford University Press.

Western Australian Tourism Commission. (1990). Kimberley Tourism Statistical Trends. Perth: Western Australian Tourism Commission.

Whittaker, Elvi. (1994). Public Discourse on Sacredness: the Transfer of Ayers Rock to Aboriginal Ownership. *American Ethnologist,* 21(2):310–334.

World Commission on Environment and Development. (1987). *Our Common Future.* Oxford: Oxford University Press.

Zubrycki, Tom (director and producer). (1990). *The Lord of the Bush.* Film by Jotz Productions, with the Australian Broadcasting Commission and Australian Film Finance Corporation Pty. Ltd.

3

Tourism, Cultural Authenticity, and the Native Crafts Cooperative: The Eastern Cherokee Experience

BETTY J. DUGGAN

In evaluating research related to the human consequences of tourism, it is important to consider the scope and level of analysis of any particular contribution. Compare this chapter by Betty Duggan, describing the successful development of a crafts cooperative by the Eastern Band of Cherokees in North Carolina, with Elvi Whittaker's account of tourism in an Australian town. It should become clear that much the same article could have been written about either region, although the conclusions of these two authors are quite different. Here, Duggan's research is directed to the ability of one Cherokee group to benefit from tourism without sacrificing their sense of cultural integrity. What is remarkable is that they have done this in a regional environment in which the misrepresentation of Native American heritage is commonplace. Duggan credits these happier circumstances to the Cherokees' ability to take advantage of outside mediation (in this case the efforts of representatives of the United States federal government) while maintaining traditional modes of production and decision-making. This article also encourages us to consider what we mean when we ask whether an object or event is "authentic." While Duggan offers examples in which local crafts might have been adapted to the tastes of tourists, the authenticity of these productions does not seem in doubt. An authentic culture is not one that remains unchanged, which seems impossible under any condition, but one that retains the ability to determine the appropriateness of its adaptations.

Introduction

Cherokee, North Carolina, is the seat of government for the Eastern Band of Cherokees, an incorporated Native American group which recognized 9,590 members in 1990. The Eastern Cherokees are descendants of the largest tribe resident in the southeastern United States during the eighteenth century, and, in particular of those Cherokees who avoided removal to Indian Territory in the 1830s. Today, the town of Cherokee (Yellow Hill community) also serves as the eastern gateway to the Great Smoky Mountains National Park, which has a yearly visitation of over ten million people (Finger, 1991).

The Eastern Band has been chastised in textbooks and professional journals, and even in their own newspaper, by a number of scholars, visitors, and Native American activists for allowing development of an opportunistic tourist landscape along Cherokee's major highways (e.g., French, 1977; Smith, 1982). Critics often fail to note the bleak economic conditions which led to initial tourist development. Four major tourist attractions that fit more subtly into the natural and built environments near the tribal administrative complex of the Eastern Band of Cherokees are also frequently omitted from these critiques. These latter enterprises—a museum which interprets Cherokee culture from prehistoric to modern times, a living history village devoted to eighteenth century Cherokee lifeways, an outdoor drama about the Trail of Tears, and an arts and crafts cooperative—offer examples of planned tourism that are economically profitable, yet culturally informed.[1]

This article focuses exclusively on the fourth attraction, the Qualla Arts and Crafts Mutual, Inc., a cooperatively-owned native enterprise that has tapped the burgeoning tourist market successfully for half a century (Blankenship, 1987; Duggan and Riggs, 1991). Today, Qualla Arts and Crafts is the most economically successful and long-lived tribal crafts cooperative in the United States (Robert Hart, personal communications, 1992). Previous researchers variously attributed the success of the Co-op, as the organization is known locally, to external factors: federal assistance programs, a regional crafts revival, specific individuals, and/or the expanding tourist market (e.g., Blankenship, 1987; Hill, 1991; Leftwich, 1970).

Long-term participation in the Qualla Arts and Crafts cooperative by Eastern Band members, however, appears to have been influenced by internal cultural factors as well. It is now considered a point of ethnic pride to be accepted into the organization's membership. This attitude reflects the perception that the Co-op is a Cherokee institution, not just a successful tourist business. The acceptance and esteem accorded

Qualla Arts and Crafts by its membership and by the Eastern Band exists also because its organizational history, structure, programs, and benefits reflect traditional Cherokee values, responses to cultural crisis and change, and historic patterns of crafts production and exchange.

From Trade to Tourism

In *Hosts and Guests: The Anthropology of Tourism,* Valene Smith (1977a) demonstrates that type of visitors (e.g., explorer, elite, offbeat, unusual, incipient mass, mass, charter) and visitor expectations and numbers, all play significant roles in determining how a local culture is affected by tourism. Previous acculturation also plays an important role in indigenous response to tourism. Smith suggests that prior to the onset of incipient mass tourism, when steady visitation becomes important but not central to the local economy, there are few consequential effects on the host group.

For the Cherokees, nearly four hundred years of culture contact with Western societies before the advent of mass tourism made them masters in the transformation of foreign institutional, economic, and technological models to fit the needs of Cherokee society (cf. McLoughlin, 1986; Pillsbury, 1983). In fact, the Cherokees developed cottage industries in several traditional crafts and introduced crafts a century before incipient mass tourism began locally (Duggan and Riggs, 1991; Hill, 1991).

Spanish military expeditions under Hernando DeSoto (1540) and Juan Pardo (1566–1568) are believed to have passed through Cherokee lands (Hudson, 1990). Later, when Europeans established sustained relations with the Cherokees around 1670, the Cherokees controlled a vast territory that stretched over 40,000 square miles of land now included in the states of Virginia, Tennessee, Kentucky, North Carolina, South Carolina, Georgia, and Alabama. Their eighteenth century villages clustered in four distinct locales—the Lower, Valley, Middle, and Overhill Towns—situated near the headwaters of the Savannah, Hiwassee, Tuckasegee, and Little Tennessee Rivers (Mooney, 1900). All Cherokee villages were linked through the tribe's matrilineal clan system (Gilbert, 1943). Social distinctions between these subregions were marked by minor dialect differences and probably by stylistic preferences within certain crafts traditions, such as basketry and pottery (Duggan and Riggs, 1991; Egloff, 1967; King, 1972).

Indigenous crafts produced by the Cherokees in the eighteenth century reflected the mixed economic base of hunting, slash-and-burn agriculture, and gathering that sustained their villages. Cherokee women wove river cane splints into a variety of double and single weave baskets and matting for domestic use and public structures (Duggan and Riggs, 1991). By finger-weaving strands of mulberry bark, bison hair, or opossum hair, and tanning and working hides, they produced clothing for the Principal People, as the Cherokees referred to themselves. Pottery jars and bowls used in Cherokee homes were made by the women. Men of the tribe generally manufactured stone, wooden, and cane tools, such as knives, axes, celts, awls, pipes, and blowguns, which were associated with hunting, land clearing, ritual, and warfare activities (Bloom, 1942).

During the first half of the eighteenth century, the Principal People traded enormous quantities of deerskins and other pelts to the British for imports, such as firearms, metal tools, housewares, salt, rum, looking glasses, pigments, jewelry, cloth, and kaolin pipes (Goodwin, 1977; McDowell, 1955). The introduction of these exotics quickly led to decreased production of some traditional crafts, including stone tools, blowguns, and featherwork (Bloom, 1942). On the other hand, stone pipe manufacturing flourished in the Cherokee villages after Contact (Roberts, 1980; Witthoft, 1949).

A few Cherokee crafts, including double weave baskets, pipes, and native-made blankets, became popular trade items in the British coastal settlements and abroad (Adair, 1775; Bushnell, 1906). Some British manufactured goods in turn became raw material resources for Cherokee craftspeople. Recycled brass, silver, tin, and iron from imported metal implements were refashioned into arrowheads, tools, and jewelry, while glass beads gradually replaced shell, bone, lily seed, and clay bead production (Raymond Fogelson, personal communication, 1994; Harmon, 1986; Newman, 1986).

By the 1790s, reliance on external trade, severe loss of life due to foreign diseases, international and colonial warfare, and land cessions led to the economic and military domination of the Principal People, first by the British and then the Americans (Goodwin, 1977). At the beginning of the nineteenth century, the United States government and missionary societies instituted formal "civilization programs" aimed at enculturating Cherokee adults and children in Western values and skills so that they might become model citizens of the young republic. Influenced by these programs, many Cherokees adopted and modified elements of the Anglo-American agrarian lifestyle, including mastery of associated domestic and mechanical arts (McLoughlin, 1986; Malone, 1956).

By the 1830s, it was not uncommon for a Cherokee farm family to have one or more members who practiced introduced crafts, including loom weaving, spinning, and blacksmithing (McLoughlin and Conser, 1977; Riggs, 1987). Despite these additions, some traditional Cherokee crafts were invigorated by a new barter trade with Anglo-American farmers who were settling within or adjacent to Cherokee lands (Freeman-Witthoft, 1977). One in-progress dissertation, which analyzes Removal Era household inventories and archaeological sites, reveals that many Cherokee families regularly used and/or made traditional pottery and baskets in the 1830s (Brett H. Riggs, personal communication, 1995).

In less than three decades, the Cherokees made remarkable strides in adapting Western agricultural and domestic practices, political and religious institutions, and literacy models to their own social and political needs (McLoughlin, 1986). These accomplishments, however, did not stop certain Anglo-American factions spearheaded by President Andrew Jackson from lobbying for the removal of the Cherokees (and all Eastern tribes) to a new Indian Territory (Oklahoma). In 1838, approximately 16,000 Cherokees were forced to abandon their farms, fields, and personal property to make the 800 mile journey to Indian Territory. At least 4,000 of this number perished waiting in the stockades or en route (Mooney, 1900).

After the "Trail of Tears," as the Cherokees called Removal, only about 1,400 Cherokees remained east of the Mississippi River. The largest enclave, some 700 people, lived in a cluster of dispersed communities on lands in and around the vicinity of modern day Cherokee. Smaller Cherokee settlements were located in southwestern North Carolina, eastern Tennessee, northern Georgia, and in northern Alabama (Finger, 1984).

Most Eastern Cherokees subsisted on the margins of the upland South's economy as small-scale farmers; some hired out as temporary agricultural, timber-industry, or domestic laborers when needs dictated. Widespread peddling of traditional and introduced crafts to Anglo-American farmers and storekeepers became an economic imperative for many Eastern Cherokee families in the second half of the nineteenth century. Extra corn, meat, clothing, and, occasionally, cash were obtained in this manner, especially from bartering basketry. This non-Indian market for Cherokee functional crafts continued well into the twentieth century, until subsistence agriculture declined as the region's economic mainstay (Duggan and Riggs, 1991; Hill, 1991).

Sometimes crafts exchanged in these transactions were second-hand items from Cherokee homes or farmsteads (Duggan and Riggs,

1991). Families and individuals also deliberately stockpiled new goods, including baskets, chairs, and wooden utensils, for long-distance peddling (Greene, 1984; Witthoft, 1979). Occasionally, crafts, such as river cane baskets, were made on the spot for customers during trips (cf. Armstrong, 1842–49). Certain modifications to traditional forms, including the addition of handles to smaller river cane baskets, may have been made specifically to fit the tastes and needs of Anglo-American customers (Duggan and Riggs, 1991).

A few elite tourists ventured into Cherokee settlements during the eighteenth and nineteenth centuries (e.g., Bartram, 1791; Davis, 1875; Lanman, 1849). These isolated visits, however, probably had little impact on the Eastern Cherokee economy or lifeways. A new kind of visitor, one who took great interest in native crafts, did enter the Eastern Cherokee domain shortly after the Civil War. This was the museum collector-ethnologist.

The Smithsonian Institution's Bureau of American Ethnology sent Edward Palmer to the Cherokee settlements in 1881, and then sponsored a series of trips by ethnologist, James Mooney, beginning in 1887. Both obtained examples of traditional and introduced crafts, as well as ritual paraphernalia (Duggan and Riggs, 1991). The work of these and later ethnologists indicate that only a handful of specialists in traditional pottery-making, the difficult double weave basketry technique, and stone pipe carving remained active around the turn of the twentieth century (Fewkes, 1944; Harrington, 1909; Speck, 1920).[2]

The federal Indian Office began urging Native Americans to produce tribal crafts for commercial sale to tourists and collectors about this time (Schrader, 1983). Soon there was clear economic incentive for the Cherokees to explore this possibility. A succession of critical events—the opening of a railroad spur line into Cherokee, North Carolina in 1909, the appearance of automobiles in western North Carolina in 1914, and the founding of the annual Cherokee Indian Fair, also in 1914—broke the relative isolation of the local Indian settlements. A handicrafts revival spreading through western North Carolina also drew the attention and money of well-heeled, urban dwellers to the region.[3]

At first, a few wealthy tourists from Asheville and other fashionable mountain resorts took one-day railroad trips to the town of Cherokee. New roads into the area soon allowed more people to attend the Cherokee Indian Fair each fall, making it one of the area's most popular events (Chiltoskey, 1979; Finger, 1991; Law and Taylor, 1991). By the mid-1920s, cash prizes and sales at the Fair offered tribal craftspeople a seasonal alternative to the shrinking agricultural barter trade (Duggan and Riggs, 1991). Incipient mass tourism had come to Cherokee.

The new regional tourist market, which placed the Eastern Cherokees in competition with Appalachian craftspeople, accelerated change in some Cherokee crafts during the first quarter of the twentieth century. For instance, in their basketry tradition several new forms were borrowed from Anglo-American and European sources, and elaboration in color combinations and design fields occurred on traditional forms. Materials preparation and technical execution sometimes suffered as basket weavers increased their tempo to meet the demands of the expanding clientele who now sought them out and paid in much needed cash (Duggan and Riggs, 1991).

The Great Depression devastated the economies of many Indian reservations; conditions were particularly grim for the Eastern Cherokees. Crafts production for the fledgling tourist market became even more important for many families. A 1931 census of 475 Cherokees found that most were subsistence farmers who earned little money, but 25 basket weavers, 30 bead workers, and 20 potters did supplement their families' cash incomes (Page, 1931). In fact, the average annual income of basket weavers that year was higher than that of others interviewed. Another study conducted later in the decade identified a number of Cherokees who worked steadily at a craft, including 21 basket weavers, 11 bow makers, 2 blowgun makers, 16 potters, and 13 bead workers (Bloom, 1945). The formal establishment of the Great Smoky National Park in 1934, and the promise of increased tourism after its projected opening, probably seemed especially appealing to these craftspeople. The Eastern Band, however, was determined to benefit from park visitation on its own terms, and swiftly rejected a government plan to include their people as a tourist attraction within the national park boundaries (Finger, 1991; Perdue, 1989).

During the 1930s, federal assistance became available to Native Americans through the "Indian New Deal" programs instituted by the Commissioner of Indian Affairs, John Collier. Abandoning decades of assimilationist policies, these programs sought to help native peoples regain control over their lands, economies, and lifeways (Schrader, 1983). On Eastern Cherokee lands, roads and bridges were built, truck and horse trails repaired, and the tribal offices and boarding school facilities expanded by Cherokee laborers employed through New Deal programs (cf. *The Smoky Mountain*, 1934; Finger, 1991).

In keeping with the spirit of New Deal philosophy, which placed considerable emphasis on cooperative ventures, the Bureau of Indian Affairs (BIA) superintendent for the Eastern Cherokees suggested that the tribal council operate a cooperatively-owned hotel, crafts shop, trading post, gas station, store, canning factory, and camping facilities.

This plan was contested vigorously by some private landowners, and by county officials who saw the proposed cooperatives as threats to their own tourism plans (Bauer, 1970; Stucki, 1984).

While many Indian New Deal recommendations did not materialize, one of Collier's programs was extremely important to Eastern Cherokee craftspeople. This was the Indian Arts and Crafts Board (IACB) (cf. Schrader, 1983). The Eastern Band of Cherokees became one of the first clients of this new federal agency, which had a mandate to assist native leaders to develop crafts training and work programs, set authenticity standards, and operate sales outlets that reflected and met local needs (Robert Hart, personal communication, 1992; Richmond, 1987).

Local interest in Cherokee arts and crafts production and preservation was already in place. Just prior to the Depression, the Eastern Band tribal council had set aside $500 "for perfecting an organization known as 'handcraftworkers among the Indians of the Eastern Band of Cherokees'" (Eastern Band, 1927). On April 1, 1932 "the Cherokee Indians," after submitting "examples of their work, including basketry, pottery, bows and arrows, blow-guns, and Indian game materials," were admitted to membership in the Southern Highland Handicraft Guild (Eaton, 1937:247). One reference suggests that a Cherokee Guild affiliate operated a shop next to the tribal offices in 1933 (Southern Highland, 1958). Several senior Cherokees craftspeople who produced crafts during the period, however, attest that no official tribal crafts organization existed at that time, and that there was never a Guild shop in Cherokee.

In the mid-1930s representatives of the Eastern Band of Cherokees, BIA, Department of Agriculture, and IACB pushed for the addition of crafts instruction to the curriculum of the Cherokee Boarding School.[4] The program for students and adults which resulted featured classes in basketry, woodworking and carving, bead work, loom weaving, and metal work, taught by tribal craftspeople as well as non-Indian crafts professionals. Later, a small sales outlet was opened at the school to cater to tourists who routinely included the facility on their Cherokee visit (Arnold, 1952; Mollie Blankenship and G. B. Chiltoskey, personal communications, 1993, 1995).

The long anticipated surge in tourism finally occurred with the end of gas rationing and the onset of a post-World War II economic boom that sent an expanded American middle class out in their automobiles in search of leisure-time activities. Cherokee was catapulted into the arena of mass tourism (Finger, 1991). Many private, mostly non-Indian, investors acquired long-term leases from the Eastern Band and erected shops and motels on tribal land, especially during the early 1960s (Hill, 1991; Kupferer, 1966). Heaviest development occurred in the Yellow Hill community, although today even more remote Big Cove has a few, Cherokee-owned seasonal campgrounds.

Entrepreneurs have competed aggressively for a share of the expanding tourist market in Cherokee. As early as 1946, businesses employed the stereotypic Plains Indian advertising motif that tourists often associate with "real Indians." To lure customers, these owners hired Cherokee men to pose as "chiefs" beside teepees located outside shop doorways. Inside, many offered fake Indian souvenirs manufactured in Asia alongside inexpensive Cherokee-made souvenirs (Ballas, 1962; Finger, 1991; Stucki, 1984). Today, this type of business persists, blended with newer tourist meccas—specialty shops, bargain outlets, games and diversion parks, restaurants, and motels—all leading up to the national park entrance sign at the edge of town. While the Eastern Band of Cherokees derives fees from these private enterprises, a much larger percentage of the tribe's income today is derived from tribally-owned or sponsored industries, service contract operations, and bingo and gambling enterprises. The Band uses profits from these activities to enhance their social, educational, and medical programs.

The Qualla Arts and Crafts Mutual, Inc.

In 1946 fifty-three Cherokee craftspeople organized the Cherokee Indian Crafts Co-op.[5] A number of the founders had participated in the Cherokee Boarding School crafts program, or sold through its sale shop. Nearly half of the early Co-op members were female basket weavers. Other early members produced wood carvings and sculptures, woven textiles, pottery, rag dolls, base and precious metal articles, and beadwork (Arnold, 1952; Blankenship, 1987; Duggan and Riggs, 1991). Perhaps as many as three-quarters of the founders spoke Cherokee or were bilingual, indicating a high degree of cultural conservatism in the early membership (Mollie Blankenship, personal communication, 1995; also cf. Gulick, 1960). Membership soon included people from all of the Cherokee area communities and the Snowbird settlement fifty miles to the south (Flanagan, 1955–1961).

Qualla Arts and Crafts was a financial success from the beginning, grossing $7,000 during its first year of operation. Seven years later the organization was debt-free. For the first few years, the Co-op was technically under BIA supervision because federal funds were used in the start-up (Qualla Arts and Crafts, 1955). In 1954 the cooperative incorporated under a North Carolina charter as a non-profit organization called the Qualla Arts and Crafts Mutual, Inc. That year it had a net worth of $31,000. Three years later, when the Co-op joined the Cherokee Chamber of Commerce and the Cherokee Better Business Association, membership included 176 craftspeople. In 1960, the group marked two more milestones: a land donation and a loan from the Cherokee Tribal Council allowed Qualla Arts and Crafts to build its own permanent shop and storage facility; and, the Co-op assisted senior members for the first time to register for Social Security benefits as self-employed workers (Blankenship, 1987; Flanagan, 1955–1961; Indian Arts, 1965; Qualla Arts and Crafts, 1955).

Since its founding, formal decisions about the governance and management of Qualla Arts and Crafts have been approved through an executive board, shop manager, and/or general membership that consists of Cherokees only. However, in the Co-op's early years, the Indian Arts and Crafts Board, the BIA's Cherokee Agency, the crafts program at the Cherokee Boarding School, as well as the Eastern Band played supportive roles (Blankenship, 1987; Hill, 1991; Indian Arts, 1965).

The Indian Arts and Crafts Board's first Southeastern field representative had been employed by the BIA as a home economics teacher and crafts advisor at the Cherokee Boarding School since the 1930s (Robert Hart, personal communication, 1992; Hill, 1991). She interpreted the IACB's directive for technical assistance very broadly, and supervised the Eastern Cherokee manager and staff on-site in day-to-day matters during the Co-op's first decade (cf. Flanagan, 1955–1961; Shearin, 1965). In contrast, the second (and final) IACB field representative served as an *ad hoc* advisor and facilitator when called upon by the Cherokee executive and management staffs (Robert Hart and Stephen Richmond, personal communications, 1992; Richmond, 1987).

This shift to solely Cherokee direction occurred in the early 1960s, a period in which tourism increased dramatically in the region. A number of changes were also instituted at this time. A new pricing structure, training workshops taught by senior craftspeople,[6] extra display space, an interpretive exhibit, and an inter-tribal sales area were added to the organization's programs and shop facilities (Blankenship, 1987; *The Cherokee One Feather*, 1975; Indian Arts, 1965). During the past three decades, revenues and membership in the Co-op have grown steadily. Currently, 335 Cherokee craftspeople belong to Qualla Arts and Crafts (Betty DuPree, personal communications, 1995).

Through the years, income derived from crafts sales through the Co-op have helped many Eastern Cherokees provide necessities and educational expenses for their families. Today, Co-op members are often employed part-time or full-time in seasonal tourist, tribal government, or off-reservation jobs. Crafts production and sales, however, continue to provide an important source of income for many members, as well as a significant means for expressing creativity. Some cooperative members also sell additional crafts to tourists directly from their homes, through work as crafts demonstrators at the reconstructed historic village, or through privately owned shops in Cherokee.

The Co-op's Emergence as a Cherokee Institution

Qualla Arts and Crafts members readily acknowledge the importance of external factors in the initiation and growth of their cooperative. Technical support from federal agencies was critical during the Co-op's first decade, and steady growth in visitation to the Great Smoky Mountains National Park provided economic incentive for Cherokee craftspeople to apply for the organization's juried membership. In addition, the distribution network of Qualla Arts and Crafts, which includes a number of museum shops and crafts events, has brought the work of selected craftspeople to the attention of national and international audiences (Duggan and Riggs, 1991; cf. Qualla Arts and Crafts, 1987).

Internal cultural factors have also played an important part in the long-term success of the Co-op. The emphasis placed on cooperation and mutual aid in the traditional Cherokee value system and economic institutions helps to explain continued participation in a cooperative organization, rather than the development of a business based on more individualistic entrepreneurial goals. Current members consider Qualla Arts and Crafts a Cherokee institution, not simply the outgrowth of a federal experiment, or just another sales outlet. It is seen as an honor to be invited into the organization's ranks.

One founding member explained this viewpoint: "The young people are inspired to belong to Qualla. This inspiration to continue these crafts is one of their goals." Another early member said, "Qualla keeps our crafts together. Its about the best thing we [Eastern Cherokees] ever done" (Anonymous informants, personal communications, 1993). These statements imply that for many Cherokees, acceptance and participation in the Co-op connotes a sense of continuity with the Cherokee past and an active expression of contemporary Cherokee ethnicity. This sentiment is sometimes stated publicly, as in this excerpt from the tribal newspaper:

> Qualla Arts and Crafts Mutual, Inc., has been primarily responsible for keeping alive the arts and crafts of the Eastern Band of Cherokee Indians. To do this, they have, first of all, encouraged the artists and

craftsmen to be creative in adapting their traditional arts and crafts to
meet the needs of the modern American society (*The Cherokee One
Feather*, 1975).

While economic success accounts for some of this ethnic pride in
Qualla Arts and Crafts, at a deeper level, it may also be rooted in the fact
that the Co-op's programs and benefits echo important Cherokee values. The late anthropologist Robert K. Thomas, a Western Cherokee
who conducted fieldwork among the Eastern Cherokees during the
1950s, characterized the central Cherokee values in the following way:

> The Cherokee tries to maintain harmonious interpersonal relation-
> ships with his fellow Cherokee by avoiding giving offense, on the neg-
> ative side, and by giving of himself to his fellow Cherokee in regard to
> his time and his mutual goods, on the positive side (Thomas, 1958:1).

Thomas also observed that harmonious relations were a minimal
behavioral standard for Cherokees, rather than an ideal behavior as
in Anglo-American society.

In the public arena, these key values are often enacted through the
expected, generous sharing of time and goods, especially through cooperative endeavors. No institution better epitomizes this than the
gadugi, or communal work groups, which labored for the economic
well-being of all members (Thomas, 1958). Cherokee woodcarver and
long-time Co-op member, Going Back Chiltoskey (personal communication, 1993) translated this word for me as: "a company of people; to
come together; to keep together." These three meanings reflect the nu-
ances of cooperative behavior in the public and private spheres for
Cherokees.

In the eighteenth century Cherokee village, many agricultural
tasks, such as the clearing, planting, and reaping of family garden plots,
were carried out by gadugi under the direction of the town chief. The
local gadugi also erected private and public buildings and assisted
other such work groups in nearby settlements. At the end of each harvest season every family was expected to give a portion of their harvest
to the town's emergency storehouse, just as the adults males of the
household were expected to contribute their labor to gadugi activities
throughout the year. This system of cooperative labor survived essentially unchanged among the Eastern Cherokees until the 1890s (Fogelson and Kutsche, 1961; Speck and Schaeffer, 1945).

Around the turn of the twentieth century, Eastern Cherokee gadugi
began to hire out as wage labor gangs to Anglo-American farmers and,
later, to timber companies as the local economy changed. During this

phase, the various gadugi elected officers, divided annual profits among members, and dispensed temporary loans to members from a common treasury. Even though gadugi now worked for non-Cherokees for cash, the primary function of the institution remained the exchange of services for the mutual economic benefit of all members. About this time, many of the social welfare responsibilities of the gadugi, such as care for the aged and infirm, help with disaster relief and funeral assistance, were shifted to separate community poor-aid societies (Fogelson and Kutsche, 1961; Speck and Schaeffer, 1945).

In 1961, Big Cove, considered the most culturally conservative of the Cherokee area communities, had three active gadugi, including one which still provided both economic and social aid (Fogelson and Kutsche, 1961). Gadugi may continue to function in a modified way today in the conservative Snowbird community in Graham County, North Carolina (Neely, 1991).[7] Many of the mutual aid functions once carried out by the gadugi organizations, however, are now implemented through a network of neighborhood and tribal-level institutions that includes community clubs, churches, and the Cherokee Boys Club (Fogelson and Kutsche, 1961).[8]

Qualla Arts and Crafts is functionally and structurally reminiscent of the gadugi institutions in a number of ways, although Co-op members point out there is no direct historical link to them. Now that tourism has replaced agriculture as the economic mainstay of the Cherokees, the Co-op provides Cherokee craftspeople with a new means to pool their skills and resources for the economic betterment of all their members and for the tribe. In 1946, this would have been particularly appealing to founders who grew up experiencing benefits of gadugi in their neighborhoods or among kin.

From a different perspective, the creation of the Co-op provides an example of another way in which cooperative behavior is traditionally used to accomplish community and tribal goals among Cherokees. Albert Wahrhaftig (1975), who studied tribal Cherokee communities in eastern Oklahoma, demonstrated that institutional innovation occurs among traditionalist Cherokees when they believe that action must be taken to protect valued tribal lifeways. If a situation occurs that threatens an important social or cultural feature, institutional change is frequently accomplished by adding educational, economic, charitable, or recreational features onto an already existing institution, such as a community church or stomp dance ground. Novel solutions and factional alliances sometimes result from this practice.

The establishment of the Great Smoky Mountains National Park simultaneously presented a potential economic boon and yet a possible threat to existing Cherokee lifeways. In response to this anticipated increase in tourism, members of the Eastern Band forged an alliance with representatives of federal and tribal agencies to exert control over how this event would effect their craftspeople. This led first to the addition of crafts classes to the existing Cherokee Boarding School curriculum. Within a few years, this action, coupled with the financial success of a small sales outlet at the school, stimulated the revival of the Cherokee basketry tradition. In less than a decade, these institutional innovations led to the founding of a new native economic institution, Qualla Arts and Crafts.

On the surface, the organizational structure of the Co-op resembles the parliamentary model of Anglo-American institutions, with a slate of elected officials headed by a president. However, Co-op officers are not perceived as part of a hierarchical chain of command. Instead, officers constitute an Executive Committee which, along with numerous other standing and special committees, share responsibility for the organization and enact the collective will of the Co-op's membership. Discussion and negotiation ensue in public committee and general membership meetings, as well as behind the scenes and even by mail, until a consensus is reached on important issues or changes. Minutes of meetings normally record motions passed unanimously, or "without dissent," not by simple majority rule as in Anglo-American procedure (Betty DuPree, personal communication, 1992; Indian Arts, 1965; Qualla Arts and Crafts, 1955).

The basis for this style of governance and approach to the distribution of power again may be rooted in Cherokee tradition. Thomas (1958) observed that among culturally conservative Cherokees it is considered immoral, and a sure source of offense, for one Cherokee to wield power over another. For this reason, he said, the Cherokees are committee "mad" (1958:8) in public matters and organizations. As was the custom in aboriginal Cherokee village councils (Gearing, 1962), more traditional Cherokees also prefer to defer decision-making, or even withdraw from participation temporarily, until unanimity is assured (cf. Gulick 1960).

Day-to-day operation of the Co-op (including buying, marketing, benefits allocation, and training and educational programs) is implemented through the cooperative's manager and staff, who, one might say, operate as yet another committee. These individuals form an interface between cooperative members, who range from traditional to contemporary artists, and interested outsiders, who include potential customers, journalists, researchers, and crafts exposition developers. The present manager, who has held the position since the 1960s, is known for her broad knowledge of Cherokee crafts and as a skilled businesswoman. Taken as a team (or committee), the manager and staff have ties to most Eastern Cherokee social groups and communities.

A primary adaptive strategy for the Cherokees historically has been the use of intermediaries to deal with situations of potential crisis or conflict that threaten traditional values or lifeways (Kupferer, 1966). One renowned example was the use of Western-educated, bicultural or highly acculturated Cherokees as go-betweens by conservative local leaders of the old Cherokee Nation in their dealings with the federal government in the 1820s-1830s. Similarly, Eastern Cherokee tribal and community leaders granted their Anglo-American business advisor great power in negotiations between themselves and government officials after the Trail of Tears, but not in local matters. The Qualla Arts and Crafts organization and its management also act as intermediaries. They must interpret and balance traditional limitations placed on aesthetics and production patterns in the various Cherokees crafts with expectations of customers, who may be tourists, art collectors, non-Indian educational or cultural institutions, or Eastern Cherokees.

In 1952, the president of the Co-op listed the organization's main purposes as "(1) to encourage better quality crafts, (2) to provide a year round market, (3) to increase income of craftsmen by paying him [sic] a fair price for his work" (Arnold, 1952:6). These goals reflect a strong influence from the Indian Arts and Crafts Board's charter (cf. Schafer, 1983). However, the specific manner in which they have been implemented by the Co-op follow a distinctly Cherokee pattern. This may be one reason for the organization's success in fulfilling their original objectives, something which long-time members believe has occurred.

Traditional Cherokee concerns about non-competitiveness, respect for elders,[9] and ways for dealing with mutual aid during times of economic and personal distress can be seen in several Co-op programs and benefits. Training and marketing practices have simply been added onto the informal system of folk instruction and family-based production and distribution that have characterized the manufacture of Cherokee crafts for generations. For example, promotional efforts, demonstrations, workshops, and exhibitions generally feature respected elders who have proven their skill over a lifetime, or family groups who work within the same craft tradition (cf., Duggan and Riggs, 1991; Indian Arts, 1965; Qualla Arts and Crafts, 1987). By defining "authenticity" for juried membership standards broadly to include both traditional crafts and reintegrated foreign crafts (cf., Graburn, 1976), Qualla Arts and Crafts fosters the dynamic nature that has characterized and preserved Cherokee crafts traditions for more than four centuries (cf., Duggan and Riggs, 1991). While quality control standards exist for each craft, there is enough leeway in the buying and pricing structures (e.g., merchandise ranges from good quality, inexpensive souvenirs to *objets d'art*) to allow craftspeople with different levels of expertise to benefit from sales.

Benefits for Co-op members include ones common to many cooperatives, and others that appear to reflect adaptations to local circumstances and Cherokee values. Buying practices allow members to have a reliable income source throughout the year, not just during the peak tourist season. Craftspeople are paid immediately for work purchased; however, they are directed to private shops that are buying when the Co-op has a stock surplus in their craft, or items do not meet the cooperative's standards. Members also accumulate equity in the cooperative, receive biannual dividends and periodic equity payments based on the profits their wares have generated, and all members receive a three percent equity payment each Christmas (Betty DuPree, personal communications, 1991; *The Cherokee One Feather*, 1975). Retired members continue to draw equity. When an active or retired member dies, heirs are assisted with funeral costs, and then receive any remaining equity accumulated by the deceased. On a more informal basis, in the case of a craftsperson facing a medical emergency or other extenuating circumstances, the Co-op may make extra purchases or allow additional equity draw-outs (Betty DuPree, personal communications, 1991; *The Cherokee One Feather*, 1975).

Conclusions

The rise of mass consumption in Western societies in conjunction with the development of a global economy after World War II has elevated tourism from the pastime of select individuals to a billion dollar industry (Jules-Rosette, 1984; Pi-Sunyer, 1982). Tourism of this magnitude acts as a powerful agent of social change for both local cultures and the visitors who come seeking leisure, entertainment, and/or knowledge of the "exotic other" (Graburn, 1977; Smith, 1977b). Negative effects of opportunistic mass tourism—overcrowding, labor shortages, prostitution, crime, environmental degradation, and loss or replacement of authentic cultural traditions—now unfortunately appear worldwide (cf., MacCannell, 1984; Oliver-Smith, et al., 1989; Parlow, 1976).

Other research suggests that mass tourism has the potential to create new jobs, encourage economic growth in other sectors, raise tax revenues, and foster understanding and better relations between different cultures. When introduced gradually with local cultural groups actively involved in planning and decision-making, tourism has produced positive results. In some cases, culturally informed tourism development has led to increased ethnic pride, and even cultural revitalization, among indigenous peoples (cf., Esman, 1984; Graburn, 1969; Swain, 1977).

In Cherokee, North Carolina, opportunistic tourism is immediately apparent along its highways. Commercial enterprises flagrantly vie to out-advertise competitors. A less visible negative effect of tourism is the fact that employment opportunities are mainly in low-skill, low-wage, seasonal jobs. Off-season unemployment rates among the Eastern Cherokees frequently soar to thirty or forty percent (Finger, 1991; French and Hornbuckle, 1981). Today, several tribally-owned industries or tribally-sanctioned enterprises, including Qualla Arts and Crafts, work to provide year-round income sources for Eastern Band members. A few private and religious-based crafts enterprises share this goal.

The Cherokees experienced several centuries of acculturation and external trade in their crafts traditions before incipient mass tourism began for them during the first quarter of the twentieth century. This earlier experience in producing crafts for a non-Cherokee market gained over many generations, when combined with New Deal initiatives and increased regional tourism, inspired a revival in Eastern Cherokee arts and crafts, including the formation of a tribal cooperative.

Qualla Arts and Crafts benefited greatly from federal and tribal assistance over the years, especially from the Indian Arts and Crafts Board. The Eastern Band of Cherokees, a society in which cooperation and mutual aid are core values for individuals and indigenous institutions, became one of the first clients of this federal agency which, itself, was created in a political and intellectual climate that revered cooperative ventures (cf., Howell, 1991; Mertz, 1978). This collaboration of like minds led to the development of a cooperative organization firmly rooted in traditional Cherokee values and New Deal idealism.

Folklorist Janet Becker (1990) recently examined the first decade of existence of the Southern Highland Handicraft Guild, another twentieth century cooperative venture headquartered in Asheville, North Carolina, about an hour away from Cherokee. This successful organization is a federation of crafts cooperatives and craftspeople in the Southern Appalachian region which was founded in 1929. Its original purposes were to preserve and revive Appalachian crafts and home-based production patterns.

Becker notes, however, that in an effort to increase income for craftspeople, the Southern Highland Handicraft Guild profoundly affected the nature and meaning of local crafts by encouraging the manufacture of articles designed to appeal to the tastes of urban consumers and tourists. Detailed instructions from professional designers to members, who often labored in workshop settings, led to the creation of recognizable "Southern Highlands" style objects, which then were marketed as "authentic" mountain crafts. Today, many of the Guild's members are professionally trained artists and crafts specialists, rather than traditional craftspeople of the region.

Increased production of Cherokee arts and crafts for consumption by tourists and collectors followed a very different route. Members of the Eastern Band of Cherokees joined with federal representatives to first create a crafts education program for their secondary school and later a tribal crafts cooperative when it became evident that mass tourism was at hand. The cooperative that emerged is an institution whose structure, programs, and benefits are rooted in traditional Cherokee values and production patterns, yet informed by centuries of economic exchange with Western societies. Qualla Arts and Crafts has built a reliable, economically improved marketplace for Cherokee craftspeople, raised production standards, and encouraged preservation of traditional crafts. Yet, it has not discouraged members from individually experimenting with new materials and forms, or from participating in alternate local and regional markets, where seasonal demand, pricing, and standards may vary widely.

Anthropologist Sharlotte Neely (1991) suggests that in the conservative Cherokee community of Snowbird, crafts are an integral part of a chain of signals that marks the ethnic and social boundaries between themselves and non-Cherokees. The Qualla Arts and Crafts Mutual Inc., through its role as widely-known and respected purveyor of the material symbols of Cherokee culture to the outside world, also plays a pivotal, public role in reinforcing modern Cherokee identity for all tribal members. In the private sphere, individual Co-op members, who produce for tourist and art markets, also fashion crafts that are used by fellow Cherokees as personal adornment, gifts, keepsakes, and religious paraphernalia (Duggan and Riggs, 1991).[10]

The Qualla Arts and Crafts Mutual, Inc. has experienced remarkable financial success in tapping into the mass tourism market that burgeoned in Cherokee, North Carolina after World War II. The organization's ability to recognize traditional economic and social values that underlie and reinforce continued production of Cherokee crafts has contributed significantly to its emergence as the oldest and most successful Native American crafts cooperative in the United States. In both respects, the Co-op provides a fine example of the positive economic and social benefits that tourism can engender when it is culturally informed and indigenously controlled.

Acknowledgments

I owe special thanks to Benita Howell who asked me to present a paper on this topic in her symposium at the 1992 Southern Anthropological Society meeting, and then brought my work to Erve Chambers' attention. Qualla Arts and Crafts Mutual, Inc. members—Betty DuPree (manager), Mollie Blankenship (founding member), G. B. Chiltoskey (early member and former school crafts instructor), and Robin Swaney (staff)—provided crucial information and comments. Drs. Howell, Raymond Fogelson and John Finger, as well as fellow graduate students, Brett Riggs and Maureen Hays, gave insightful comments on various drafts. Numerous discussions with Brett, during preparation of a jointly edited publication on Cherokee basketry, greatly informed the present work. Robert Hart (director) and Stephen Richmond (retired Southeastern field representative) explained Indian Arts and Crafts Board and inter-agency contributions. Hart also provided copies of early field reports. Joan Greene, Museum of the Cherokee Indian archivist, brought several important documents to my attention. Celine O'Brien of the Southern Highland Handicraft Guild kindly checked their files for references to the Co-op.

Notes

1. The first three attractions were created over the years by the Cherokee Historical Association (CHA), a non-profit organization originally started in 1947 by a consortium of primarily non-Indian businessmen and county governments in Western Carolina. All three CHA attractions employ numerous Eastern Cherokees seasonally, and a few on a full-time basis. The museum, which opened in 1976, is governed by a board of directors that includes an equal number of Eastern Band and CHA representatives. In recent years scholars have questioned the historical accuracy of the CHA's popular outdoor drama (Finger, 1979, 1991; King, 1979; Stucki, 1984).

2. Mooney (1900) reports that the Cherokee pottery tradition was almost extinct by the end of nineteenth century, having been replaced by Catawba pottery introduced by members of that tribe who lived among the Eastern Cherokees for a time. Harrington (1908, 1909) and Fewkes (1944) describe

the differences in manufacture and style between the two traditions. Bloom (1945) found that only one of the sixteen full-time Eastern Cherokee potters that he interviewed during the 1930s produced traditional Cherokee pottery. The rest followed the Catawba tradition.

3. Early Cherokee fairs featured both Appalachian and Cherokee music, performance, and crafts, but after a few years participation in this annual fall event was restricted to Cherokee-only performers, demonstrators, agricultural displays, and crafts competitions (Chiltoskey, 1979). For discussion of the Handicrafts Revival, crafts cooperatives and guilds, and folk festivals in the Southern Highlands during the same period, see Davidson (1989), Duggan and Riggs (1991), Eaton (1937), Hill (1991), Law and Taylor (1991), Shapiro (1978), and Whisnant (1983). One survey, which excluded the Cherokees, indicates that at least 10,000 "mountain people" were working through 105 craft centers in the Southern Appalachian region in 1933 (Becker, 1990).

4. Various researchers and Eastern Cherokees attribute development of the school's crafts program to the sponsorship of one or more of these groups (cf., Finger, 1991; Hill, 1991; Indian Arts, 1965). Discussions with Robert Hart (IACB), Steve Richmond (former IACB Southeastern field representative), and members of the Co-op strongly suggest to me that the school program resulted from a broad-based initiative.

5. Several different original membership counts have been published. These vary from a low of fifty (Flanagan, 1955–1956) to a high of sixty people (Chiltoskey, 1979; Hill, 1991). My count is based on an early handwritten list on file at the Qualla Arts and Crafts office (Qualla Arts, n.d.).

6. In the mid-1960s, the IACB even arranged for Cherokee instructors in river cane basketry and woodworking to conduct workshops with Choctaw craftspeople in Mississippi (Indian Arts, 1965).

7. Two elderly residents of Big Cove told me in 1994 that formal gadugi no longer operate in that community, although kin often join together to plant gardens and accomplish other labor intensive tasks around their homes and neighborhoods. Sharlotte Neely (1991), ethnographer of the conservative Cherokee community of Snowbird in Graham County, North Carolina, believes that the Snowbird Community Development Club has absorbed the public functions of formal gadugi locally. She says, however, that gadugi in the sense of "working together" still continue, often with former gadugi officers taking an active role. In 1993, a middle-aged member of this community told me in passing that there were still gadugi in Snowbird. It was not clear in the context of that conversation which meaning she used.

8. The Cherokee Boys Club is a non-profit organization that is now designated as a Cherokee Tribal Enterprise. It began in 1932 as a student organization at the Cherokee Boarding School. Today, it runs many on- and off-reservation social and economic programs once operated by the fed-

eral government. These include management of the tribal children's home, food pantry, hospital laundry service, and the Cherokee school system, as well as trash collection for the Great Smoky Mountains National Park (Hill 1991).

9. Like the leaders of the ancient village peace councils, Co-op officers, demonstrators, and classroom crafts instructors are often senior experts respected for their traditional knowledge and skill. Gilbert (1943) and Marino (1988) have addressed the place that respect for elders is accorded in Cherokee society.

10. This is true, in particular, for Cherokee baskets, which Duggan and Riggs (1991) argue are the most prominent material symbol of tribal identity employed by Eastern Cherokees today. Tribal members routinely use native baskets and matting in a variety of situations and ways, such as purses, diaper bags, household storage containers, cherished heirlooms, gifts, and as altar decorations and collection plates in at least one church.

References

Adair, James. (1775). *History of the American Indians*. London.

Armstrong, Drury Paine. (1842–49). Diary. Typewritten copy of original manuscript on file, McClung Historical Collection, Lawson McGhee Library, Knoxville, Tennessee. 182 pp.

Arnold, Dorothy Andora. (1952). Some Recent Contributions of the Cherokee Indians of North Carolina to the Crafts of the Southern Highlands. Unpublished M. S. thesis, Knoxville: The University of Tennessee.

Ballas, Donald J. (1962). The Livelihood of the Eastern Cherokees. *The Journal of Geography*, 61 (November):342–50.

Bartram, William. (1791). *Travels through North & South Carolina, Georgia, East & West Florida, the Cherokee Country, the Extensive Territories of the Muscogulges, or Creek Confederacy, and the Country of the Chactaws*. Philadelphia: James & Johnson.

Bauer, Fred B. (1970). *Land of the North Carolina Cherokees*. George E. Buchanan, Brevard, North Carolina.

Becker, Jane S. (1990). Selling Tradition: The Southern Highland Handicraft Guild and Southern Mountain Culture, 1929–1942. Paper presented at the annual meeting of the American Folklore Society, Oakland, California.

Blankenship, Mollie. (1987). History of Qualla Arts and Crafts Mutual, Inc. In *Contemporary Artists and Craftsmen of the Eastern Band of Cherokee Indians*, pp. viii.Cherokee, North Carolina: Qualla Arts and Crafts Mutual, Inc.

Bloom, Leonard.
    (1942). The Acculturation of the Cherokee: Historical Aspects. *The North Carolina Historical Review,* 19 (4):323–358.

    (1945). A Measure of Conservatism. *American Anthropologist,* 47:630–35.

Bushnell, David I., Jr. (1906). The Sloane Collection in the British Museum. *American Anthropologist,* 8(n.s.):671–685.

Chiltoskey, Mary Ulmer. (1979). *Cherokee Fair & Festival: A History thru 1978.* Asheville, North Carolina: Gilbert Printing Company.

Davidson, Jan. (1989). Introduction. In *Mountain Homespun,* Frances Louisa Goodrich, pp. 1–47. Reprint. The University of Tennessee Press. Originally published 1931, New Haven, Connecticut: Yale University Press.

Davis, Rebecca Harding. (1875). Qualla. *Lippincott's Magazine of Popular Literature and Science,* 41 (November):576–86.

Duggan, Betty J. and Brett H. Riggs. (1991). Cherokee Basketry: An Evolving Tradition. In *Studies in Cherokee Basketry,* Betty J. Duggan and Brett H. Riggs, (Eds.). *Occasional Paper* No. 9, pp. 22–52. The Frank H. McClung Museum, The University of Tennessee, Knoxville.

Eaton, Allen H. (1937). *Handicrafts of the Southern Highlands.* New York: Dover Publications.

Eastern Band of Cherokees. (1927). Tribal Minutes, February 1, 1927. Microfilm copy on file, Museum of the Cherokee Indian, Cherokee, North Carolina.

Egloff, Brian T. (1967). An Analysis of Ceramics from Historic Cherokee Towns. Unpublished M. A. thesis, Department of Anthropology, University of North Carolina, Chapel Hill.

Esman, Majorie E. (1984). Tourism as Ethnic Preservation: The Cajuns of Louisiana. *Annals of Tourism Research,* 11:451–467.

Fewkes, Vladimir J. (1944). Catawba Pottery-Making, with Notes on Pamunkey Pottery-Making, Cherokee Pottery-Making, and Coiling. *Proceedings of the American Philosophical Society,* 88:69–124.

Finger, John R.
    (1984) *The Eastern Band of Cherokees 1819–1900.* Knoxville: The University of Tennessee Press.

    (1991) *Cherokee Americans: The Eastern Band of Cherokees in the Twentieth Century.* Lincoln: University of Nebraska Press.

Flanagan, Gertrude C. (1955–1961) Annual Reports of Gertrude C. Flanagan, Specialist, Indian Arts & Crafts Board. Manuscripts on file. United States Department of Interior, Indian Arts and Crafts Board, Washington, D. C.

Fogelson, Raymond and Paul Kutsche. (1961). Cherokee Economic Cooperatives: The Gadugi. In *Symposium on Cherokee and Iroquois Culture,* William N. Fenton and John Gulick, editors. *Smithsonian Institution, Bureau of American Ethnology, Bulletin,* 180, pp. 83–123, *Paper* 11. Washington, D. C.: U. S. Government Printing Office.

Freeman-Witthoft, Bonita. (1977). Cherokee Indian Craftswomen and the Economy of Basketry. *Expedition,* 19(3):17–27.

French, Larry. (1977). Tourism and Indian Exploitation: A Social Indictment. *The Indian Historian,* 10(4):19–24.

French, Larry and Jim Hornbuckle. (1981). The Cherokee—Then and Now. In *The Cherokee Perspective,* Larry French and Jim Hornbuckle, editors, pp. 3–43. Boone, North Carolina: The Appalachian Consortium Press.

Gearing, Frederick O. (1962). Priests and Warriors: Social Structures for Cherokee Politics in the 18th Century. *American Anthropological Association Memoir* 93. Menasha, Wisconsin: American Anthropological Association.

Gilbert, William H. (1943). The Eastern Cherokees. *Smithsonian Institution, Bureau of American Ethnology Bulletin,* 133, *Paper* 23, pp. 169–413. Washington, D. C.: United States Government Printing Office.

Goodwin, Gary C. (1977). *Cherokees in Transition: A Study of Changing Culture and Environment Prior to 1775.* Department of Geography, *Research Paper No.* 181. The University of Chicago.

Graburn, Nelson H. H.
(1969). Art and Acculturative Processes. *International Social Science Journal,* 21:457–468. U. N. E. S. C. O., Paris.

(1976). Introduction. In *Ethnic and Tourist Arts: Cultural Expressions from the Fourth World,* Nelson H. H. Graburn, editor, pp. 1–33. Berkeley: University of California Press.

(1977). Tourism: The Sacred Journey. In *Hosts and Guests: The Anthropology of Tourism,* Valene Smith, editor, pp. 17–31. Philadelphia: University of Pennsylvania Press.

Greene, Joan (editor). (1984). The Story of My Life as Far Back as I Can Remember as Written by Aggie Ross Lossiah. *Journal of Cherokee Studies,* 9 (2):89–99.

Gulick, John. (1960). *Cherokees at the Crossroads.* Institute for Research in Social Science, Chapel Hill: University of North Carolina.

Harmon, Michael Anthony. (1986). Eighteenth Century Lower Cherokee Adaptation and Use of European Material Culture. *The South Carolina Institute of Archaeology and Anthropology, Volumes in Historical Archaeology, No.* 2. Columbia: The University of South Carolina.

Harrington, Mark Raymond.
  (1908). Catawba Potters and Their Work. *American Anthropologist,* 10 (n.s.):398–407.

  (1909). The Last of the Iroquois Potters. *Education Department Bulletin, Museum Bulletin* 133, University of the State of New York. New York State Museum, Annual Report, 1908, 61(1):222–27.

Hill, Sarah H. (1991). *Cherokee Patterns: Interweaving Women and Baskets in History.* Unpublished Ph. D. dissertation, The Graduate Institute for Liberal Arts, Atlanta, Georgia: Emory University.

Howell, Benita J. (1991). The New Deal for Tenant Farmers: Government Planning and Indigenous Community Development on the Cumberland Plateau. In *Southern Appalachia and the South: A Region within a Region,* John C. Inscoe, editor. *Journal of the Appalachian Studies Association,* 3:82–97.

Hudson, Charles. (1990). *The Juan Pardo Expeditions: Exploration of the Carolinas and Tennessee, 1566–1568.* Washington, D. C.: Smithsonian Institution Press.

Indian Arts and Crafts Board. (1965). Qualla Arts and Crafts Mutual, Inc. *Smoke Signals,* 44:14–15.

Jules-Rosette, Bennetta. (1984). *The Messages of Tourist Art: An African Semiotic System in Comparative Perspective.* New York: Plenum Press.

King, Duane H.
  (1972) An Analysis of Aboriginal Ceramics from Eighteenth Century Overhill Cherokee Sites in Tennessee. Unpublished M. A. thesis, Department of Anthropology, Athens: University of Georgia.

  (1979). The Origin of the Eastern Cherokees as a Social and Political Entity. In *The Cherokee Indian Nation: A Troubled History,* Duane H. King, editor, pp. 164–180. Knoxville: The University of Tennessee Press.

Kupferer, Harriet J.
  (1966). The "Principal People" 1960: A Study of Cultural and Social Groups of the Eastern Cherokee. *Smithsonian Institution, Bureau of American Ethnology, Bulletin,* 196, pp. 215–324, Paper 78. Washington, D. C.: U. S. Government Printing Office.

Lanman, Charles. (1849). *Letters from the Allegheny Mountains.* New York.

Law, Rachel Nash and Cynthia W. Taylor. (1991). *Appalachian White Oak Basketmaking: Handing Down the Basket.* Knoxville: The University of Tennessee Press.

Leftwich, Rodney L. (1970). *Arts and Crafts of the Cherokee.* Cherokee, North Carolina: Cherokee Publications.

MacCannell, Dean. (1984). Reconstructed Ethnicity: Tourism and Cultural Identity in Third World Communities. *Annals of Tourism Research*, 11:375–391.

McDowell, William L., Jr. (editor). (1955). Journals of the Commissioners of the Indian Trade, September 20, 1710–August 29, 1718. *Colonial Records of South Carolina*. Columbia: South Carolina Archives Department.

McLoughlin, William G. (1986). *Cherokee Renascence in the New Republic*. Princeton: Princeton University Press.

McLoughlin, William G. and Walter H. Conser, Jr. (1977). The Cherokees in Transition: A Statistical Analysis of the Federal Cherokee Census of 1835. *The Journal of American History*, 64 (December):678–703.

Malone, Henry T. (1956). *Cherokees of the Old South: A People in Transition*. Athens: University of Georgia Press.

Marino, Cesare. (1988). Honor the Elders: Symbolic Associations with Old Age in Traditional Eastern Cherokee Culture. *Journal of Cherokee Studies*, 13:3–19.

Mertz, Paul E. (1978). *New Deal Policy and Southern Rural Poverty*. Baton Rouge: Louisiana State University Press.

Mooney, James. (1900). Myths of the Cherokee. *Smithsonian Institution, Bureau of American Ethnology, Nineteenth Annual Report*, 1897–98, Part 1, pp. 3–576. Washington, D. C.: U. S. Government Printing Office.

Neely, Sharlotte. (1991). *Snowbird Cherokees: People of Persistence*. Athens: The University of Georgia Press.

Newman, Robert D. (1986). Euro-American Artifacts. In Overhill Cherokee Archaeology at Chota-Tanasee, Gerald F. Schroedl, editor. *Department of Anthropology, Report of Investigations*, 38, pp. 415–468. Knoxville: The University of Tennessee.

Oliver-Smith, Francisco, Jurdao Arrones, and José Lisón Arcal. (1989). Tourist Development and the Struggle for Local Resource Control. *Human Organization*, 48(4):345–351.

Page, L. W. (1931). Census of the Eastern Cherokee Tribe of the Eastern Cherokee Reservation of the Cherokee, N. C. Jurisdiction, as of April 1, 1931. Manuscript on file, Museum of the Cherokee Indian, Cherokee, North Carolina.

Parlow, Anita. (1976). The Land Development Rag. Southern Appalachian Ministry of Higher Education, Knoxville, Tennessee.

Perdue, Theda. (1989). *The Cherokee*. New York: Chelsea House Publishers.

Pillsbury, Richard. (1983). The Europeanization of the Cherokee Settlement Landscape Prior to Removal: A Georgia Case Study. *Geoscience and Man*, 23:59–69. Baton Rouge.

56   *Betty J. Duggan*

Pi-Sunyer, Oriol. (1982). The Cultural Costs of Tourism. *Cultural Survival Quarterly,* 6(3):7–10.

Qualla Arts and Crafts Mutual, Inc.
(n. d.). Membership Lists Accompanying Articles of Incorporation. Manuscript on file, Qualla Arts and Crafts Mutual, Inc., Cherokee, North Carolina.

(1955). Minutes of the Executive Committee and Annual Meetings, January 27, 1955. Manuscripts on file, Qualla Arts and Crafts Mutual, Inc., Cherokee, North Carolina.

(1987) *Contemporary Artists and Craftsmen of the Eastern Band of Cherokee Indians.* Arts and Crafts Mutual, Inc., Cherokee, North Carolina.

Richmond, Stephen M. (1987). Introduction. In *Contemporary Artists and Craftsmen of the Eastern Band of Cherokee Indians,* Mutual, Inc., pp. viii. Qualla Arts and Crafts Mutual, Inc., Cherokee, North Carolina.

Riggs, Brett H. (1987). Socioeconomic Variability in Federal Period Overhill Cherokee Archaeological Assemblages. Unpublished M. A. thesis, Department of Anthropology, Knoxville: The University of Tennessee.

Roberts, Wayne D. (1980). Lithic Analysis at Chota-Tanasee. Paper presented at the 37th Southeastern Archaeological Conference, New Orleans.

Schrader, Robert F. (1983). *The Indian Arts & Crafts Board: An Aspect of New Deal Indian Policy.* Albuquerque: University of New Mexico Press.

Shapiro, Henry. (1978). *Appalachia on Our Mind.* Chapel Hill: University of North Carolina Press.

Shearin, Majorie. (1965). A Study of Craft Programs in North Carolina Art Museums, Colleges and Universities, Craft Organizations, and Recreational Craft Centers. Unpublished M. S. thesis, Department of Anthropology, Knoxville: The University of Tennessee.

Smith, M. Estelli. (1982). Tourism and Native Americans. *Cultural Survival Quarterly,* 6(3):10–12.

Smith, Valene. (1977a). Introduction. In *Hosts and Guests: The Anthropology of Tourism,* Valene Smith, editor, pp. 1–14. Philadelphia: University of Pennsylvania Press.

Smith, Valene (editor). (1977b). *Hosts and Guests: The Anthropology of Tourism.* Philadelphia: University of Pennsylvania Press.

Southern Highland Handicraft Guild. (1958). *Crafts in the Southern Highlands.* Southern Highland Handicraft Guild, Asheville, North Carolina.

Speck, Frank G. (1920). Decorative Art and Basketry of the Cherokee. *Bulletin of the Public Museum of the City of Milwa. kee* 2, pp. 53–86. The Trustees, Milwaukee, Wisconsin. Reprinted in *Studies in Cherokee Basketry,* Betty J. Duggan and Brett H. Riggs, editors. *Occasional Paper No. 9,* pp. 6–20, The Frank H. McClung Museum. Knoxville: The University of Tennessee, 1991.

Speck, Frank G. and C. E. Schaeffer. (1945). The Mutual-Aid and Volunteer Company of the Eastern Cherokee: as Recorded in a Book of Minutes in the Sequoyah Syllabary, compared with Mutual-Aid Societies of the Northern Iroquois. *Journal of Washington Academy of Sciences,* 35(6):169–179.

Stucki, Larry R. (1984). Will the 'Real Indian' Survive? Tourism and Affluence at Cherokee, North Carolina. In *Affluence and Cultural Survival,* Richard F. Salisbury and Elisabeth Tooker, editors. Washington, D. C.: American Ethnological Society.

Swain, Margaret Byrne. (1977). Cuna Women and Ethnic Tourism: A Way to Persist and an Avenue to Change. In *Hosts and Guests: The Anthropology of Tourism,* Valene Smith, editor, pp. 71–81. Philadelphia: University of Pennsylvania Press.

The Cherokee One-Feather staff. (1975). "Qualla Mutual Preserves Rich Cultural Heritage." *The Cherokee One-Feather.* Wednesday, December 3rd issue.

The Smoky Mountain Indian Trail staff. (1934). "Our 'New Deal' Superintendent." *The Smoky Mountain Indian Trail,* 1(14)5, 8–9.

Thomas, Robert K. (1958). Cherokee Values and World View. Manuscript on file, Institute for Research in Social Science, Chapel Hill: University of North Carolina.

Wahrhaftig, Albert L. (1975). Institution Building Among Oklahoma's Traditional Cherokees. In *Four Centuries of Southern Indians,* Charles Hudson, editor. Athens: University of Georgia Press.

Whisnant, David E. (1983). *All That is Native and Fine: The Politics of Culture in an American Region.* Chapel Hill: University of North Carolina Press.

Witthoft, John.
(1949). Stone Pipes of the Historic Cherokees. *Southern Indian Studies,* 1:43–62.

(1979). Observations on Social Change Among the Eastern Cherokees. In *The Cherokee Indian Nation: A Troubled History,* Duane H. King, editor. Knoxville: The University of Tennessee Press.

4

Urban Tourism in Revitalizing Downtowns[1]: Conceptualizing Tourism in Boston, Massachusetts

R. TIMOTHY SIEBER

Anthropologists have tended to study tourism in places that are remote from their own communities, among people where the distinctions between tourists and their "hosts" seem clear. In this chapter, R. Timothy Sieber challenges this preference and asks whether the discipline's usual choice of subject has in some ways limited the usefulness of its conclusions. In his study of tourism in Boston, Massachusetts, Sieber demonstrates how a shift to a more familiar, urban setting draws into question many of the assumptions that are often made about the industry. Not the least of these is the relative ease by which most investigators delineate the categories of "tourist" and "host". We can note many instances in this volume in which the assumption of a more traditional host/guest relationship is transformed by the realities of a thoroughly mediated hospitality industry. Sieber takes us one step further in suggesting that, at least in urban settings, tourists and hosts (i.e., residents) may not even be distinguishable by their behaviors, or in their enjoyment of "tourist" facilities. These observations bring us a step closer to considering the extent to which modern social relations and public spaces are beginning to be wrested from once powerful metaphors of residentiality and neighborhood, to be shaped instead by newer images of travel and visitation.

Introduction: The Case of the Missing Tourists

This is a discussion of the peculiarities of urban tourism, and how most of the generalizations that anthropologists have recently advanced about the nature of tourism and tourists do not seem to be that useful in capturing the complexities of cities as tourist sites. I would like to begin the discussion by telling a story. Its title might be, "The Puzzle—or the Case—of the Missing Tourists."

As part of a broader project on waterfront redevelopment in Boston, in 1988 I set out to study the city's major history and heritage festival, Harborfest, which takes place over the long fourth of July weekend (Sieber, 1990). Considered by Bostonians as a major tourist event, Harborfest was explicitly designed to attract tourists to the city's hotels, restaurants, and museums during a time of the year usually short on visitors. Futhermore, in 1988, Harborfest had been high-lighted as one of the nation's most important tourist events—one of the "One Hundred Most Exciting Events in America"—by the American Bus Association, which compiles such lists annually. The festival's opening ceremonies were set at Faneuil Hall Marketplace, a commercial center attracting fourteen million visitors a year, and crowded with perhaps 10,000 people on this particular Friday afternoon at the beginning of the long holiday weekend. The opening events included a jazz band, music and singing, clowns, children's balloons, and a fire truck. Afterwards, a local television reporter with her cameraman sought to capture some footage for a news spot on the festival. First she filmed her concluding remarks:

> The city says one million people will be coming to Boston for this, and according to the Greater Boston Convention and Tourist Bureau, the city will make sixty million dollars from it. Between the Esplanade and the Harborfest, it will be a fun-packed weekend, so get out and enjoy it. At Faneuil Hall Marketplace, this is Juanita Barker reporting for News 56 at 10."

The reporter then set about to find some tourists to interview, for a human interest angle. She and her cameraman surveyed the crowd, but could spot no obvious tourists among the many hundreds of people milling about. After a few moments of unsuccessful inspection, she called out loudly, "We need people from out of town!" There was no response. "Are you here for Harborfest?" she asked one young couple. They mumbled, "Well, not really . . . " and turned away. "Anyone here for Harborfest?" she called out again. One man she looked at said, "No,

I'm local." "No one?" the reporter called out again. "We're natives," someone else remarked. She finally identified a young couple from Florida, and the camera began to roll. "This is dubbed to be one of the most exciting events in America, in the top 100. What will you be doing?" she asked. They said nothing. It seems they did not know there was a festival going on. She prompted them: "It's pretty exciting. You're here at the kickoff today." Finally the young woman responded, "Well, it really is so exciting to be here—the people, the action, the activities around here. It's so great around here, so exciting." Her next and final statement, however, ruined the interview. Not really understanding what it was that she as a tourist was supposed to be commenting on, she gave the festival the wrong name, saying "Yes, the people here are great, and *Clownfest* too!"

Why did the reporter have such trouble finding tourists, that is, people from someplace else, people who were—as Dennison Nash (1981) and others have suggested—strangers to their host settings? Why was it so difficult to find tourists who, in their turn, were following their role of seeking out the non-ordinary, the activities explicitly designed for tourists (MacCannell, 1989)? Why, further, were most of the people at this supposed tourist event not even strangers to the city? These questions all point to a number of peculiarities about urban tourism in general, and especially tourism in post-industrial cities, those cities that have typically revitalized their downtowns at least partly with the aim of developing strong tourism industries.

Tourism in these city settings, I will argue, has special qualities, boundaries, and significances, and it poses special problems of analysis that most conventional cultural models of tourism do not handle well. Conventional definitions such as Nash's (1989), for example, regard metropolitan zones as sending areas for tourists, rather than sites of tourism, and see tourism as typically occurring in more rural, more "natural" settings. As Bruner says, "Tourists long for the pastoral, for their origins, for the unpolluted, the pure, and the original" (1989: 439). Surely he's not discussing cities. Tourists are, further, supposed to be "strangers" in the tourist setting (Nash, 1989; Smith, 1989; Graburn, 1989), to have arrived there only after travel from distant places, and once they are in the setting to be devoted to leisure rather than work (Graburn, 1989). Because of its supposed non-work and non-ordinary character, tourism as an activity is sacred, liminal, or ritual, rather than profane, for the actor (Graburn, 1989). Tourists and tourism, in short, constitute a sharply bounded cultural domain in terms of identity, activity, values, and setting.

In cities like Boston, however, categories of opposition such as those of tourist and local, stranger and friend, leisure and work, and sacred and profane are not so clearly separated as they seem to be in more conventional tourist locales. Urban tourism increasingly produces images of heritage and identity that are consumed as much by residents as by visitors. Although they may drive there in Volvos, or take Amtrak, today's urban travelers may be—like the proverbial urban peasant migrants of our past anthropological studies—much more acculturated to the city, and much longer under its sphere of influence, than our cultural models of tourism would lead us to believe. It is essentially the urban context itself, I will argue, that gives tourism in that locale its peculiar qualities.

In addressing general issues of urban tourism in revitalizing downtowns, I will rely on case materials from my own study city of Boston. Research on tourism in Boston was completed as part of a broader field study, taking place throughout the late 1980s, of the city's changing public culture, in domains such as tourism, architecture and design, education, urban planning, parks and recreation, and public celebration, that resulted from dramatic redevelopment of the city's central business and historic districts, and particularly its waterfront zone (see Sieber, 1990, 1991, 1993), during this time period. Longstanding trends toward deindustrialization of the port, corporatization of the economy, and residential gentrification intensified then, and downtown public space and facilities were increasingly transformed to accommodate a more upscale blend of newcomers and visitors from outside the city, including conventioneers, business travelers, suburbanites, and tourists. My fieldwork entailed active participant observation in a wide range of relevant public events and activities, designed for tourists and other types of visitors, and ongoing formal and informal interviewing of participants at all levels. Though my data concern Boston in particular, I believe the generalizations to follow are applicable to other post-industrial cities, at least in North America (Sieber, 1991), and have implications for the understanding of urban tourism cross-culturally.

Cities are inherently supra-local

The supra-local functions of cities have always entailed their serving as transportation and travel nodes. Nearly two decades ago, when John Gulick published his list of seven urban essentials—that is, the critical defining features of urban places across time and space—his list included several that relate travel to and from cities to the brokerage functions that these settlements play in broader regional and inter-urban contexts. He notes, for example, that in cities:

1. There are local residents and institutions that serve as brokers between the larger society of which the settlement is a part and the immediate region that the settlement dominates by reason of the brokerage functions located in it. The brokerage functions are concerned primarily with governmental administration, transportation, communication, and commerce.

2. In connection with these brokerage functions, persons considered to be strangers or outsiders to the settlement regularly visit it. The presence of these strangers and outsiders is a normal condition of life in the settlement . . .

4. Members of the uppermost class, in particular, have various personal connections and associations in other larger cities. These connections impart prestige and probably usually imply power. They may also be accompanied by behavior and attitudes that are, in the context of the particular culture, sophisticated, cosmopolitan, cultivated, universalistic, and urbane . . . (Gulick, 1980: 73–74 [1973]).

These generalizations articulate long-standing themes in the anthropological analysis of urban centers and their place in complex societies. As Anthony Leeds pointed out so well (e.g., 1976, 1980, 1994), cities have long served as nodes in multi-level sociocultural systems, as sites of transaction and linkage, involving flows of information, people, and control between both city and hinterland, and between city and broader urban hierarchy. Travel among localities, especially among elite sectors, is an inevitable part of the functions these groups play in supra-local coordination of broader metropolitan, regional, and international systems. In recent years, Rollwagen (1980, 1988) and Wolfe (1980, 1986) have extended our understanding of the system scale—now multi-national and global—within which these flows of people, information, and contact operate.

As part of the supra-local roles they play, cities have always hosted many visitors and contained an infrastructure to support travel, especially by elite groups. The kind of visiting we might gloss as "business travel," in particular, has always been an important ingredient to cities' functioning as centers of economic, political, and even ideological control. These sorts of urban function, and their implications for travel and visiting, are still quite applicable to that category of today's cities variously termed "corporate" (Gordon, 1977), "informational" (Castells, 1989) or "post-industrial" (Mollenkopf, 1983; Sieber, 1991). These cities, as a rule high on the urban hierarchy, play critical coordinative roles in regional, national, or global systems of management. They also, not surprisingly, are the sites of most urban tourism today, and the cities where tourism infrastructure and marketing are most developed.

Such cities are located particularly in post-industrial regions of the world—Japan, Western Europe, and North America—whose economies are based primarily in the service or information sectors, and whose downtowns host those legions of office towers that function as centers of decision-making, coordination, and control (Plotnicov, 1988), in the corporate and governmental arenas. These are cities whose transitions to centers of corporate control since World War II have normally been accompanied by downtown revitalization—not only the construction of the office towers themselves, but associated public amenities—such as parks, restaurants, "cultural" and entertainment institutions like museums and sports arenas, and hotels. In addition, broader infrastructural developments have occurred, particularly with new and renovated housing, and transportation, through new auto, air, and rail linkages. Finally, new retail commercial development, typically festival marketplaces and specialty marketing, complete the picture. As Judd and Collins pointed out long ago, the development of infrastructure and marketing for tourism is a central ingredient of all such downtown revitalizations (Judd and Collins, 1979).

Perhaps one reason for this is that business-oriented travel and an infrastructure to support it are probably more important to corporate cities than to any earlier city type. Because of revolutions in telecommunications and transportation, and the increasing integration of regional, national, and global economies, more professionals and managers than ever before are needed to coordinate such systems and to assure an orderly flow of communication within the system. There is no doubt more coming and going than ever before as these elite workers travel to realize their work as brokers and mediators, both in relation to the urban hinterland and between different levels in these broader political-economic hierarchies.

In his analyses of Pittsburgh and kindred post-industrial cities, Leonard Plotnicov has given us some suggestions of why tourism is an integral part of downtown revitalizations. Plotnicov (1986) has maintained that the corporatization of cities has increased the number of affluent urban professionals living and working in those locations. There is a wide range of lifestyle amenities, mostly in the arena of leisure and recreation, that the new urban professionals require, not only for personal fulfillment, but also as sites for business-related face-to-face networking, such as clubs and restaurants (1987: 42–43; 1989). Plotnicov goes so far as to suggest that cities' efforts to draw visitors, through the tourism and convention trade, are ways of expanding the market and financing for downtown amenities so necessary for corporate business activity (1986: 3). He also notes that in Pittsburgh most of those drawn to the city, even in conventional tourist roles, are from within the broader hinterland of the city, within 200 miles. The end result, in any event, is that resident urban professionals, business travelers, conventioneers, and tourists all are in a symbiotic relationship with one another, patronizing the same sites, amenities, and services (Plotnicov, 1986, Sieber, 1991).

Urban Tourism in Boston

It is no wonder the Boston television reporter had trouble finding tourists to interview about Harborfest. Not that many tourists—if defined as strangers—really attend its activities. Seventy-five percent of the one million people participating are actually locals, not necessarily from the inner city but from within the broad suburban ring extending some twenty-five miles from the city's core. Boston is the regional metropolis of the six-state New England region, and almost all the remaining attendees—the more conventional tourists, in fact—are in fact drawn from this broader hinterland. Harborfest's own study of its print and electronic publicity for the festival shows that almost all festival advertising was placed in metropolitan and near regional media markets, mainly within fifty miles of Boston. Most of the one hundred thousand schedule brochures were distributed to supermarkets, banks, department stores, and movie theaters in the broader metropolitan region. Less than one percent were sent out of state in response to requests (Benson, 1988). In other words, most of Harborfest's "tourists" are metropolitans who already enjoy at least some familiarity with the Boston area.

Looking at statistics for all types of visitation to Boston over the year helps to put into perspective how little conventional tourism actually occurs in the city. Boston does receive some conventional out-of-town tourists who stay in hotels and lack local roots, but they probably make up a minority of the approximately 4.25 million annual visitors who say they are making a pleasure trip to the city. Metropolitans, that is, suburbanites account for most of these pleasure visitors. In addition to all so-called pleasure travelers, the city's Convention and Visitors Bureau also records almost as many visitors, another four million, who come to the city as conventioneers or business travelers. Probably a greater number of these are genuine strangers to the city, although not there mainly for leisure purposes.

In other words, in the general realm of urban tourism, it is hard to separate activities and places according to whether they involve suburban visitors, suburban commuters who work downtown, independent tourists who are genuinely strangers and accommodated in hotels, resident professionals, conventioneers, or business travelers. In tourist Boston, the mix of these categories is the most salient feature of the situation. Most restaurants, bars, parks and other recreation sites in the downtowns, in fact, include mixes of these people. An example is the award-winning Christopher Columbus Park located squarely within a zone of Boston's newly revitalized waterfront that is generally thought of as "heavily tourist." An August 1989 survey done here at the height of the tourist season showed a fairly even mix over the day and week of neighborhood people, downtown workers—mostly suburban commuters—using the park for lunch or recreation, suburbanite daytrippers in town on errands such as shopping or doctor's appointments, and out-of-town tourists or business travelers staying in hotels (Caleskie, 1990).

Throughout Boston, mixing of this sort is commonplace. The Convention and Visitors Bureau's each year lists the city's top "tourist attractions," mostly museums, historic structures, and other points of interest located in the revitalized downtown (Greater Boston Convention and Visitors Bureau, 1991).[2] Interestingly, *all visitors* at these sites are counted as tourists, and as a rule are offered the same programming, even though attendance actually includes a mix of the above groups. Faneuil Hall Marketplace's fourteen million annual visitors, for example, include a majority of suburbanites and downtown workers eating and socializing in the dozens of restaurants and bars located there. At the New England Aquarium, the city's fourth greatest attraction, where yearly tourist visitation is listed as 1,300,000, staff acknowledge that almost 20% of the total are local school and community groups, and another 27% are from suburbs within 25 miles of Boston. At the John Hancock tower and observatory, sixth on the attraction list with 332,000 visitors yearly, staff say about 25% of visitors are local residents and those they have brought with them—mostly from suburban locations. The most traditional tourist-oriented activity available, not on the list of the top twenty, are the guided sightseeing tours on special trolleys. Even here, guides estimate 15–20% of the patronage from locals, mostly suburbanites.

It is also important to note that many truly non-metropolitan visitors do not approach the city as total strangers because their visits are mediated through their friends or relatives who are local residents. Although Boston figures are not available, the Massachusetts-wide figures are suggestive. Of all travelers to the state, 35% stay with friends or family when visiting; only 53% stay in paid accommodations; and, fully 48% of all visitors choose to visit the state because it is convenient to their residences or because their friends or relatives live there (Massachusetts Office of Tourism, 1988). Sharing touristic experiences with out-of-town guests, in fact, seems to be a major avenue for locals themselves to participate in tourist activities.

In the same way as tourism is embedded in the broader economic infrastructure of the city—and is clearly not a distinct sector—it should also be pointed out that in the urban context most people who actually work to service tourists or other visitors never interact personally with them, as hosts might do in serving guests. They do not even have the chance to treat them impersonally or stereotypically, as hosts are supposed to do in sites of mass tourism (Nash, 1989). Even in the thickly touristic environment of hotels, as union president Domenic Bozzotto told me, most employees are not "gratuity workers" and do not have face-to-face relationships with visitors. The majority work behind the scenes in kitchens, laundries, and as housekeeping staff. As a hotel cook noted, "Back in the kitchen, no one ever sees the customers, and no one really cares if they like the food or not." Even for gratuity workers, Van Kemper has questioned whether distinctions among categories of guests are that relevant in hosts' perceptions of them: "For instance, does a waiter in a Manhattan restaurant distinguish between tourists and other classes of customers? Does the Hilton Hotel (anywhere in the world) differentiate between business travelers and tourists? Indeed, as anthropologists we are likely to mix business with leisure during our field trips or conventions . . ." (Kemper, 1980: 472–473). Most people serving tourists do not necessarily recognize them as such, and do not have to make the cultural adjustments Nash has also suggested are always incumbent upon hosts in tourist situations (Nash, 1989).

Another feature of urban tourism that deserves note is the mix of work and play, business and pleasure to which Kemper alludes. As we have seen, much of the city's allure is that it allows these to be combined in creative and interesting ways. The business traveler can, by evening, visit relatives, a museum, or a theater, or bring along family to sightsee while he or she attends meetings. The suburban commuter with a downtown job can meet friends after work for dinner, or a concert. Businesspersons can consummate deals over cocktails. Conventioneers can escape meetings for a walk through the arboretum or art museum. The suburbanite in town for a doctor's appointment can catch a late run movie afterward. This definition of post-industrial cities as places of work and play, and as exciting places because of it, makes them more amenable to work and residence by the urban professionals central to their economies (Plotnicov, 1990). As I have argued elsewhere, this mixing of work and play in the city also heralds the passing of industrial-era images of cities as working-class places of work and toil, in favor of more bourgeois constructions of work and of quality of life that infuse tourism programming as well as broader public urban culture (Sieber, 1990, 1991).

Finally, let me address the issue of tourism programming, and the manner in which the commodification and representation of place have so permeated the public culture of many post-industrial cities. In earlier work, I have argued that in Boston's case, most of the people who now inhabit, work in, or visit the downtown are essentially newcomers to the city. Half of Boston's families have, for example, lived in the city less than five years (Ganz and Konga, 1989: 136), and a full 60% of those working in the city are suburban commuters (Ganz and Konga, 1989: 134). Virtually everyone now in the downtown area lack old or permanent ties to the area, or a developed sense of their connection to local place, history, and tradition. Local residents—especially professionals—and suburban commuters enjoy consuming the same representations of the city's "authentic" history, heritage, and local color that are the mainstay of tourist programming.[3]

Mobility, migration, and radical differentiation of urban space render all metropolitans, to some degree, strangers in their home environments. In the same vein, the kind of sophisticated, detached, cosmopolitan frame of mind that Gulick noted is so characteristic of urban elites, and urban places, is now a more generalized, mass-based feature of the public culture of the city. As MacCannell (1989) and John Urry have both suggested (1990), the tourist gaze is an important element of general contemporary urban sensibility, and the tourist the prototype of the contemporary urbanite. If the tourist blends so well into today's social landscape, it may be because that social landscape is so fundamentally touristic itself.

Rethinking Tourists and Tourism

The economy of cities—usually multifunctional and highly differentiated—then, can never be so strongly dominated by the tourism sector as tourist sites are in more conventional leisure settings, such as resorts, tourist zones where almost all infrastructure supports hospitality, recreation and service of temporary visitors. Perhaps cities never can develop beyond that intensity of tourism that Smith calls, "incipient mass tourism," where "the tourist industry is only one sector of the total economy, and hotels usually have a mix of guests including domestic travelers and businessmen as well as tour groups" (Smith, 1989:13).

Perhaps cities also diverge as tourist sites for another reason. Within the greater panoply of tourism types, they have always served as magnets for more education-related, as opposed to leisure-related, forms of travel. For instance, historical tourism is commonly associated with large cities, where relevant historic sites are more likely to exist (Smith, 1989: 5; Sieber 1990). And, as Cate Cameron has noted in her own work on cultural tourism and urban revitalization, cities in Europe and the United States have long distinguished themselves in cultural tourism, because of their high concentration of performing arts, museum, and architectural attractions (Cameron, 1990). Urry (1990) also notes the strong prevalence of educational definitions of today's tourism.

None of these considerations would come as a surprise to those managing and planning the tourism industry itself. A broader system-wide perspective on urban visitation, like that suggested by these urban anthropological considerations, in fact, already informs the view of specialists and officials in urban tourism. In their treatment of urban tourism in the *Handbook of Tourism Research*, for example, Blank and Petkovich note:

> Tourism for most urban areas diverges markedly from popularly held concepts of tourism . . . commonly thought of as vacation travel. Most urban tourism, in contrast, is complex and heterogeneous . . . Most travel to cities is *multi-purpose*. That is, most travelers undertake more than one activity while there (Blank and Petkovich, 1987: 166; italics in original).

They note that people visit the city for many purposes other than leisure strictly defined, and they recommend that tourism managers and officials think of "all non-residents who enter the city"—except job commuters—as tourists for purposes of marketing and programming (Blank and Petkovich, 1987: 167)

In Boston, conversations with officials at the Convention and Visitors Bureau indicate that they too take a view of urban tourism much broader than that suggested by conventional notions of tourism, whether in the popular press or in anthropology. Larry Meehan, Public Affairs Director of the Bureau, for example, outlined several new markets his bureau has recently identified in their planning and marketing efforts. In each case, visitors use tourist services during their multi-purpose stays in Boston. These new markets are also indirectly generated by growth in the city's service sector industries, such as education and health care.

(1) Visitation connected to the 87 colleges and universities in the Boston region—both parents visiting their children there as students, and also the extensive springtime alumni class reunion traffic connected to these institutions.

(2) Visitation connected to hospitals and the city's role as a health services center of regional, national, and even international scope. Family members accompanying and supporting sick relatives, in other words, use tourist services.

(3) Technical education and consulting travel, often related to the region's wealth of high technology industries, where business or professional groups travel to the area to receive technically-related tours, orientation, and training in matters covering the gamut from pollution control to data processing.

In its own efforts to increase local tourism, and to win recognition of its full contributions to the local economy, the Bureau often has to combat popular stereotypes of tourists as strangers. As Meehan explained:

So many visitors don't look like tourists and don't act like strangers. The foreign tourists, especially the Japanese tourists, get the most press. They look strange, and they travel close together in groups; but there are some really nice Belgian people who are also there in that restaurant who don't get counted.

The standard industry measure for determining a tourist, seemingly generous, is that anyone traveling from over fifty miles is one. While this standard may seem loose in terms of popular and perhaps anthropological perceptions, the Boston Bureau sees the standard as overly restrictive, and points out that it assumes a less dense metropolitan arrangement than Boston or most other contemporary cities actually have. Many locals and metropolitans are people from far closer than fifty miles who use tourist services, and are counted as tourists by business and government. In fact, as Meehan noted, "those crowds of people you see, those tourists—they're really us."

Perhaps the many ambiguities displayed by urban tourism—the lack of clear boundaries between tourist and host, work and leisure, distance and closeness, backstage and frontstage—are not simply anomalies, but rather point to the labile, the multivalent, even contested meanings these distinctions have in a wider range of tourist settings. Perhaps a more critical, constructivist approach to these distinctions may help to capture more of complexity of tourism, and its embeddedness in broader contemporary cultural and social process.

Most tourism in the world, for example, is probably domestic rather than transnational. Many nations and world regions have their own middle and upper classes who engage actively in internal tourism, as can be seen in the heavy patronage of Cancun, Mexico, for example, by middle class visitors from Mexico itself and elsewhere in Latin America. More studies of such nearer-range tourism could illuminate class and regional relations that are too seldom discussed in anthropological studies of tourism. Anthropology's long preoccupation with colonial and post-colonial settings is understandable given the history of the discipline, and its sensitivity to the cultural dynamics involved. As often it might do so, however, international tourism does not always reenact the clear imperialist frame—as it does in Bruner and Kirshenblatt-Gimblett's recent study of Maasai performances for European tourists in Kenya (1994), for example—that is so often stressed in the literature as the prototype of all tourism. Such a construction mistakenly implies that only westerners tour, and that everyone else mainly serves as objects of their gaze. The heavily Portuguese immigrant city of New Bedford, Massachusetts, to cite only one contrary example, strongly promotes itself as a tourist destination not only for residents of Portugal, but for residents of the thriving Portuguese immigrant communities in the developing nations of Brazil and Venezuela.

On the global plane, tourism may also be hard to distinguish from temporary return migration, or other types of visiting that are not necessarily leisure-oriented; and, some international travel that is actually leisure-oriented may be done by people who are going home, rather than away. For example, many international travelers immersed in the tourist flow are migrants returning home, whether to India, Portugal, or Colombia, for short-term visits with kin, sometimes for family rituals or simply for holidays. Other kinds of temporary sojourners, who also may not regard themselves as conventional tourists, such as missionaries, anthropologists, students, aid workers, and business people, may nonetheless extensively use tourist services, and be classified and even treated as tourists by a variety of locals. In any part of the world, who is a tourist may not be a matter easily agreed to by the parties involved, and there may be value in examining how these disparate definitions relate to one another.

Finally, of course, who are the hosts? Perhaps, here too, the case of urban tourism prompts some critical questions about conventional understandings. Need hosts always interact in face-to-face service of tourists? In performances for visitors, do hosts always present a sharply bounded frontstage, or "picture" (Bruner and Kirshenblatt-Gimblett, 1994), that is different from their everyday lives backstage?[4] Do hosts, in fact, always perform for visitors? It could be that anthropology's strong ethnographic orientation, and predilection for study of ritual behavior, focus analysis too exclusively on these kinds of transactions.

In every tourist economy, probably the majority of tourism workers never interact directly with visitors, for example, the dishwasher in the hotel kitchen, the truckdriver who delivers vegetables to the restaurant, the peasant at home who manufactures crafts that will be later sold to visitors by someone else, or the planner who oversees restoration of historic city buildings, or the construction of a new road to the seashore, or even the construction laborers on those projects. The full place of tourism is not completely visible at the point of interpersonal contact between host and guest. The medium of tourism display today is much broader than personal service or ritual performance, in any case, since place, the built environment, and landscape everywhere have also become commodified and managed as tourist attractions, as much in the countryside as in the city. Today's differentiated and complex economy of tourism challenges anthropology to devise more complex methods for its study—at the least, multi-site ethnography, and as so many in urban anthropology have long suggested, the supplementing of ethnography with more serious contextualizations of tourism within political economy and historical process. Surely the world's largest industry demands no less.

Notes

1. This chapter derives from a paper delivered as part of a panel on "Tourism and Cultural Conservation," organized by Erve Chambers, at the 1991 Annual Meeting of the Society for Applied Anthropology in Charleston, South Carolina. The investigation was supported by the Faculty Development program and sabbatical funding from the University of Massachusetts/Boston. For their assistance in this research, I extend special

thanks to Larry Meehan, Public Affairs Director of the Greater Boston Convention and Visitors Bureau; Domenic Bozzotto, President of Local 26, Hotel, Restaurant, Institutional Employees and Bartenders Union, AFL–CIO; Cynthia Mackey, Public Affairs office, New England Aquarium; and the officers and organizers of Harborfest, Inc. Andrew J. Gordon has also aided in general conceptual and theoretical clarification. Leonard Plotnicov read and carefully commented on an earlier version of the paper. Erve Chambers made many useful, challenging editorial suggestions that have strengthened the paper. At various stages, the following have assisted in my research on Boston Harbor developments and I also offer them my grateful thanks: Mary Concannon, James Lonergan, Diane Caleskie, Charlotte Gorman, Christine Buckley, Christine Chaisson, Marjorie O'Neill, and Dimitra Doukas. Of course, I alone am responsible for the analysis presented here.

2. Of the twenty-five metropolitan-area sites, thirteen are located in the city's downtown area. Eleven, mostly in the downtown area, are waterfront sites or attractions. Twenty-one are located in Boston proper, and four in the nearby metropolitan area (Cambridge and Salem). The historical and "cultural" character of Boston's tourism is reflected in the fact that thirteen of the twenty-five sites are museums, and seven are historic structures or monuments. The top ten sites, beginning with the most popular, are: Faneuil Hall Marketplace, Museum of Science, Museum of Fine Arts, New England Aquarium, USS Constitution [historic ship], Bull & Finch Pub [model for television program, "Cheers"], Old North Church, John Hancock Observatory, Boston Tea Party Ship and Museum, and John F. Kennedy Library and Museum. Despite the historical cast of the city's tourist sites, ten of the top twenty-five sites [mostly museums] interestingly date from the city's post-World War II period, the era of its most significant post-industrial development.

3. Johnson and Metzger (1983) have suggested, in their studies of seaport towns in California and Florida, that in a culture deeply valuing the work ethic, leisure itself gains acceptability for tourists when elements of work are visible in tourist sites, particularly when that work is "authentic" craft work such as fishing (Johnson and Metzger, 1983). Bruner has also remarked on the desire of the international tourist to apprehend the "disappearing primitive" (1989: 441) as a symbol of cultural authenticity. Within the context of western post-industrial society, the analogous symbol of authentic culture and connection to nature might well be the pre-industrial craft worker (e.g., fishermen, farmers, etc.). whose presence is thought to give background and local color to so many tourist attractions.

4. Anthropologists may be wrong in suggesting so often that visitors are deceived by these performances, and heed John Urry's claim (1990) that today's tourists are cognizant of their artificiality, and in fact enjoy watching them as forms of cultural production.

References

Benson, Mary Jane. (1988). Boston Harborfest Marketing Analysis: 1982–1987. Boston: Boston Harborfest, Inc.

Blank, Uel and Michael D. Petkovich. (1987). Research on urban tourism destinations. In *Travel, Tourism, and Hospitality Research: a Handbook for Managers and Researchers.* J. R. Brent Ritchie and Charles R. Goeldner (Eds.). Pp. 165–176. New York: John Wiley & Sons.

Bruner, Edward M. (1989). Of cannibals, tourists, and ethnographers. *Cultural Anthropology,* 4(4): 438–445.

Bruner, Edward M. and Barbara Kirshenblatt-Gimblett. (1994). Maasai on the lawn: tourist realism in East Africa. *Cultural Anthropology,* 9(4): 435–470.

Caleskie, Diane. (1989). Uses of Christopher Columbus Park and North End Park. Unpublished manuscript. 6 pp.

Cameron, Catherine M. (1989). Cultural tourism and urban revitalization. *Tourism Recreation Research,* 14(1): 23–32.

Castells, Manuel. (1989). The Informational City: Information Technology, Economic Restructuring and the Urban-Regional Process. Cambridge: Blackwell.

Collins, Thomas W. (1980). Wider linkages in the urban setting. In *Cities in a Larger Context.* Thomas W. Collins, (Ed.). Pp. 1–5 Southern Anthropological Society Proceedings, No. 14. Athens, Georgia: University of Georgia Press.

Ganz, Alexander and L. Francois Konga. (1989). Boston in the world economy. In *Cities in a Global Society.* Richard V. Knight and Gary Gappert, (Eds.). Pp. 132–140. Urban Affairs Annual Review, Vol. 35. Newbury Park: Sage.

Gordon, David M. (1977). Capitalist development and the history of American cities. In *Marxism and the Metropolis: New Perspectives in Urban Political Economy.* William K. Tabb and Larry Sawers, (Eds.). Pp. 25–63. New York: Oxford University Press.

Grayburn, Nelson H. H. (1989). Tourism: the sacred journey. In *Hosts and Guests: the Anthropology of Tourism,* 2nd Ed., Valene Smith (ed.). Pp. 21–36. Philadelphia: University of Pennsylvania Press.

Greater Boston Convention and Visitors Bureau. (1991). Area's largest tourist attractions (ranked by 1990 attendance). *Boston Business Journal,* 10(47): 12 [January 14, 1991].

Gulick, John. (1980). Urban domains: environments that defy close definition. In *Urban Place and Process.* Irwin Press and M. Estellie Smith, (Eds.). Pp. 61–77. New York: Macmillan.

Johnson, Jeffrey and Duane, Metzger. (1983). The shift from technical to expressive: the "play-full" harbors of Southern California. *Coastal Zone Management*, 10(4): 429–441.

Judd, Dennis R. and Margaret Collins. (1979). The case of tourism: political coalitions and redevelopment in central cities. In *The Changing Structures of the City*. Urban Affairs Annual Review, No. 16. Gary A. Tobin, (Ed.). Pp. 179–199. Beverly Hills, California: Sage.

Kemper, Robert Van. (1980). Comment on "Tourism as an Anthropological Subject." *Current Anthropology*, 22(5): 472–473.

Leeds, Anthony. (1976). Urban society subsumes rural: specialties, nucleations, countryside and networks: metatheory, theory and method. Atti del XL Congresso Internazionale degli Americanisti, Roma, 1972, Vol. 4. Pp. 171–182. Genova: Tilgher.

(1980). Towns and villages in society: hierarchies of order and cause. In *Cities in a Larger Context*. Thomas W. Collins, (Ed.). Pp. 6–33. Proceedings of the Southern Anthropological Society. Athens, Georgia: University of Georgia Press.

(1994). Cities, Classes and the Social Order. Roger Sanjek, (Ed.). Ithaca: Cornell University Press.

MacCannell, Dean. (1989). *The Tourist: A New Theory of the Leisure Class*, Rev. Ed., New York: Schocken Books.

Massachusetts Office of Travel and Tourism. (1988). Travel & Tourism in Massachusetts: Economic Impact and Visitor Demographics, 1987–1988. Boston: Massachusetts Office of Travel and Tourism.

Mollenkopf, John H. (1983). *The Contested City*. Princeton: Princeton University Press

Nash, Dennison. (1980). Tourism as an anthropological subject. *Current Anthropology*, 22(5): 461–468

(1989). Tourism as a form of imperialism. In *Hosts and Guests: the Anthropology of Tourism*, 2nd Ed. Valene Smith, (Ed.). Pp. 21–52. Philadelphia: University of Pennsylvania Press.

Plotnicov, Leonard. (1986). Selling Camelot: the orchestration of fun and games in Pittsburgh. Paper delivered at the Annual Meeting of the American Anthropological Association, Philadelphia.

(1987). The political economy of skyscrapers: an anthropological introduction to advanced industrial cities. *City & Society*, 1(1): 35–51.

(1990). Work and play: an urban lifestyle ideally portrayed. *City & Society*, 4(1): 3–19.

Rollwagen, Jack R. (1980). Cities and the world system: toward an evolutionary perspective in the study of urban anthropology. In *Cities in a Larger Context.* Thomas W. Collins, (Ed.). Pp. 123–140. Southern Anthropological Society Proceedings, No. 14. Athens, Georgia: University of Georgia Press.

(1988). New directions in urban anthropology. In *Urban Life,* 2nd Ed. George Gmelch and Walter P. Zenner, (Eds.). Pp. 149–160. Prospect Heights, Ill.: Waveland Press.

Sieber, R. Timothy. (1990) Selecting a new past: emerging definitions of heritage in Boston Harbor. *Journal of Urban and Cultural Studies,* 1(2):101–122.

(1991). Waterfront revitalization in post-industrial port cities of North America. *City & Society,* 5(2): 120–136.

(1993) Public Access and the Urban Waterfront: a Question of Vision. In *The Cultural Meaning of Urban Space.* Pp. 175–193. Robert Rotenberg and Gary McDonogh, (Eds.). Westport, CT: Bergin & Garvey.

Smith, Valene. (1989a). Introduction. In *Hosts and Guests: the Anthropology of Tourism,* 2nd Ed. Valene Smith, (Ed.). Pp. 1–17. Philadelphia: University of Pennsylvania Press.

(1989b). *Editor, Hosts and Guests: the Anthropology of Tourism,* 2nd Edition. Philadelphia: University of Pennsylvania Press.

Urry, John. (1990). The tourist gaze: leisure and travel in contemporary societies. Newbury Park: Sage.

Wolfe, Alvin W. (1980). Multinational enterprise and urbanism. In *Cities in a Larger Context.* Thomas W. Collins, (Ed.). Pp. 76–96. Southern Anthropological Society Proceedings, No. 14. Athens, Georgia: University of Georgia Press.

(1986). The multinational corporation as a form of sociocultural integration above the level of the nation state. In *Anthropology and International Business.* Studies in Third World Urban Societies, No. 28. Hendrick Serrie, (Ed.). Pp. 163–190. Williamsburg, Virginia: College of William & Mary.

5

Women as a Category of Analysis in Scholarship on Tourism: Jamaican Women and Tourism Employment

A. LYNN BOLLES

Unlike many industries, in which opportunities for labor are limited to the manufacture or extraction of a particular product that is produced at a specific manufacturing site, the tourism industry is complicated by the fact that tourists can serve as both the products and consumers of the industry, and their activities can be directed and controlled with only limited success. While the greater economic benefits to be derived from the production of tourists are generally realized by those who have large amounts of capital to invest in the industry, there is also more than usual opportunity for entrepreneurs who have little capital or, in some cases, just their labor to invest. This can make it difficult to weigh the relative costs and benefits of tourism to any segment of the "host" community. In this chapter, A. Lynn Bolles explores another relatively neglected area of anthropological research related to tourism—the consequences of the industry for local women who, as Bolles points out, figure prominently in both the imagery and economics of tourism in countries like Jamaica. Bolles' conclusions point to some of the anomally presented by the industry. On the one hand, she finds that the employment opportunities normally available to Jamaican women are inequitably limited by patterns of gendered exploitation in which tourism follows the course of earlier colonial activity. On the other hand, many of the women Bolles interviewed report that they are satisfied with their employment in the tourism sector and express the feeling that they would be worse off should such opportunities not be available to them.

According to a very well-worn and often quoted Chinese proverb, women hold up half of the sky. In the tourist industry, women hold up more than their share, as hosts, as workers, as images of touristic adventure. Jamaica, one of the earliest sites of modern-day tourism, is a well-known destination, particularly for United States based travelers. The success of such a tourism is often based on the quality and the quantity of service rendered to the consumer. In Jamaica, and elsewhere in the world, women are engaged in activities that provide service for the tourist area. Given this scenario, perhaps there is no other better place than Jamaica to describe and analyze women's roles in this industry that is based on consumers visiting a place away from home for the purpose of experiencing a change or adventure (Smith, 1991:1).

There are two items on the agenda in this chapter. The first is to contribute to the tourist ethnography of Jamaica. The second is to begin to locate women in the research on tourism by analyzing tourism from a female gendered perspective. In this way, women as tourist workers and how they are or can be effected as residents of communities where tourism is an important economic enterprise comes into focus.

Reasons for calling for the inclusion of women as critical agents in tourism results from a three point perspective. First, in my general overview of cross-cultural touristic literature, when women are not missing from the scene, they were housed literally in the domestic sphere alone. For example, there was little discussion of the gendered effects in works in tourism that focused on environmental or economic development issues. Second, when women are the topic of research, it is usually in the study of sex tourism in South East Asia, or elsewhere that female bodies are a tourist commodity to be sampled by paying visitors. Although sex tourism is an important phenomenon to examine, it is just one of the many roles that women play in the tourist arena. Finally, women as hosts and folks provide a multiplier impact on tourism: they supply usually poorly paid domestic service, and other forms of wage labor; they supply artistry; they supply advertising images; they supply entrepreneurial skills to the economic sector; and they supply their sexuality for sale. A change of scenery for a visitor has multiple meanings when women as hosts, native girls, and folk are concerned.

The discussion is divided into three parts. In the first, I argue that women as a category of analysis must be considered in the theory and method of anthropological studies of tourism. Second, I explain that when women are at the core of the analysis, our understanding of tourism increases in dramatic ways. Both genders of the human species are represented, which underscores the sexual division of labor in other aspects of culture. Finally, some of my findings are outlined from my fieldwork on women tourist workers in Negril, Jamaica.

Women as a Category of Analysis

In the early stages of familiarizing myself with the anthropological studies on tourism, I quickly discovered *Hosts and Guests*, edited by Valene L. Smith. This volume provides a wealth of information concerning the discipline's two decades of analyzing and understanding the cultural, social and economic interaction between hosts and their paying guests—the tourists. In that work, Swain (1990:83–104) examines the differential impact of indigenous tourism on the Kuna of Panama. The focus is on two activities marketed for tourist consumption—ecological tourism and "mola" production. Both of these enterprises reflect the gendered division of family labor among the Kuna. The bottom line is, "in general, local tourism development . . . differentially affects women and men (Ibid.)." This chapter is the only one in this very influential volume that really makes that definite statement about women and tourism. Other contributors discuss the impact of hotels, tours, and various forms of contemporary cultural phenomena that connotes the new economic and symbolic power of tourism. But none of the other authors look at how tourism reaches into the core of the social structure and rearranges or confirms certain gendered roles.

In the book's section on theory, Nunez (1990:274) comments on touristic studies by anthropologists, and the level of maturity of the scholarship within the field; "As a subject of scholarly study, tourism may be new, but it may be treated within traditional methods and theories of anthropological research of the present and will benefit from the application of more recent, more sophisticated models as data and understanding accumulate." No better rallying call has ever been made!

Continuing the discussion, I would like to build upon Nunez's statement by citing another assessment of the discipline. This one was made sixteen years earlier than the first edition of *Hosts and Guests*. In her introduction to her edited volume *Toward an Anthropology of Women*, Rapp (1975:16) states "Focusing first on women, we must redefine the important questions, reexamine all previous theories, and be critical in our acceptance of what constitute factual material. Armed with such a consciousness, we can precede to new investigations of gender in our own and other cultures." Of course, Rapp's statement was one of the earliest articulations of feminist anthropology; a perspective now known for its cutting edge theories, innovative methodologies in field-work and recasting old concepts. Perhaps the sophisticated models alluded to by Nunez included a feminist anthropological perspective.

The development of a feminist anthropology, I would argue, followed in-roads and innovations made by African American and other anthropologists' of color, Marxist, and critical thinkers of the discipline in their examinations of anthropology—the child of imperialism (B. Valentine, 1978; Jones, 1970; Hymes, 1979; Leacock, 1971; Green, 1970). Feminist anthropology discourse was not, as Moore (1989) reminds us, a critique based on the neglect of women in traditional ethnography. Most of the anthropological literature did not deny the female of the human species. However, most of the ethnographic record definitely contributed to female invisibility. Women were hidden from the overall social analysis, misrepresented, and positioned in arenas of action that were not necessarily accurate in terms of the culture and society under study. Sometimes, whole clans, families, groups, villages, and towns were analyzed and described without women! Furthermore, what women actually did in a social system in comparison to men was sometimes lacking in the analysis. Without an appropriate examination of the sexual division of labor the analysis resulted in absence, neglect, and misrepresentation. It was this basic point of view that began the call for an anthropology of women, outlined by Rapp and others in the early 1970s.

Jumping over the interceding years, feminist anthropology and other under-represented "native" anthropologies have brought other frames of reference to the discipline; efforts in the decolonizing of anthropology. Harrison (1991:9) notes that "decolonized anthropology articulates theoretical explanations that seek to be acted upon in creative, socially responsible, human-centered ways." Therefore, in many ways, feminist anthropology is a mode of decolonizing the discipline, particularly in reference to the study of gender. For feminist anthropology, the next stage is not only promoting the study of women, but the study of gender. The goal is to reveal the complexities within and among women's histories, experiences, and activities cross-culturally and how this broadens the scope of studying social systems. By examining these gendered differences we can build theoretical constructs which analyze the variations among women, the overlay of class, race, ethnicity, religion, sexual orientation, and so forth as they form an understanding of a female position in culture and society. A feminist anthropology must be also involved in reformulating feminist theory, which relies too often on the obvious, or the obtuse (see Mascia-Lees et al., 1989; Bolles, 1992).

Feminist anthropological research is not without its own problems: there is a tendency to reflect a Eurocentric and class bias (Bolles, 1995).

The history of Western elite class bias is addressed by Ong (1988). In her discussion of research on women and work in export processing zones in the developing world, Ong aptly remarked "Western feminists have made non-Western women the "other." The concept of "otherness" comes from the work of Simone De Beauvior, the feminist existentialist philosopher. She argued that men rendered women voiceless, subordinated, and inconsequential to the things that really count; an oppositional referent between the genders. Western feminist researchers and academics positioned non-Western women in that same "other" mode; they represented what the researcher is not. As Lamphere (1991:1) noted, the native peoples became "different," that is unlike those in the hegemonic culture (meaning EuroAmerican or European, and middle-class). Women "othering" other women based on a wide variety of differences, is definitely a challenge facing feminist anthropology, and other feminists who work in and outside of the academy. Clearly feminist anthropology must meet and provide the mode for redressing the situation. As diverse fields contribute to the scholarship on cross-cultural understandings of women's roles in culture and society, it is imperative that an anthropological perspective lead the way. Such an area, that has sparked the interest in a number of disciplines, and is in need of feminist inputs is the anthropological study of tourism.

Theory Building in Tourist Studies

A goal of feminist anthropology is to reformulate theories and approaches to the study of gender, examining the differences and commonalties of women cross-culturally. Touristic studies are in need of developing new modes of conceptualizing and approaching the study of tourism (Kinnaird, Kothari and Hall, 1994:1–43). Therefore, two theoretical and methodological spaces open up in feminist anthropological studies of tourism. Not only is gender a category of analysis for tourism studies, but it can also provide a mode of analysis to show the range of variation of female experiences in the complex arrangements fostered in tourist industries. Further, this kind of analysis is critical for comparative research.

All of the bodies of theories that are used by cultural analysts do not necessarily all fall together nicely, nor so neatly in touristic studies. Given the "frontier" nature of the field of study, I would like to suggest a particular approach for feminist touristic discourse. This perspective presents a way whereby the women under study are referents to their own self-defined social and cultural position. Moreover, this mode of research also defines a special role for the feminist researcher in this endeavor. It follows Collins's (1989;1990) development of black feminist thought. This viewpoint focuses on the alternative ways women produce and validate knowledge. It envisions methodologies that illustrate such experiences. Although Collins's work focuses on U.S. black women, it does have applicability elsewhere, partiularly among poor and oppressed women.

Collins argues that there are two levels of the way black women express their standpoints. One is the everyday, taken-for-granted knowledge of women of the African Diaspora—the majority of whom are usually poor and working class. Their knowledge may be expressed and produced in words, songs, organizations, quilts and in other forms. These everyday, taken-for-granted expressions convey social and cultural meaning that demonstrate how a woman deals with the world around her. An example that comes to mind is the way African American novelist Alice Walker described her mothers' flower garden as a horticultural representation of the poems her mother did not have the time to write down on paper.

The second level of knowledge is the specialized knowledge furnished by experts who are a part of the group, that is to say, also black and female. The experts express the everyday views of the women under study in a formal, specialized (academic, artistic) format. The role and the responsibility of this black feminist researcher is to create new modes of articulating that black women's everyday knowledge in a way which does not appropriate the message, but brings it to another audience outside of the community. In the realm of the academy, and in anthropology, the audience consists of colleagues, readers of published works donor agencies, and the like. For scholar-activists, or applied researchers, the audience is configured accordingly.

It is suggested here that women hosts and residents of tourist communities be approached in the fashion outlined by Collins's black feminist thought. The everyday, taken-for-granted expressions of women hosts and tourist workers produces knowledge about the world around them, and are valid in their own right. The role of the feminist researcher expert is to negotiate the meanings of that everyday female perspective so it can be brought to a larger audience of experts or the academy, funding agency and so forth.

Ordinary women's experiences should not be used as just a set of data acquisitions gathered in the fieldwork situation. Instead, the intruding, educated woman from the outside should position herself squarely in terms of her own role, and represent the women under study on their own terms. A feminist researcher should begin her inquiry from that standpoint, which also requires much self-reflection. Advocating a black feminist thought approach is not an easy one.Furthermore, this position is contrary to the premises of western based scientific thought (see Harding, 1987). Taking on this perspective requires a scholar to unlearn what has been a well-learned process.

The production and knowledge validation of the majority of women works across class, race, ethnicity and other boundaries. It will also add to the examination of commonalties and differences among the world's women. Following this line of reasoning, what it means to be female in certain social, economic, and cultural settings can truly become credible.

Tourism research on women can really benefit from this theory of how women as hosts, workers, and residents produce and validate knowledge. Mary Castelberg-Koulma (1991:197) notes "Few studies address themselves to the effects that tourism has on the local female population." She then goes on to describe and analyze peasant Greek women's cooperatives in terms of the impact of mass tourism on working-class and poor communities. In the boom and bust cycle of Greece's seasonal tourism, members of the poor and working-class involved in the business display exaggerated gendered roles. Men exhibited an exaggerated masculinity for the benefit of European and EuroAmerican-American female tourists. In contrast, Greek women became far more chastened in the domestic sphere than culturally expected. Women were also not given opportunities to expand their access to resources and skills in the tourist sector. By looking at the role of women in society, and locating the direction and nature of those social changes, Castelberg-Koulma analyzed tourism in terms of the differential impact on peasant Greek women and men.

Gender, as discussed in the case study from Greece, is viewed not as a unified category, but a many faceted one, that is open to change and variation (Ginsburg and Tsing, 1990:2). Negotiating gender is the manner by which terms and social relations are debated and redefined by the people themselves. This is a critical element to consider when people are pursuing particular and often conflicting interests. In the introduction to *Uncertain Terms*, Ginsburg and Tsing make the following analogy. The way women and men negotiate their lives, locations, and ideas is similar to negotiating a river—trying to swim and keeping from sinking. This kind of gendered perspective enables feminist researchers to examine the diverse situations of power struggles, and to analyze to the full extent, any social processes which produces, challenges, or confirms gender categories.

Jamaican Tourism and Women

My research on women in tourism focuses on Jamaica. That country is one of the major players in the Caribbean tourist industry, with a long history in the business. In recent times, tourism has become one of Jamaica's largest sources of revenue, and in 1993 was the largest earner of foreign exchange (PIJ, 1993). In the same year, tourists spent approximately U.S. $ 950 million (PIJ, 14:1). Of all U.S. travelers to the Caribbean, sixty percent visited Jamaica (PIJ, 1992:14:2). As this short list of facts shows, tourism contributes significantly to the welfare of the country's economy. Furthermore, the tourist sector employs countless number of women across different categories of work.

Jamaican women as hosts, residents, and tourist workers, in tourist-economy communities are spread throughout the population, but are dramatically concentrated on the north coast of the island. The following analysis is based on fieldwork conducted in Negril, a tourist community located on the most Northwestern tip of the island. The work examines the role women play in the tourist sector of Negril, across boundaries of class and race. In this study, tourism becomes a vehicle for exploring the differences and commonalties among women.

Negril is a unique location to study the impact of Jamaica's tourism on the lives of women workers for a number of reasons: its late entry as a major destination; its wide range of accommodations—cottages, villas, and hotels of various sizes; its history as a vacation area for Jamaicans; its new-age health and sports tourism; a low-paced atmosphere indicative of its fishing village origins; and its high rate of returning visitors, connected to the personal relations developed between the folk and guests. The transformation of Negril from a fishing village to a hot tourist spot occurred over twenty some years. During that time, women's income-generating activities expanded, so that a range of jobs exists stemming from traditional ones like fruit vending to contemporary ones such as managing a multinational-owned resort.

Advertisements for Jamaica usually feature a Caucasian man and woman sitting on a white sandy beach taking in the sun (consumer identification is a critical marketing response). Often photos show men dressed in military garb reminiscent of the colonial past. But always, there are images of smiling faces of black or brown women as nannies, flower vendors, or as exotically costumed female entertainers bending under a "limbo" bar, camera angle focused on the area between their legs. The men are manly and the women are welcoming and available in their femininity (Enloe, 1990:32). Not only are women the majority of

workers in the tourist industry, but without their image, visitors would-
n't be lured to these "exotic" locales.

Tourism is a labor-intensive industry. It requires a high ratio of employees to paying customers; people who come as tourists need and also
expect a lot of service. Furthermore, the kinds of jobs typed as labor-
intensive are also unskilled work categories that assume the worker
already knows how to perform the tasks required by the job. Most of the
jobs in the tourist sector are viewed, in most societies and definitely in
the Caribbean, as ones that women not only know how to do, but that
comes "naturally" to them. Therefore, housekeeping, doing laundry,
cooking, serving and so forth, are female dominated jobs.

Most Jamaican working-class women have the sole responsibility of
rearing and financially supporting their children and other dependents
(Bolles, 1988). The notions of financial autonomy, independence (which
includes fulfilling obligations to a domestic network) and authority figure importantly in women's position in relation to men in Jamaica.

Many poor women rely on informal tourist work. Under the broil-
ing sun, women vendors walk up and down the beach, trying to sell
crafts, or fruit or to braid the hair of visitors, at the same time being ha-
rassed by hotel security guards because they do not have a vendor's license issued for a fee by the Chamber of Commerce. Seven days of the
week, for many hours per day, women do this kind of work with no
guarantees of meeting expenses. According to D'Amico-Samuels (1986),
women vendors in Negril's tourist area are engaged in creating economic opportunity in the narrow space between the "rock" of doing
poorly-paid scarcely available wage labor and the "hard place" of living in abject poverty.

Working-class women employed in hotels, restaurants, or other
businesses depend on child care provided by their network of family
and friends. Often items left by guests in their rooms find their way to
workers' homes. What is discarded or of little consequence to carry back
to the States is a useful good to maids and their family members. When
salaries are small and employment is bounded by the dates of the official high tourist season, December 15th to April 15th, any supplement
is appreciated.

D'Amico-Samuels' study also noted that middle-class and upwardly mobile working-class women have made significant contributions to Negril's successful tourist business. This group of women
as proprietors of cottages and guest houses are crucial to Negril's per-
son-to-person ambiance. Middle-class women and those who aspire to
be so have reaped the rewards of doing good business. Women with

advanced training certificates and higher education degrees are welcomed in the tourist industry.

Tourism, therefore, has provided decent and in some instances,
fairly substantial livelihoods for Jamaican women. One cannot assume
that the impact of a developing tourist sector always results in negative
consequences for the women or their communities. The question is,
what causes the differences between success stories and horror stories
and points in between?

According to GOJ statistics, fifty-eight percent of the total employment was in direct relation to the growth of tourism in the wider Negril
community (JIP, 1989:13.5). Four years later, sixty percent of women's
employment gains was in the hotel and restaurant services (JIP,
1993:18.1). Further, Negril experienced a seventy one percent rate of hotel room occupancy in comparison to Montego Bay (57.2%) and Ocho
Rios (66.4%), the other two major north coast tourist centers. It is not
surprising then to discover that hotel domestic work employs the most
women in the area.

However, as mentioned earlier, women play other roles in the
tourist trade besides being chambermaids. They are cooks, tourist
market vendors, artists, recreational supervisors, nannies, barkeeps,
waitresses, and nightclub entertainers. They braid hair, sell T-shirts,
coconuts, crafts and straw, snacks and fruit in vendor's cooperative
markets and on the beach. Women are travel agents and sell fine
jewelry and Waterford crystal in fashionable boutiques/duty-free
shops. Women also manage cottages, villa complexes and hotels (usually as assistant managers), but in some small units, CEOs. Women
work as cooks and as food and beverage managers in large hotels, They
are agents for car rental services and they serve as tellers in local banks.
In Negril, women work as accountants, bookkeepers, bankers, nurses,
and are culinary arts, hospitality, and recreation experts. This list of
job types is informative of how women fulfill a variety of employment
categories in the tourist sector on the north coast of Jamaica.

The employment types exemplify the tremendous range of differences among women workers involved in Jamaican tourism. These
jobs demonstrate the varied levels of education, skills, and training
among Jamaican women. Implicit then are class differentials, and in
the Jamaican context, class often correlates with skin color. Historically,
due to the legacy of slavery and maintained by a colonial and neocolo-
nial system, the majority of the Jamaican middle-class are of a lighter
skin color than their black skinned country person of more humble origins. Since Jamaica's independence in 1962, however, education, one of
the factors that maintained the status quo, has become more available

to the population at large. Education, an important component for upward mobility helped to increase the size of the black middle-class. Looking at gender and education, it is clear that girls have also benefited. Approximately seventy-two percent of all students enrolled in public secondary schools were girls (JIP, 1993: 20.7). However, when the majority of girls leave school and enter the workforce, the types of jobs that await them are decidedly sex-segregated and low paying that in turn reproduces the class system, as the list of tourist related jobs mentioned above implies.

Jamaican women, across class boundaries, have high percentages of labor force participation (62.4%)—one of the highest in the world (JIP, 1993:18.9). Across job categories, the female labor market is highly sex-segregated, following traditional lines of what is considered "women's work". Women are the majority of domestic service workers as well as being a major force in clerical, sales, and lower level managerial positions. The tourist industry incorporates all of those categories of female work, and uses gender segregation rationalization in the pay scales. Wage discrimination is against the law, but traditional job categories imply the credo that women's wages are supplemental to a primary male breadwinner. The reality is, however, that nearly half of the households in Jamaica are headed by women. Across class lines, women are a part of the household income generating pool. However, the wages they receive are often related to the kind of work (domestic, or service sector) and the legitimization of unequal pay for women.

Making a Living in Tourism

My study of women and tourist work began very modestly by visiting friends of friends in Negril. I sounded out these tourist workers about the problems they faced in their lives and work situations. After those preliminary discussions, I concluded that what I perceived to be important questions were indeed compelling issues for those in the community. So, I began to conduct fieldwork in Negril for a total of nine months over three years. I made the acquaintance of women workers through a variety of channels—references from the Chamber of Commerce, mutual friends, and basic brazen anthropological techniques of hanging out and starting up a conversation. The goal of the larger project was: to bring the role of the women tourist workers into the light of the industry; to analyze tourism as an industrial sector that employs women; and to document the broad range of tourist related work because the sector is providing the financial mainstay of the country. My sample of fifty women is relatively small, but it reflects the range of experiences of women in the business across social categories.

Negril is composed of three distinctive sections; its famous seven mile stretch of white sandy beach; the west-end or the cliffs, and Negril Centre. Each area has its sense of community, or lack of one, and all are work sites for women. The three women featured here represent each section of town. Their stories convey the range of variation for women's work and family life.

The Beach

Negril's beach came as a windfall. The coconut blight of the 1950s ravaged the groves leaving behind a gleaming white stretch of beach of exceptional beauty. According to the law, hotels cannot block public access to the beach. In the 1970s, vendors of all sort of goods strolled the beach looking for customers, some of whom took issue at being unduly pressured to buy. In response to consumer complaints, public access to the beach was challenged by the hoteliers. Hotel security forces question anyone walking across the sand adjacent to the resort who is not a guest in the establishment. They question all vendors, particularly those who are known as too poor to pay for a vendor's license issued by the Chamber of Commerce. Not only is the license costly for most poor people, it is clearly a way of social control—keeping the local public at bay. One unlicensed vendor, who skirts the control mechanism, is Gloria. She has made friends out of many of the hotel security patrols, and sets-up "shop" just outside of the hotel's parameter on public land.

> Gloria braids hair on the beach as an unlicensed itinerant vendor. She walks up and down the Negril beaches asking women tourists if they want their hair styled in a fashion made popular a decade ago by actress Bo Derek. Armed with elastic bands, beads, bobby pins, combs and clips, and a mirror, Gloria braids quickly and efficiently, using an artists' eye to provide the most becoming hair style for her clients. She approaches groups of women tourists, cajoles them, and gets them to try it. She does a fast, professional job which pleases, and then entices the friends of the woman or those lookers-on to enjoy in the "look." At the end of the day, Gloria can make (during the high season) US $20–30 representing about six clients due to competition by other hair braiders. She had to learn how to manage "the thin little hairs of the white women," but now she considers herself one of the best hair stylists on the beach. Gloria was fortunate that her mother babysat her children when they were young, while she "worked the beach."

The West End

Before Negril was discovered by international visitors, it was the vacation spot for the urban Jamaican middle-class. Families traveled from Kingston to Negril for a relaxing vacation "in the country," where amenities were often far and few between. On the West End Road, that runs from Negril Centre to the Lighthouse, there are cottages for rent. Some of these cottages are now a part of a hotel compound, all family owned and operated. Originally, families in Negril built extra rooms onto their own homes to accommodate the Jamaicans who were on family holidays, who tended to repeat their visit. However, as the visitors started to come from outside of Jamaica, Negrillians took advantage of this cottage industry. The accommodations were not luxurious, but very family-centered, and very welcoming, particularly on the part of the woman of the house who was in charge of the visitors. Soon families were building cottages with tourists from Jamaica and abroad in mind. And with time, the amenities came too.

> Mrs. Cuthburt owns and manages three cottages. She is the sole owner of one cottage, and the other two she owns with her husband. Mrs. "C" started out renting cottages to Jamaican middle class families who vacationed in Negril in the early 1960s. She did all the cooking, laundry, maid service, desk clerk, "every little striking thing." Mrs. Cuthburt saved her money as business was good because of referrals from returning guests. She acquired the two additional cottages with her husbands financial contribution provided by wages as a low-level manager on a nearby sugar estate. Mrs. Cuthburt bore five children. All of her children played with the guests, and the guest kids. They also helped their mother change linen, clean rooms and run errands. Since they are now all grown-up, they live either in the United States, or Kingston with their own children.

Negril Centre

Negril Centre is marked by the circular roundabout that ends the road from Montego Bay, begins the West End Road toward the Lighthouse, and the road that comes from Sav-La-Mar, the urban center of the parish of Westmoreland. Banks, supermarkets, shops, bus stops, the American Express office, the Chamber of Commerce office, and a variety of other enterprises are located there. The first hotels built in Negril for tourists are Jamaican owned and located in the vicinity of Negril Centre. The owners of these first hotels are not native Negrillians, but do have family connections in this part of the country. The following discussion centers around the history of one family's resort.

Marie was the food and beverage manager of a large hotel close to Negril Center. She graduated form a prestigious girls' high school in Kingston, and attended The University of London. When Marie returned home to Jamaica in the late 1970s, she became a Rasta (Rastafari is a religion and accompanying life-style that professes the importance of being African, being closer to nature, and revering Haile Selassie, late emperor of Ethiopia as the messiah). As a result of her father's prodding, Marie moved to Negril to work in his hotel, located on the beach. She was hesitant to enter the tourist sector given her religiosity, but found out she enjoyed the business. However, Marie worked hard as the food and beverage manager. In that job, she had to procure foodstuffs for the American clientele, as well as to buy from local farmers, all at a good price. Marie has three children that are taken care of by domestic help.

Conclusion

The descriptions of these three female tourist workers in Negril illustrate the range of women's jobs in the industry. Each woman takes advantage of wage earning opportunities available according to their skill and educational level, and to their access to capital. How they negotiate the tourist business rests on their own hard work, and on a network of kin, business associates, and employees whom they rely on to make their economic activity a possibility and hopefully a success. All three women work a double day; that is, they tend to the care of children and families after their paid job is done, or incorporate them into the family business.

The heterogeneity of women's lives and experiences in this Jamaican example clearly shows that tourism is a gendered industry, and that the division of labor is a critical operational factor. The role of women, as a category of analysis, makes the anthropological study of tourism more inclusive, and close to the reality it represents—the world's fastest growing industry.

References

Bolles, A. Lynn. (1988). *My Mother who Fathered Me and Others: Gender and Kinship in the English-speaking Caribbean*. East Lansing, MI: *Women and International Development Working Paper Series, #175*.

————. (1992, December). "Standpoints and Knowledge of Black Women." A paper presented at the American Anthropological Association. San Francisco, CA.

————. (1995, November). "Decolonizing Feminist Anthropology." A paper presented at the American Anthropological Association. Washington, DC.

Castelberg-Koulma, Mary. (1991). "Greek Women and Tourism: Women's Cooperatives as an Alternative Form of Organization." In *Working Women*. Edited by N. Redflift and M.T. Sinclair. Pp. 197–212. New York: Routledge.

De Beauvior, Simone. (1952). *The Second Sex*. New York: Bantam rpt. 1970.

D'Amico-Samuels, Deborah. (1986). "You Can't Get Me out of the Race: Women and Economic Development in Negril, Jamaica, West Indies." Unpublished Ph.D. dissertation, Graduate Center of City University of New York.

Enloe, Cynthia. (1990). *Beaches, Bananas, and Bases*. Berkeley: University of California Press.

Ginsburg, Fay, and Anna Tsing. (Eds). (1990). "Introduction." In *Uncertain Terms*. Pp. 1–27. Boston: Beacon.

Green, Vera. (1970). "The Confrontation of Diversity within the Black Community." *Human Organization*, 29:4:267–272.

Harding, Sandra. (Ed). (1987). "Introduction: Is There a Feminist Methodology?" In *Feminism and Methodology*. Pp. 1–14. Bloomington, IN: Indiana University Press.

Harrison, Faye V. (Ed.). (1991). "Anthropology as an Agent of Transformation." In *Transforming Anthropology*. Pp. 1–14. Washington, DC: American Anthropological Association.

Hymes, Dell, (Ed.). (1979). *Reinventing Anthropology*. New York: Vantage Press.

Jones, Delmos. (1970). "Towards a Native Anthropology." *Human Organization*, 29:4:251–259.

Kinnaird Vivan, Uma Kothari and Derek Hall. (1994). "Tourism: gender perspectives." In *Tourism a Gender Analysis*. Edited by V. Kinnaird and D. Hall. Pp. 1–34 Chichester, UK: Wiley Publishers.

Leacock, Eleanor B. (Ed.). (1971). *The Culture of Poverty: A Critique*. New York: Simon and Schuster.

Mascia-Lees, Frances et al. (1989). "The Postmodernist Turn in Anthropology: Cautions from a Feminist Perspective." *Signs, 15*:1:7–33.

Moore, Henrietta. (1988). *Feminism and Anthropology.* Minneapolis, MN: University of Minnesota Press.

Nunez, Theron. (1990). "Touristic Studies in Anthropological Perspective." In *Hosts and Guests.* Edited by V.L. Smith. Pp. 265–280. Philadelphia: University of Pennsylvania Press.

Ong, Aiwah. (1988). "Colonialism and Modernity: Feminist Re-presentations of Women in Non-western Societies." *Inscriptions,* Nos. 3/4. Pp. 86–95.

Planning Institute of Jamaica. (1989, 1993). *Economic and Social Survey.* Kingston, Jamaica: Planning Institute of Jamaica.

Rapp, Rayna. (1975). *Towards and Anthropology of Women.* New York: Monthly Review Press.

Smith, Valene L. (1990). *Hosts and Guests: The Anthropology of Tourism.* Philadelphia: University of Pennsylvania Press, 2nd Edition.

Swain, Margaret Byrne. (1990). "Gender roles in Indigenous Tourism: Kuna Mola, Kuna Yala, and Cultural Survival." In *Hosts and Guests,* Edited by V. L. Smith. Pp. 83–104. Philadelphia: University of Pennsylvania Press.

Valentine, Betty Lou. (1978). *Hustling and Other Hard Work.* New York: The Free Press.

6

Cultural, Economic, and Environmental Impacts of Tourism Among Kalahari Bushmen[1]

ROBERT K. HITCHCOCK

As the human and environmental risks often associated with tourism development have become more apparent, increased attention has been paid to strategies for encouraging a more sustainable approach to tourism that will permit planners to encourage development without jeopardizing the resources upon which the industry depends. In this chapter, Robert Hitchcock provides an appraisal of several such efforts as they impinge on the lives of the Kalahari Bushmen, a people who have long intrigued Western visitors. Hitchcock concludes that the Bushmen have both benefitted from "sustainable" tourism programs and realized several unanticipated costs associated with increased tourist activity. These costs have included greater social stratification, community factionalism, and environmental harm. The benefits appear to be greatest where Bushmen have had the opportunity to participate in decision-making related to tourism development, leading Hitchcock to suggest that there is likely to be a close link between goals of sustainability and the equal expression of human rights. This chapter introduces the reader to another subset of tourism's many mediators—those government officials and professionals who, while generally not involved as investors in tourist enterprises or as direct employees of the industry, have begun to play important roles in determining both the direction and ideology of tourism's future.

Introduction

Tourism has been recommended as a strategy for promoting sustainable development by both southern African governments and international development agencies (Republic of Botswana, 1990; Ministry of Finance and Development Planning, 1991; Ministry of Wildlife, Conservation, and Tourism, 1992a, b:70–74; USAID, 1989; USAID/ Namibia, 1992). As *Namibia's Green Plan* notes, the country's challenge is "to develop a sustainable tourism industry that will complement and not harm the attractions which draw tourists to Namibia" (Ministry of Wildlife, Conservation, and Tourism, 1992b:74). Planning tourism activities that are sustainable requires an integrated, systemic, and multifaceted approach (Smith and Eadington, 1992; Boo, 1992).

Much of the tourism in southern Africa is nature tourism or, as it is termed by many of the companies marketing tours in the region, ecotourism. Ecotourism is considered to have substantial benefits for those who take part in it, both tourists themselves and those whose areas they visit (Boo, 1990, 1992; Kiss, 1990; Whelan, 1991; Giannecchini, 1993). There is, however, evidence to indicate that tourism can have negative environmental and socioeconomic impacts (Smith, 1989a, b; Johnston, 1990; Savage, 1993; Pleumarom, 1994). Non-government organizations involved in assessing the impacts of tourism and people in tourist-affected areas are learning that tourism is by no means the benign, non-polluting, and economically beneficial development approach that it is often made out to be by the World Tourism Organization (WTO) and tourism agencies.

Smith (1989a:3) points out that tourism can be a significant factor in bringing about cultural change. This is particularly true of what Smith (1989a:2) defines as "ethnic tourism," visits paid to traditional or indigenous populations who reside in remote places and who retain, at least to a certain extent, many of their unique customs and lifestyles. The effects of tourism on people who live in out of the way places are often substantial (Smith, 1989b; Johnston, 1990).

Tourism can sometimes be problematic for local people, especially in situations where the host population is extremely poor (Enloe, 1989; Smith, 1989b). Resident populations sometimes go to extraordinary lengths to meet the needs of tourists. In some cases, local households give up other kinds of economic activities such as agriculture or hunting in an effort to take advantage of employment opportunities in the tourist industry. There are also situations where people abandon their values and shed their dignity in their quest for the cash that tourists provide. Tourism also brings about dependency of poorer people on wealthy individuals and companies. Thus, there are differences of opinion among groups visited by tourists as to the balance between benefits and costs.

In recent years, greater emphasis has been placed on "alternative tourism," recreational activities that pose little threat to the habitats or

the societies that are visited. This kind of tourism is supposed to be designed in such a way that it actually enhances the quality of life for the
hosts while providing educational benefits to the guests (Smith and
Eadington, 1992). It is this kind of tourism which most local people
would prefer to be involved in. Tourism can have positive effects if local people are able to participate in tourist related enterprises and if they
receive an equitable share of the revenues.

The social, economic, and environmental impacts of tourism on local populations in rural areas are subjects that are receiving increasing
attention from scientists and development planners (Wu, 1982; Crick,
1989; Smith, 1989b; Smith and Eadington, 1992). A number of investigations have been done of the social, economic, and environmental impacts of tourism among various indigenous groups, ranging from the
Cuna (Kuna) Indians of Panama (Wright, Houseal, and de Leon, 1985;
Swain, 1989; Chapin, 1990; Ventocilla, Herrera, and Nunez, 1995) to
American Indians in the southwestern United States (Browne and
Nolan 1989), and from Australian Aborigines (Altman, 1989) to the Hill
Tribes of Thailand (Cohen, 1989) and the Toroja of Indonesia (Volkman,
1990). These studies have shown that tourism often has significant ef-
fects, and that the poorer and more remote the population, the greater
the impacts.

In the majority of cases where indigenous peoples have been exposed to sizable numbers of tourists, the costs have tended to outweigh
the benefits. Most tourism operations tend to involve indigenous peoples only to a limited extent. Poverty and hardship are all too often the
result of commercial tourism. It is for this reason that indigenous communities have pushed for a greater say in decisions regarding the fre-
quency, number, and types of tourists who enter their communities and
the kinds of tourism that are promoted.

This chapter addresses the effects of tourism among the Bushmen,
the indigenous peoples of the Kalahari Desert region of southern
Africa.[2] Drawing on data collected among rural communities in the
Kalahari over a period of nearly twenty years (1975–1995), the chapter
considers the cultural, economic, and environmental impacts of tourism
among a set of populations who are well-known to the public through
extensive popular and scientific coverage (Marshall, 1976; Lee, 1979,
1993; Silberbauer, 1981; Biesele, 1990; Biesele; Guenther, Hitchcock,
Lee, and Macgregor, 1989). Tourism has brought about substantial
socio-economic and environmental changes among Kalahari communities (Almagor, 1985; Gordon, 1990; Hitchcock and Brandenburgh, 1990).
As I will attempt to demonstrate, there is significant variation in the
kinds of impacts that tourism has had among Bushmen, and there are

differing opinions at the local and national levels concerning the nature
and effects of these changes.

Tourism among Kalahari Bushmen

The countries of Namibia and Botswana (Figure 1) provide useful
illustrations of the socioeconomic and environmental impacts of
tourism in remote areas. Tourism companies market both countries as
being "unspoiled Edens" where people can see large numbers of elephants, lions, and other wildlife as well as groups of people who sup-
posedly continue to hunt and gather "as they have always done." A
significant proportion of the tourists who visit the rural parts of the two
countries are people who tend to place high value on viewing wildlife
and people in their "natural state." Today, there are at least a half dozen
companies that market "Bushman tourism" on the internet, and numerous other companies both in southern Africa and elsewhere use
brochures that display Bushmen in various ways.

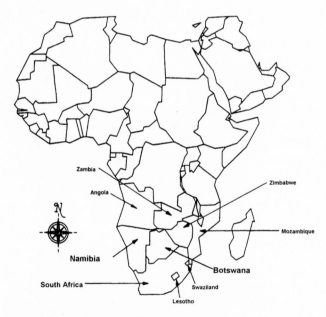

Figure 1. Map of Namibia, Botswana and Adjacent
Nations

There are many tourists who visit Namibia and Botswana in order to see "exotic" peoples, particularly the Bushmen of the Kalahari and the Himba of the Kaokoveld. Excited by the prospect of viewing what are marketed as "some of the world's most traditional peoples," tourists arrange with safari companies to go to remote communities. The purpose of these visits, according to many of the tourists who make them, is to experience an exotic culture and to see people who still pursue their "age-old lifestyles."

The tourism industry in both Namibia and Botswana is based largely upon natural resources, especially wildlife and remote and exotic habitats. As a result, the major tourist destinations tend to be the Kalahari and Namib Deserts, the Kaokoveld, the Okavango Delta, and the various national parks and game reserves in the two countries (Campbell and von Richter, 1976; Johnson, 1976; Pfotenhauer, 1991; Ministry of Wildlife, Conservation, and Tourism, 1992a). Since the numbers of people living in these areas tend to be small, most of the contacts between tourists and resident populations consisted of situations in which local people served as guides, helpers, or photographic subjects (Almagor, 1985; Gordon, 1990; Hitchcock and Brandenburgh, 1990).

A primary reason cited by Namibian and Botswana government planners for increasing tourism is that it generates employment and income (Ministry of Finance and Development Planning, 1991; Ministry of Wildlife, Conservation, and Tourism, 1992a:70). In 1991, 6,000 people were employed in tourism-related industries in Namibia. Tourism generated approximately 200 million Rand (US $80 million) to the country's Gross Domestic Product (GDP). Tourism was identified as one of the most promising sectors for future growth in the Botswana economy (Ministry of Finance and Development Planning, 1991:49, 295–301). In the northwestern part of the country, forty percent of all formal sector jobs were linked to tourism (Ministry of Finance and Development Planning, 1991:295). Tourism also provided people in the rural areas of both countries with a market for their products, thus facilitating the flow of cash into local communities.

One of the suggestions made during the course of discussions of tourism in Namibia and Botswana is that "model villages" might be set up in which local people would perform such "traditional" activities as hunting, gathering, skin processing, and handicraft manufacture (Lilly- white and Lillywhite, 1991; Domestic Technology International, 1992). When asked whether or not they would like to participate in such efforts, a number of local people said that they would; they hastened to add, however, that they did not want to be mistreated or given small amounts of money for their work. There were other local people who said that such an approach would simply create or reinforce negative stereotypes of local people. As one of them said, "We do not want to have to perform for tourists. It is not right that we should be treated like animals in a circus."

Tourists who expect to see hunter-gatherers in rural Namibia and Botswana are often amazed, if not taken aback, at the variety of activities in which people participate. While foraging does represent a fairly significant means of obtaining subsistence and generating income in some remote areas, many of the people also raise livestock, grow crops, and work as herders, field hands, and wage laborers (Marshall and Ritchie, 1984; Hitchcock, 1988; Biesele et al., 1989; Wilmsen, 1989; Biesele, 1990; Gordon, 1992; Lee, 1993). There are also people who leave the remote areas temporarily in order to seek employment in towns or in the mines, often returning to their homes laden with consumer goods such as radios, bicycles, and blankets.

Socioeconomic Impacts of Tourism

Tourism poses a number of dilemmas for local people. On the one hand they have the opportunity to get jobs and generate some cash through sales of crafts or demonstrations of activities such as dancing or gathering wild plants. On the other hand, tourists sometimes interfere with local people's daily activities, and they are not always aware of the appropriate ways to behave. Ethnic tourists often come in to remote places with preconceived notions of what to expect. Not always finding what they hoped for, they occasionally resort to bullying tactics. One of the difficulties faced by local people is that they had little ability to control the manner of their contact with outsiders.

Tourists were sometimes aware of the impacts that they had on local people. One advantage of tourism, according to some of the visitors, was that it provided local residents with sources of income that they would not have otherwise. Some of the tour operators said that the most important impact of tourism was that it provided jobs. Assessment of the actual numbers of remote area dwellers with jobs in the tourism industry in the Kalahari, however, suggests that at present there may not be as many positions available as some people claim.

In Namibia, analyses of tourism suggest that community-based tourism holds much promise for profits and sustainable economic development (Ashley, Barnes, and Healy, 1994; Ashley and Garland, 1994). Detailed analyses of tourism at the local level, however, suggests that many of these benefits have yet to be realized (Thoma, 1993; Garland, 1994; Hitchcock and Murphree, 1995). In Eastern Bushmanland, for example, there are only a dozen Ju/'hoansi who are employed directly in the tourism industry. The overall total of twelve tourism-related jobs is relatively insignificant when compared to the numbers of people involved in foraging and agriculture, which provides food, income, or employment for the vast majority of households in Eastern Bushmanland (Hitchcock, 1992).

One of the difficulties of a tourism-based industry is that the breadth of participation in the benefits tends to be somewhat skewed. The people who benefit the most tend to be adult males who are multilingual and who have had some experience in dealing with outsiders. It is these people who often end up working for tour operators or providing assistance to visitors. In the Ovambo and Caprivi areas of Namibia, the people who interacted most frequently with tourists were men who had worked on the mines in South Africa and who spoke Afrikaans. Interviews of women and children in the remote areas revealed that they felt left out when it came to direct benefits from tourism. There were differential gender impacts of tourism in the Kalahari, with adult males tending to benefit more than adult females, particularly in terms of employment.

Inflows of cash into communities can sometimes cause disagreements, especially when the distributions of the benefits are inequitable. This is all too often the case when tourism companies employ men to work for them, and women have little, if any, access to jobs. Such situations can result in social tensions, something that has occurred among the Himba of northwestern Namibia (Jacobsohn, 1991; Biesele, Green, and Hitchcock, 1992). There are also situations where some members of the community have greater access to tourism company benefits because of longstanding arrangements with them, something that has caused conflicts in Eastern Bushmanland in Namibia and in the southeastern and southwestern Kalahari Desert regions of Botswana (Hitchcock, 1991, 1992, 1993; Hitchcock, Masilo, and Monyatse, 1995).

In the early 1990s in Botswana, only sixty three Bushmen had full-time employment in the tourist industry, although a greater number, perhaps 300–400 people, had seasonal employment. The problem was, as a number of Bushmen noted, that the jobs they had usually tended to be ones where they were required to perform menial tasks for other people. These tasks ranged from cleaning toilets to collecting firewood and heating up water for tourist showers.

Most of the Bushmen interviewed in Botswana who had worked for tourism companies served either as hunting guides or camp laborers. These activities were sometimes carried out at some risk to the individuals involved. One !Xo from the southern part of Ghanzi District in Botswana told me that he was asked by the company for which he worked to run along in front of the vehicle looking for animal spoor. His worst nightmare, he said, was that the drunk hunters in the truck would shoot him instead of the animals they were after. Alternatively, he noted, there was a chance that the animal he was following would double back and attack him, something that has resulted in the deaths of several Bushmen in the past twenty years.

An assessment of the data on personnel in safari companies and tour groups in Botswana and Namibia reveals that there are virtually no Bushmen in management positions. None of these companies is owned or operated by Bushmen. According to some Namibian and Botswana Bushmen, tourism is literally out of their hands. It is controlled, they maintain, by private companies who prefer to hire trained managers from outside the local area. This was the case in Eastern Bushmanland, where a safari company, Anvo Hunting Safaris, had the concession to bring hunters and tourists into the area (Hitchcock, 1992; Thoma, 1993).

Rural people in the Kalahari were divided in their opinions about tourism. Some people felt that tourism was useful in that it enabled them to make some extra money. Others felt that they had little control over the actions of tourists, and they resented the intrusions in their lives.

Tourism in the Kalahari has served to expand the number of marketing opportunities for local handicrafts and other items. A kind of renaissance in crafts has occurred, with numerous groups producing baskets, ostrich eggshell bead necklaces, skin bags, and other items. While the handicraft industry has helped to rekindle interest in producing traditional goods, it has also had some negative economic effects, tying people to an unstable world market system. A common refrain heard in the Kalahari is that prices paid to producers are low and that profits go mainly to middlemen, some of them private companies owned by people from other countries or parastatal companies such as Botswanacraft in Botswana.

Stresses occur in rural communities when the numbers of visitors are substantial. Some people dislike the fact that outsiders, including anthropologists, come into their villages uninvited. Others note their lack of appreciation for the fact that they occasionally are requested to do disagreeable chores for tourists such as washing their clothes or cleaning up their campsites. Often the tourists give them little in the way of recompense. As one tourist put it, "What good is it to give Bush-men money? They don't understand its value." He went on to say, "Be-sides, there is no place to spend it out here anyway." Another tourist said that she refused to give cash to local people because, she said, "they would just spend it on beer."

It is important to note that some remote groups have had excellent working relationships with tourism companies. One tour operator who visits people in the southeastern and central Kalahari areas of Botswana is always welcome, according to Kua and G//ana informants, because he provides much needed employment. The owner of the company uses some of his profits to invest in developments in local villages. For one group he helped purchase a donkey cart which is used to haul water in drums to their homes. He bought seeds and tools for another group so that people could expand their agricultural activities. He sometimes purchases crafts beyond his own immediate needs and sells them in South Africa, later returning with the profits. This individual, along with members of a few other safari companies, lobbied the government on behalf of local people, recommending that land be set aside for them and that they be provided with water, social services, and employment opportunities.

Cultural Effects of Tourism

One of the cultural effects of tourism in the Kalahari is that it served to increase the awareness of local people of the customs and ideas of other societies. In some cases, local people became more ambivalent about their own ways of doing things. A few individuals said that they thought that hunting and gathering was "primitive" and it would be preferable if they could get jobs that would provide them with money for good clothing, food, and cars. At least two people said that tourists made them more aware of their own poverty, and as a result they be-came resentful of development workers who sometimes appeared to be incapable of providing them with the knowledge necessary to make them more successful economically and politically.

According to a number of local people, tourism tends to reinforce and amplify the distinctions between rich and poor. "Why is it," I was asked repeatedly, "that Europeans have so many things while we have so few?" Some individuals suggested that tourism fuels class aware-ness and causes resentment. One person noted that tourism benefits tend to flow towards the elite, leaving the majority of people either the same or worse off than they were before. Another said that young people have begun to desire Western goods such as bicycles and radios. In order to acquire these items they leave home in order to seek their fortune in towns and urban areas such as "Johanni" (Johannesburg). A reduction in labor availability and a breakdown in family structures sometimes results.

Some local people in rural Namibia and Botswana felt that they were in a kind of "human zoo" in which they were the objects of scrutiny by rich outsiders. A few people indicated that they disliked being thought of as "Bushmen" when in fact they were members of other groups. There were also people who made efforts to fit into the tourists' stereotypes of Bushmen, dressing-up intentionally in skins and carrying bows, arrows, and digging sticks, thus posing as "pure" hunter-gatherers. One non-government organization suggested that tourism has done more to promote hunting and gathering than all the efforts of anthropologists put together. Fitting in to outsiders' stereotypes does have its downside, however. In one community in the Caprivi, conflict broke out between Bushmen and members of another group, the Mbukushu, because some of the Mbukushu felt that the Bushmen were receiving preferential treatment from tourists (Chief Kipi George, personal communication).

Tourism can be culturally disruptive when it causes heightened desires for economic gains that are difficult, if not impossible, to attain. In interviews of a sample of people in six different communities in Eastern Bushmanland, it was found that a number of them hoped to move to town and to get well-paying jobs (Hitchcock, 1992). When asked what they wanted in their future, several of them said, "Toyota Land Cruisers, just like the ones that tourists drive." A few of them remarked that they looked forward to having the chance to sit outside their tents in tourist camps, eating sumptuous meals and enjoying iced drinks. While there is inherently nothing wrong with these aspirations, the chances of people obtaining them are relatively remote given the prevailing socioeconomic conditions in the Kalahari.

Discussions with Ju/'hoansi and other Bushmen in the Kalahari revealed that they were sometimes asked to remove their Western clothing so that they might be photographed in what tourists felt to be their "traditional" garb, something which many of them resented (Hitchcock, 1991, 1993; Hitchcock and Brandenburgh, 1990). Tourism played a role, they said, in people learning to attach even greater significance to Western-oriented perceptions of status and role. A question that sometimes was brought up during the course of interviews was why tourists so often looked for "traditional" people as opposed to those who were perceived as being successful in the local economy. Cattle owners sometimes said that they did not appreciate the fact that tourists sought out people who foraged. In the northern Kalahari, a man expressed his discomfort with the idea that tourists visited his area solely to see grass huts with people processing wild plants and making beads in front of them. Some people at Zutswa in the Kgalagadi District of Botswana suggested that the drying trays for salt, an important source of income for local people, be dismantled because they made the village look "too modern" for tourists' tastes.

A number of people said that they felt that tourism was useful to some people but not others, and they disliked those people who the tourists tended to focus their attention on. In some parts of the Kalahari, tourists trained their cameras on elderly women with tattoos, much to the chagrin of elderly men and young people. Thus, tourism has contributed to a process of rising social cleavages at the local level in Namibia and Botswana. While tourism may indeed expand incomes and create additional employment opportunities, it also causes social stratification and exacerbates problems of factionalism in local communities.

Some people in remote areas wanted to restrict tourism, and efforts were sometimes made by local development personnel to keep visitors away from local communities. This was the case in Ka/Gae in western Botswana, for example, where visitors were handed a sheet stating "We do not want you here." Others were anxious to interact with tourists and they even went so far as to produce brochures outlining prices for handicrafts.

It was not unusual to see individuals or families flocking toward tourist vehicles with handicrafts in hand. In Tjum!kui, the administrative center in Eastern Bushmanland, and in Ghanzi in Botswana, some poverty-stricken individuals begged tourists for food, something which left the visitors feeling uncomfortable. A government development worker in Botswana observed that some rural people had become so tourist-oriented that they refused to work on community projects, preferring instead to wait for visitors to come and give them food and money.

There are also cases of people who eschewed contact with tourists. When they heard the rumble of a Land Rover, they simply picked-up and left until the tourists disappeared over the horizon. As one tourist who had been on a lengthy trip across the Kalahari noted, "Whenever we got close to a Bushman village, we could see people scurrying away."

A significant cultural problem of tourism in the Kalahari is interpersonal conflict between members of the host communities and visitors. Numerous people mentioned that they resent tourists who do not greet them or come to them personally to explain what their purpose is in coming to their areas. A common complaint is that tourists do not treat local people as they would members of their own groups. "Why is it," they ask, "that we are requested to take off our clothes so people can take pictures of us? We don't see the tourists changing their clothes for photographs." This perceived inequity contributed to a feeling of distaste for tourists and for outsiders generally, something that made development work by government officials more difficult than would have been the case otherwise.

It is clear that tourism is viewed differently, depending upon the perceptions that local people have of its costs and benefits. In contrast to the notion that rapid modernization brings about a kind of acculturation that destroys local traditions, a number of Kalahari Bushmen have become actively engaged in perpetuating customary activities. Tyua groups along the Nata River in northeastern Botswana have more initiation rites and dances than they did in the past, in part, according to local informants, because they wish to differentiate themselves from their non-Tyua neighbors and visitors.

People in several parts of the Kalahari have requested help from Botswana's National Museum and Art Gallery in setting up their own museums and libraries. Some of them have also asked anthropologists to provide them with information on indigenous customs they can use in the writing of brochures to be handed out to visitors. The Ju/'hoansi of Eastern Bushmanland have worked closely with linguists, anthropologists, and educators in developing curricula to be used in local schools (Hitchcock, 1992; Thoma, 1993; Garland, 1994). In this sense, tourism can be viewed as having played a role in cultural conservation among Kalahari Bushmen.

At the national level, there are differences of opinion about the effects of tourism. Some government planners note that tourism will be useful because it will help to diversify the rural economy. Another benefit tourism will bring, they suggest, is that it will enhance people's pride in their own culture. Others say that tourism will have negative effects in that it will serve to reduce cultural variety and cause social problems. One Botswana official told me that while he thought that tourism was useful, he was concerned that increased numbers of visitors in rural areas of the country could overtax the local environment. He also expressed reservations about ethnic tourism, saying that it might give foreigners the impression that everyone in the Kalahari was poor, an image that he did not want people in the developed world to have of his country.

Environmental Impacts of Tourism

The environmental impacts of tourism in the Kalahari have varied, depending in part upon the kinds of tourism being promoted and the numbers of people involved. According to a number of informants, tourist vehicles sometimes destroyed the plants upon which they depended for part of their subsistence. The sounds of Toyota Land Cruisers and Land Rovers crashing through the bush on their way to remote communities also frightened away game. In some cases, tourists swam in the water reservoirs belonging to local communities, something that caused resentment and raised concerns about potential health problems. Tourists often had a negative effect on firewood supplies, particularly since, in the opinions of a number of Bushmen, they did not know how to build proper fires and tended to use wood at a prodigious rate.

In some of the remote areas where Bushmen reside, water is scarce most of the year. Women obtain moisture from rain pools and springs in the rainy season, but in the dry season they must resort to using water-bearing parts of plants for moisture. It is these plants which tourists want Bushmen to dig up so that they can photograph them doing "traditional" activities. The cost of this activity, from an economic standpoint, is that it limits their availability for subsistence purposes. From an environmental standpoint, it means that the reproductive parts of plants are not available for plant growth.

There were situations reported in which tourists went to remote parts of southern Africa with few supplies, hoping that they could "rough it," or, if necessary, ask local people for food and water. For people who saw themselves as having few resources, having rich tourists ask them for what little they had was extremely disconcerting.

Sometimes the actions of tourists in driving or walking around the landscape had both environmental and cultural effects. In some parts of the Kalahari, people who wished to remain anonymous could hardly do so after being visited by a group of tourists in a large vehicle. Other tourists would see the tracks and follow them in to the Bushman camp. A major problem cited by local people was that tourists rarely, if ever, asked permission to visit their communities; instead, they simply drove in and began walking around their homes. As a consequence, people complained that their privacy was being invaded. Local leaders sometimes approached tourists and requested that they treat people with respect but more often than not, they said, they were rebuffed.

Social tensions rose in situations where tourists camped close to Bushman communities and played loud music, disturbing the peace and tranquility which Bushmen valued so highly. Resentment was also generated when tourists left large amounts of litter. As one man asked, "What is it about tourists that makes them so unwilling to clean up after themselves?" Some people did point out that they did not mind the litter too much if it contained useful items such as tin cans and pieces of cloth.

A socioecological impact of tourists was the effect of their vehicles, horse-riding, and walking across old village sites. In some cases, these village sites contained materials that Bushmen recycled for later use. In other cases, the old camps had the graves of people from nearby communities. Several Bushmen said that they did not want to have tourists disturbing the graves of their loved ones. An additional problem of tourist presence was that it sometimes led to the removal of vegetation cover through purposeful action such as burning off areas in which to camp or inadvertent action such as driving across fragile land surfaces, a process which exacerbated soil erosion.

The sale of handicrafts to tourists is a major source of income in many if not most Bushman communities in the Kalahari. The commercialization of handicraft production has had spinoff environmental impacts, with wild plant species such as palms (*Hyphaene ventricosa*) beginning to disappear in areas where there is extensive marketing of crafts (Cunningham and Milton, 1987).

Safari hunting also had effects on the resource base and safety of local people. In areas where guns were used, hunters using traditional weaponry were often at a competitive disadvantage since the potential prey would stay long distances away from people in order not to be hit by gunfire (Hitchcock, Masilo, and Monyatse, 1995). Safari hunters sometimes wounded game but did not always follow-up the injured animal. This animal then became a potential threat to local people, something that was particularly problematic if it was a dangerous species such as an elephant, buffalo, or lion. On the very day that I first arrived in the northeastern Kalahari in August 1975, I was told by a hunter not to proceed any further up the road because he had wounded an elephant and had to leave it because he had pressing business in town.

The health and nutritional impacts of the presence of tourists were also issues raised during the course of discussions of tourism in the Kalahari. Some Bushmen pointed out that they feared that new kinds of diseases would be introduced into their communities. In at least one case in the eastern Kalahari, measles that broke out in a local community were traced to a visitor who had camped nearby for several days. Health workers in both Namibia and Botswana expressed their fears that sexually transmitted diseases, including HIV/AIDS, could wreak havoc in remote communities. This is one of the reasons that people in the Kalahari are afraid of the potential impacts of so-called sex tourism.

From a nutritional standpoint, tourists sometimes contributed to what was felt by some Bushmen to be a deteriorating dietary situation because of their giving people large amounts of sugar. Tobacco was also sometimes provided to local people by tourists and, I should note, by anthropologists, a process which some people felt was partially responsible for rising respiratory problems. The sale or giving away of alcoholic beverages contributed to rising levels of family violence, alcohol-related accidents, and disease (Marshall and Ritchie, 1984; Nurse, Weiner, and Jenkins, 1985). It is ironic that tourists who gave people alcohol were often the same ones who turned around and criticized local people for being drunk. Overall, the health and nutritional statuses of Bushman communities has changed significantly, although to what extent these changes are directly an outgrowth of tourism remains to be determined.

Tourism and Land Rights

A significant human rights issue of current concern in both Namibia and Botswana relates to the relocation of people out of areas designated as national parks, game reserves, and other kinds of conservation areas such as national monuments. Over the past several decades, residents were required to leave a number of southern African parks and reserves, including the Kalahari Gemsbok Park in the 1930s, Namibia's Etosha National Park in the 1930s and 1940s, Botswana's Moremi Wildlife Reserve in the 1970s, and the Tsodilo Hills National Monument in 1995. Suggestions were made by a consultant for the International Union for the Conservation of Nature and Natural Resources (IUCN) that people be relocated away from the area between Nxai Pan National Park and what used to be Makgadikgadi Game Reserve, now part of Nxai Pan and Makgadikgadi National Park in Botswana.

Currently there are ten different settlements in Botswana that are being considered for relocation by the government of Botswana (see Table 1). The reasons given for the resettlement of these communities revolve primarily around habitat and wildlife conservation and promotion of tourism. From 1986 and continuing to the present, representatives of the Botswana government have held discussions with

Table 1
Remote Area Dweller Settlements in Botswana that may be Relocated for Conservation and/or Development Purposes

District Name	Name of Settlement or Project Area	Land Area Allocated	Population Size
Central	Kedia	20,000 hectares	634
Ghanzi	D'kar	600	380
Ghanzi	Groot Laagte (Qabo)	40,000	345
Ghanzi	!Xade	40,000	791
Kgalagadi	Ngwatle	40,000	135
Kgatleng	Kgomodiatsaba	6,400	540
Kgatleng	Khurutshe	6,400	223
North West	Joao	6,400	100
North West	Phuduhudu	6,400	314
North West	Tsodilo Hills	73,125	110

Note: Data obtained from the Remote Area Development Program, the Ministry of Local Government, Lands, and Housing, the various District Councils, and the Department of Wildlife and National Parks

residents of the Central Kalahari Game Reserve, the largest reserve in the country, in an attempt to convince them to move to areas outside of the reserve (see Figure 2).

Several reasons were given by government officials to local people as to why the resettlement was necessary. First, they noted that the move would help ensure conservation of the resource base, including wildlife, in the reserve. Second, they said having people move out of the reserve would enhance the tourism potential of the region. Third, they argued that the reserve contained "resources of national importance," specifically diamonds and other minerals. Fourth, they maintained that it would be cheaper to provide services to people in places that were not as remote as the central Kalahari. Finally, they suggested that if resettlement occurred, those who were moved would have greater access to economic opportunities and to government services and thus "be able to integrate with the rest of Botswana society."

One of the impacts of the resettlement will likely be a reduction in incomes and employment opportunities. Currently, at least fifty people have formal sector jobs in the central Kalahari, serving as teachers, drivers, and government workers. While it is possible that there will be some jobs created by the tourism industry in the central Kalahari, it is unlikely that many of these jobs will be made available to people from

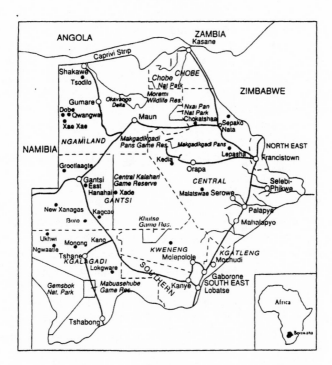

Figure 2

the resettled areas. The experience of tourism in Botswana (e.g., in Ngamiland) has been that tourism companies generally do not hire local people for the various jobs except for menial positions such as camp cleaners. The notion that tourism will provide a windfall of benefits to people on the fringes of the central Kalahari is unlikely at best, particularly given the facts that the tourism companies usually bring their own long-term employees and most of the tourism in the region will be done in small, mobile groups which will not stay in the reserve for any length of time.

The Central Kalahari Game Reserve relocation decisions appear to be part of a general pattern of Botswana government efforts to encourage or require people to leave their traditional areas. Such a strategy poses severe problems for local people. Extensive research by social and natural scientists and by development workers has shown that involuntary community relocation of people with strong ties to the land has nearly always resulted in a reduction in the standards of living of those who were moved (Scudder, 1996). While some of the people moved may temporarily be better off, over the longer term conditions can be expected to worsen, in part because of increased competition for natural resources and employment opportunities. This could be especially problematic in the central Kalahari region since the areas adjacent to the reserve do not have sufficient water supplies and other resources to support large numbers of people and their livestock. The experience with resettlement in both Botswana and Namibia indicates that people who lose access to their traditional areas experience severe social, psychological, and economic difficulties.

Tourism and Land Use and Resource Planning in Southern Africa

The desire to increase the flow of tourists has sometimes prompted African governments to set aside portions of their countries as national parks and game reserves (Anderson and Grove, 1987). Like other southern African countries, Namibia and Botswana have set aside a substantial portion of their land as reserves (see Table 2). Botswana is the world's leading country in terms of the amount of area designated as parkland per person (Wilkinson, 1978:621). In some cases, residents of these areas have been required to relocate their homes, and they have been prevented from utilizing the resources in their former territories (Marshall, 1984; Gordon, 1985, 1992; Hitchcock, 1985, 1988).

It seems ironic that conservation and tourism should be used as justifications for the dispossession of people in southern Africa and elsewhere. In recent years there have been more and more calls for local people to be allowed to benefit directly from conservation activities. Development planners, scientists, and local people have all argued that conservation and social equity goals can best be achieved if local people are allowed to participate extensively in decisions about the various ways in which development should proceed (Boo, 1990, 1992; Brown and Wyckoff-Baird, 1992; Wells and Brandon, 1992; Ministry of Wildlife, Conservation, and Tourism, 1992a, b).

Namibia and Botswana are now in the process of planning and implementing programs aimed at promoting resource conservation while at the same time enhancing economic benefits for local people. Namibia has recommended the establishment of conservancies in communal and commercial areas (Ministry of Wildlife, Conservation, and Tourism, 1992b). In Botswana, besides national parks, game reserves, and national monuments, land was zoned as Wildlife Management Areas (WMAs), areas of the country where wildlife conservation, utilization, and management represent the primary forms of land use. These areas tend to be ones with few livestock, and they generally contain populations that depend in part upon natural resources (Kalahari Conservation Society, 1988).

According to policy papers on wildlife conservation and tourism (e.g., Republic of Botswana, 1986, 1990; Ministry of Environment and Tourism, 1994a, b, 1995a, b), emphasis will be placed upon wildlife-related activities in the Wildlife Management Areas of Botswana and the conservancies in the communal areas of Namibia. Activities will include consumptive game utilization, photographic tourism, and game ranching. The idea behind this kind of approach is that both conservation and development would be enchanced. There are questions, however, as to the sustainability of integrated conservation and development projects (Gibson and Marks, 1995). There are also questions about the gender effects of tourism and natural resource management projects (Enloe, 1989; Hunter, Hitchcock, and Wyckoff-Baird, 1990; Jackson, 1993; Mehra, 1993).

In Botswana it is argued that rural development would be enhanced through an expansion of employment opportunities and the generation of additional household income (Republic of Botswana, 1986, 1990). Settlement and non-wildlife related activities would, however, be limited (Carter, 1983). This was the case in the Central Kalahari Game Reserve, for example, where people were told by Department of Wildlife and National Parks personnel in the 1980s that they could no longer hunt and gather because, it was noted, those kinds of activities would have negative effects on wildlife that tourism came to the reserve to see.

A major question issue being addressed today is whether or not residents of the wildlife conservation areas will be allowed to exploit resources at the same rates and using the same technology as they have in the past. People who depended heavily on wild resources in both countries were allowed to continue to hunt as long as they used traditional weaponry. In recent years, the situation in Botswana evolved to the point where people with Special Game Licenses (subsistence hunting licenses) were able to use guns to hunt (Hitchcock, 1988; Hitchcock, Masilo, and Monyatse, 1995). This is not the case in Eastern Bushmanland, however, where people are only allowed to hunt with bows, arrows, spears, and clubs. The only people allowed to use guns to hunt in Eastern Bushmanland were people who entered the area with a safari company (Hitchcock, 1992).

Tourism and Elephants

An outgrowth of the safari tourism and hunting issue relates to the presence of elephants in the Eastern Bushmanland region (Figure 3). Ju/'hoansi have had to contend with the impacts of elephants on their

Table 2
Projects in Community-Based Natural Resource Management and
Ecotourism in Botswana and Namibia

Project	District	General Comments
Chobe	Chobe	A community-based natural resource management project involving five northern Botswana villages working with a safari company in a joint venture, employing Community Escort Guides (CEGs), and planning local development involving tourism, craft production, fisheries, and community reserve; the communities formed the Chobe Enclave Community Trust (CECT) which oversees project activities.
Kedia	Central	A game harvesting and wildlife processing project involving Remote Area Dwellers that included training of hunting units, sales of meat and leather crafts, and running of a processing facility (1986–1991).
Kuru	Gantsi	Kuru Development Trust (KDT) was established in 1986 on a farm (D'Kar) in the northern Ghanzi District; consists of five communities with some 700 people collaborating in projects ranging from art to handicrafts production and from tanning to horticulture; the development of a communal game ranch (Qaeqare) is on-going.
Mabutsane	Southern	Several rural communities were involved in a wildlife utilization, tourism, and handicrafts project from 1990 to 1992 (the Mosekaphofu Game Harvesting Project); local people were allocated a set of animals to hunt even though the rest of the district had had a hunting ban imposed by the Southern District Council. The local hunting team consisted of eleven participants, all male, who received wages for their work. Some skins were sold for craft production purposes and small numbers of tourists visited the project area.
Nata	Central	A sanctuary and ecotourism program in northern Sua Pan that is run by Nata Conservation Trust, an NGO with a board that includes four communities; it has a conservation area with birds, fauna, and camping facilities.
Tsodilo Hills	North West	A National Museum, Monuments, and Art Gallery project in which local people take part in conservation of local natural resources and tourism related to some 350 rock art sites.

Project	District	General Comments
Zutshwa	Kgalagadi	Maiteko Tshwaragano Conservation Trust (MTDT), a local NGO, is running a multifaceted development program which ranges from salt production to handicraft purchasing and from local-level training to institution strengthening.
Nyae Nyae	Eastern Otjozondjupa	A multi-faceted development program that includes tourism, farming, the raising of cattle and game, craft purchasing by a community-based organization, the Nyae Nyae Farmers Cooperative (NNFC). A campsite for tourists has been established at Makuri, and craft marketing is done on a regional basis.
Bagani	West Caprivi	A tourism and craft production program that includes a campsite and a community organization that helps in marketing of local goods.
Lizauli Village	East Caprivi	A traditional village which employs local people who work in the village during the day and who demonstrate various traditional activities to tourists, many from a nearby lodge (Lianshulu).
Mudumu National Park	East Caprivi	A bed-night levy has been instituted benefitting residents of five villages around the Mudumu Park.

Note: Adapted from Hitchcock, Masilo, and Monyatse (1995).

water sources, wild plant foods, and personal safety for a substantial period of time. Many of the residents of Eastern Bushmanland expressed their concern about the presence of elephants, which have been known to chase people and to consume most if not all of the water in natural springs and pans.

Observations of the interactions between people and elephants revealed that Ju/'hoansi had a healthy respect for the large mammals. At the same time, elephants respected people, as could be seen, for example, in situations where they waited for people to finish getting water from a trough before moving in themselves to drink. Volker Grellman (personal communication), the owner of the safari company that had the hunting concession in Eastern Bushmanland, maintains that Bushmen and elephants live "in peaceful co-existence." While some Ju/'hoansi would agree with these ideas, others are less sanguine about the presence of so many elephants in their areas.

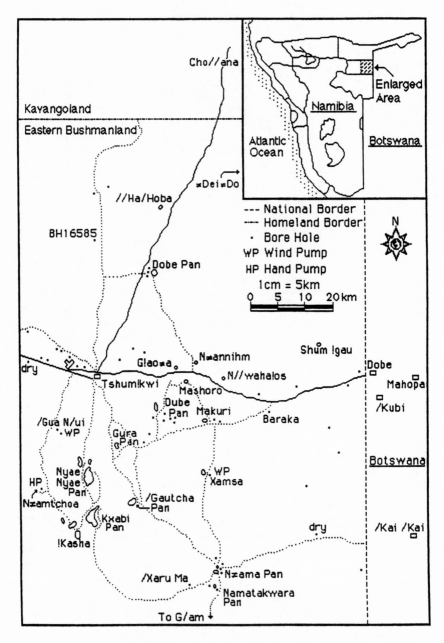

Figure 3. JU/WA Settlements in the Nyae Region, Namibia (Bixler, 1992).

According to figures obtained by Anvo Hunting Safaris and the Ministry of Wildlife, Conservation, and Tourism, there were some 300–400 elephants in Eastern Bushmanland at the time of my survey in 1992. The numbers of elephants have increased substantially over the past 10–15 years. Part of the reason for this expansion, according to Ju/'hoansi, is the presence of water points for game established by Nature Conservation.

There were a variety of opinions expressed about elephants. Some people said that they wished the government would allow hunters to take more elephants since they not only destroyed their crops and water equipment, but also frightened their children and livestock. Two people had an opposing view: they said that they hoped the government would reduce hunting by outsiders, but would still allow local people to control the exploitation of elephants. A few people said that all animals in Eastern Bushmanland should be conserved, including elephants (Hitchcock, 1992).

Elephant conservation was a topic of discussion among the Ju/'hoansi both among themselves and at meetings such as those of the Environmental Planning Committee, a regional committee in which the Ju/'hoansi of Eastern Bushmanland participated (Payne, 1992). Some people noted that scientists argued that elephants were declining in some parts of southern Africa. They insisted, however, that this trend was not evident in Bushmanland, where elephants seemed to be increasing in number. Several people noted that there were at least twice as many elephants now than there were in 1980. One reason given for this situation was the availability of water in the region. Another reason offered was that elephants had moved south from Angola because of the warfare there. A third reason given was that there was an abundance of foods in the region which are particularly well-liked by elephants, especially mangetti (mongongo) nuts (*Ricinodendron rautanenii*).

In spite of their concerns about the effects of elephants, the people of Nyae Nyae have come to appreciate the significance of their presence in terms of attracting tourists to their areas. A number of them recognized that a major reason for foreign clients wanting to come to Bushmanland to hunt was the fact that they could go after elephants. In some cases, the safari company hired local people to work with them, usually as game trackers, scouts, and skinners. The killing of elephants by safari hunters meant that there was meat available for those local people willing to eat it.

A serious problem that elephants have posed in the past decade is that they sometimes destroyed crops as well as borehole equipment, hand pumps, and fences. Elephants sometimes damaged borehole casings and lifting rods, resulting in the caving in of boreholes. They also destroyed troughs such as the one near the government camp in Tjum!kui. The people of Eastern Bushmanland have had to place large rocks around their water facilities (hand and wind pumps and storage tanks), something that requires a fairly substantial amount of labor and capital. In order to protect their facilities, people have resorted to shouting and cracking bullwhips at night in the hopes that the sounds would keep the elephants at bay.

Another animal that has tourism potential is the Kalahari lion (*Panthera leo*). As is the case with elephants, Ju/'hoansi have had to contend with problems that they cause, ranging from attacks on people to the taking of livestock. Under current Namibian law, Ju/'hoansi are not allowed to shoot lions even if they have killed some of their cattle or chased people. They are quick to point out that people who pay large amounts of money and come into Eastern Bushmanland with the safari company *are* allowed to hunt lions. The irony of this situation is vexing to the Ju/'hoansi, who claim that they are being discriminated against. Lions were a common topic of discussion among people interviewed in Eastern Bushmanland. Some of them indicated that they feared them and said that they were a threat to their livelihoods. As the former head of the Nyae Nyae Farmers Cooperative noted in one interview, "Lions are the dogs of Western conservation."

The difficulty at present is that the Ju/'hoansi have no say whatsoever in decision-making concerning elephants, lions, or any other wildlife resources in Bushmanland. Quotas for elephants were set by the Ministry of Wildlife, Conservation, and Tourism with no input from Ju/'hoansi. Complaints about problem elephants and lions were not responded to quickly, according to local informants, and the result was that often the animal that was shot was not the one that caused the damage to the fields, water points, or livestock. Meat from the elephants killed by safari hunters was not always distributed equitably. One of the most frequently cited complaints was that none of the money generated by the safari company was given to the local communities.

Like the Bushmen, tourists in remote parts of southern Africa have to contend with the fact that the physical infrastructure is relatively poorly developed and that many of these areas contain animals that can be quite dangerous. Roads are usually sand-choked tracks that sometimes are hidden by high stands of grass. The grass itself poses a danger since on occasion it gets caught beneath vehicles and then catches fire. Trucks have been burned out completely, leaving the occupants to await rescue or to undertake long treks to settlements. There are few patrols by Nature Conservation or Department of Wildlife and National Parks personnel, and many of their vehicles do not carry enough spare parts or sufficient extra fuel or water to supply tourists when they have gotten into trouble. The maps of these areas are extremely rough, and numerous changes have occurred due to drought and the impacts mineral exploration and other kinds of human activities. It is clear that extensive preparatory work will have to be undertaken before these regions can be considered safe for greater numbers of tourists.

Tourism Impacts in the Tsodilo Hills

One part of the Kalahari where tourism promotion is having substantial impacts on the well-being of resident populations is the Tsodilo Hills region of northwestern Botswana. This area attracts visitors because of the presence of unique environmental features (micaceous schist hills, rolling tree-bush savanna, and dune fields) and because they support resident groups of people who hunt and gather for part of their subsistence. The Tsodilo Hills are also important for archaeological and historical reasons. The hills contain over 3,000 rock paintings and a number of unique archaeological sites.

Two different communities exist in Tsodilo, a Ju/'hoansi group of approximately thirty people and an Mbukushu group of about twenty. According to present and former National Museum and Art Gallery personnel, in the 1980s approximately 1,000–1,500 people per year paid visits to the Tsodilo Hills. The majority of these people stopped at the local Mbukushu and Ju/'hoansi villages in order to pick up guides, purchase handicrafts, or see what living conditions were like. In the Tsodilo area, Ju/'hoansi households made as much as $600 a year from handicraft sales, while the Mbukushu groups tended to make about half of that. This difference in economic returns caused a certain amount of resentment among the Mbukushu. This situation was mitigated, however, by the fact that a man who lived with the Mbukushu served as the official guide to the Hills. The Mbukushu were also involved in the tourism activities of a local safari company that works in the Shakawe area.

Some of the Ju/'hoansi at Tsodilo were so attuned to tourists that they shed their Western clothes, put on skins, and picked-up bows or digging sticks whenever the sound of an airplane or truck was heard. One Ju/'hoan man shocked some German tourists who were examining a rock art panel when he reached into his leather pouch and pulled out a Ronson lighter and used it to light one of the men's cigars. A local woman delighted a group of Japanese tourists when she came out of her hut wearing a T-shirt that said "Have a good day" in Japanese.

Some of the people in the Tsodilo complained that there were too many tourists visiting the hills. One woman said that the tourists tended to use up all the firewood, and another noted that visitors sometimes had loud parties which lasted late into the night. At one point, she said, she went to the camp of some particularly noisy tourists and complained that the noise was disturbing the sleep of her children who had to get up and go to school the next day. One of the tourists replied that Ju/'hoansi children had no business attending school but instead should be helping do laundry and dishes in tourist camps.

Given these kinds of experiences, it is not surprising that local people did not always appreciate the presence of tourists. One of the points made by tourists who took part in these visits was that they were surprised that people were not as "traditional" as they expected. One of them even demanded his money back, saying that he should have been told that hunter-gatherers no longer existed in the northern Kalahari. Another complained that the Bushmen were guilty of having done the rock art recently in order to attract tourists.

The tourists entering these areas exacerbated already existing socioeconomic and environmental problems. Firewood is on the decline in the Tsodilo Hills. There have also been cases in which the rock paintings have been defaced. Some local people felt that they should not have to put up with the depradations of outsiders who they felt showed callous disregard for local sensibilities. Others believed that tourism was a kind of two-edged sword in that it enabled people to get greater access to cash and goods while at the same time it increased pressure on local resources.

One of the suggestions made for Tsodilo was that the Ju/'hoansi community close to the Female Hill should be moved to a place at least five kilometers away from the hills. Some of the local people who attended the *kgotla* (local council) meetings at which this recommendation was made said that it was unfair that they should lose their land and other rights to tourism development. As one Tsodilo resident put it, "Why should my family and I have to leave our home simply because a few dozen tourists from South Africa or Europe want to camp out in the desert for a day or two?" One Ju/'hoan woman who attended the meetings pointed out that tourists often had little idea of the dangers that lurked in the Kalahari. As proof of this, she noted, they slept in the open away from fires when there were lions around. She also said that some tourists took only small amounts of water and few tools with them into the bush, something that sometimes led to severe problems when they had breakdowns. More than one group of tourists in the Kalahari, she noted, has been saved by a Bushman who repaired their vehicle for them or showed them the way back to a well-travelled road. Nevertheless, as it turned out, the Ju/'hoansi of Tsodilo were resettled away from the Hills. By early 1996, it was reported by government workers that the incomes of the Ju/'hoansi had gone down significantly, that the jobs promised people had failed to materialize, and that there was a great deal of dissatisfaction among the Ju/'hoansi. One of their complaints was that their neighbors, the Mbukushu, had not been required to move, and as a result they had concluded that the Botswana government's policy was to provide benefits to non-Bushmen peoples over Bushmen. Such ideas have contributed to a rising sense of dissatisfaction with government policy on tourism and natural resource management in Botswana.

In the past several years, local people in rural Namibia and Botswana have argued that they should have the same opportunities as other groups to take part in tourism and resource exploitation activities. Some Bushmen have stressed the inequities in a system in which the majority of the funds from tourism fail to reach them. It is interesting to note, however, that even the government does not benefit to any great extent from tourism activities since most of the funds are repatriated to other countries by the tourism companies, many of which are foreign-owned. It is apparent that greater efforts must be made in Namibia and Botswana to ensure that local people benefit directly from tourism and that they are able to have a say about how tourism is conducted in their areas.

Conclusions

Analysis of the various tourist-related activities in the Kalahari indicates that tourism has both costs and benefits. On the one hand it provides people with employment and increased income generating opportunities. On the other hand, tourism causes a certain amount of resentment at the local level and it sometimes disrupts people's lives. There are indications that tourism has contributed to processes of environmental degradation as well as to an increase in social stratification.

Cultural effects of tourism include changing attitudes toward material goods and a desire on the part of some people to become more involved in the market and the national societies of Namibia and Botswana. At the same time, there have been countervailing trends, with rising pride in Bushman products and cultural traditions and enhancement of Bushman ethnic identity. Pressure has mounted among Bushmen for the development of materials that provide accurate, balanced descriptions of Bushman societies. Local people have also pushed for tourist ethics statements that dictate the kinds of respectful behavior that tourists should exhibit when interacting with Bushman peoples (Hitchcock, 1992; Thoma, 1993; Garland, 1994).

The places where Bushmen and other rural southern African people have had some say about the ways in which tourism is undertaken have seen some positive changes in household living standards and levels of social satisfaction. This was the case in the southern part of Eastern Bushmanland, for example, where several local communities interacted with a tourist for an extended period, receiving in exchange a reasonable amount of money and setting the rules under which the tourist operated. It was also the case in the Kaokoland region of Namibia, where Himba worked with tour operators and anthropologists collaborated in an effort to promote community-controlled tourism (Owen-Smith and Jacobsohn, 1989; Jacobsohn, 1991, 1995).

The Bushmen, like other indigenous peoples, have undergone major social and political changes over time. What once were described as egalitarian societies are now more stratified, with individuals in leadership positions who have some decision-making authority. It should come as no surprise that efforts are being made by a number of Bushman communities to form pressure groups and to establish their own political institutions (Hitchcock and Holm, 1995). They are doing this in part as a means of coping with greater numbers of interactions that they are having with outside agencies and individuals, some of whom are tourists. One of the goals of some of the Bushman self-help and advocacy groups is to promote what they see as responsible tourism, tourism which is not environmentally or socioeconomically destructive.

Some of the Bushmen today are seeking cultural and political autonomy, arguing that they should have the basic right of self-determination. An issue that they see as being of paramount concern is what they perceive to be social, economic, and political discrimination against them. As they put it, being a Bushman means that one must cope with tourists, low prices for goods, minuscule wages, menial jobs, and uncertain access to land and resources. If they are to be able to break completely out of the downward spiral of impoverishment, they argue, they must be able to have greater control over both the natural and social environments. Bushmen, they stress, should also have a much greater role in the identification and resolution of problems facing them. If this is not the case, say some spokespeople for Bushman communities, then they have the responsibility to themselves and their children to seek whatever means necessary to bring about transformations in the structures of domination that tourism and commercial trade represent. Sustainable development and human rights can only come about in the Kalahari if there are significant changes in the ways in which tourism, development planning, and natural resource management policies are implemented.

Notes

1. An earlier version of this paper was presented at the 50th Annual Meeting of the Society for Applied Anthropology held in Charleston, South Carolina, March 13–17, 1991. Erve Chambers invited me to be a part of that session, and I thank him for his support and for his comments, insights, and editorial suggestions. Support of the research upon which this paper is based was provided by the U.S. National Science Foundation, the Ford Foundation, the Remote Area Development Program, Ministry of Local Government, Lands and Housing, Government of Botswana, the Norwegian Agency for International Development (NORAD), and the United States Agency for International Development (USAID) offices in Namibia, Botswana, and Zimbabwe. I wish to thank the Nyae Nyae Development Foundation, the Nyae Nyae Farmers Cooperative, the Ministry of Wildlife, Conservation and Tourism of Namibia, the Department of Wildlife and National Parks of Botswana and the Remote Area Development Program of Botswana for assistance. The permission to conduct the research in Botswana was provided by the Office of the President, to whom I am grateful. I would also like to express my appreciation to Megan Biesele, David Green. Holly Payne, Axel Thoma, Magdalena Brormann, Alec Campbell, Izak Barnard, Gakemodimo Mosi, Jim Ebert, and the members of communities in Namibia and Botswana for their help and for the data, ideas, and information that they provided so willingly.

2. Anthropologists sometimes refer to the Bushmen as "San," but the people themselves do not acknowledge the term. Setswana-speaking peoples call them Basarwa, a term meaning those who lack cattle, a description some people consider to be derogatory. The majority of people refer to themselves by their own group names (e.g., G/wi, G//ana, Ju/'hoansi, !Xo, Nharo). As was stressed at a 1992 regional conference held in Windhoek, Namibia, a number of people in Botswana and Namibia prefer to describe themselves as Bushmen since the term is a generic one and it is well-known. Some of the more politically aware Bushmen call themselves simply "the dispossessed." There are a number of people who wish to be called N/oakwe, or, simply, "the first people." With bureaucratic efficiency, the government refers to these, and other rural poor living outside established villages, as Remote Area Dwellers, or RADs (Hitchcock and Holm,

1993). The term in Botswana used to refer to RADs is *Tengyanateng*, meaning, literally, "the farthest people," or, as it is sometimes translated, those
from "the deep within the deep" (Mogwe, 1992).

References

Almagor, Uri. (1985). A Tourist's "Vision Quest" in an African Game Reserve.
    Annals of Tourism Research, 12(1):31–47.

Altman, Jon. (1989). Tourism Dilemmas for Aboriginal Australians. *Annals of
    Tourism Research,* 16(4):456–476.

Anderson, David and Richard Grove. (1987). *Conservation in Africa: Peoples, Poli-
    cies, and Practice.* Cambridge: Cambridge University Press.

Ashley, Caroline and Elizabeth Garland. (1994). *Promoting Community-Based
    Tourism Development: Why, What, and How?* Directorate of Environmental
    Affairs Research Discussion Paper Number 4. Windhoek, Namibia: Min-
    istry of Environment and Tourism.

Ashley, C., J. Barnes, and T. Healy. (1994). *Profits, Equity, Growth, and Sustain-
    ability: The Potential Role of Wildlife Enterprises in Caprivi and Other Com-
    munal Areas of Namibia.* Research Discussion Paper Number 2. Windhoek,
    Namibia: Directorate of Environmental Affairs, Ministry of Environment
    and Tourism.

Associates in Rural Development. (1992). *Decentralization and Local Autonomy:
    Conditions for Achieving Sustainable Resource Management.* 2 Volumes.
    Burlington, Vermont: Associates in Rural Development and Washington,
    D.C.: U.S. Agency for International Development.

    (1995). *Facilitation and Documentation Support for The Living in a Finite
    Environment (LIFE) Program Assessment Exercise for the LIFE Project in
    Community-Based Natural Resource Management, USAID/Namibia Compo-
    nent (690–0251.73).* Burlington, Vermont: Associates in Rural Develop-
    ment and Windhoek, Namibia: USAID/Namibia.

Biesele, Megan. (1990). *Shaken Roots: The Bushmen of Namibia.* Marshalltown,
    South Africa: Environmental and Development Agency Publications.

Biesele, Megan, David Green, and Robert Hitchcock. (1992). Decentralization
    and Natural Resource Management: Namibia Field Report. In *Decentral-
    ization and Local Autonomy: Conditions for Achieving Sustainable Resource
    Management. Volume II: Appendices.* Burlington, Vermont: Associates in
    Rural Development, Inc. and Washington, D.C.: U.S. Agency for Inter-
    national Development, Research and Development Bureau.

Biesele, Megan, Mathias Guenther, Robert Hitchcock, Richard Lee, and Jean
    MacGregor. (1989). Hunters, Clients, and Squatters: The Contemporary

Socioeconomic Status of Botswana Basarwa. *African Study, Monographs,* a (3): 109-151.

Bixler, Dorinda Sue. (1992). Parallel Realities: Ju/Wasi of Nyae Nyae and South African Policy in Namibia 1950–1990. M.A. Thesis, University of Nebraska, Lincoln, Nebraska.

Boo, Elizabeth. (1990). *Ecotourism: The Potentials and Pitfalls.* Washington, D.C.: World Wildlife Fund.

(1992). *The Ecotourism Boom: Planning for Development and Management.* Wildlands and Human Needs (WHN) Technical Paper Series No. 2. Washington, D.C.: World Wildlife Fund.

Brown, Michael and Barbara Wyckoff-Baird. (1992). *Designing Integrated Conservation and Development Projects.* Washington, D.C.: Biodiversity Support Program.

Browne, RitaJean and Mary Lee Nolan. (1989). Western Indian Reservation Tourism Development. *Annals of Tourism Research, 16*(3):360–376.

Campbell, A. C. and W. von Richter. (1976). The Okavango Delta and Tourism. In *Proceedings of the Symposium on the Okavango Delta and Its Future Utilization* (pp. 245–247). Gaborone: Botswana Society.

Carter, Judy M. (1983). The Development of Wildlife Management Areas. In *Which Way Botswana's Wildlife?,* Kalahari Conservation Society (pp. 63–73). Gaborone, Botswana: Kalahari Conservation Society.

Chapin, Mac. (1990). The Silent Jungle: Ecotourism among the Kuna Indians of Panama. *Cultural Survival Quarterly, 14*(1):42–45.

Chr. Michelsen Institute. (1995). *NORAD's Support of the Remote Area Development Program (RADP) in Botswana: An Evaluation Report.* Report to the Royal Norwegian Ministry of Foreign Affairs. Bergen, Norway: Chr. Michel Institute Development Studies and Human Rights and Oslo, Norway: Royal Ministry of Foreign Affairs.

Cohen, Erik. (1989). "Primitive and Remote" Hill Tribe Trekking in Thailand. *Annals of Tourism Research, 16*(1):30–61.

Colchester, Marcus. (1994). Salvaging Nature: Indigenous Peoples, Protected Areas, and Biodiversity Conservation. *United Nations Research Institute for Social Development Discussion Papers, 55.* Geneva: United Nations Research Institute for Social Development.

Crick, Malcolm. (1989). Representations of International Tourism in the Social Sciences: Sun, Sex, Sights, Savings, and Servility. *Annual Review of Anthropology, 18*:307–344.

Cunningham, A. B. and S. J. Milton. (1987). Effects of Basket-Weaving Industry on Mokola Palm and Dye Plants in Northwestern Botswana. *Economic Botany, 41*(3):386–402.

Domestic Technology International (DTI). (1992). *Botswana Low Impact Ecotourism Development Plan*. Evergreen, Colorado: Domestic Technology International and Washington, D.C.: U. S. Agency for International Development.

Enloe, C. (1989). *Bananas, Beaches, and Bases: Making Feminist Sense of International Relations*. Berkeley and Los Angeles: University of California Press.

Garland, Elizabeth. (1994). *Tourism Development in Eastern Bushmanland: Final Report*. Windhoek, Namibia: Nyae Nyae Development Foundation of Namibia.

Giannecchini, Joan. (1993). Ecotourism: New Partners, New Relationships. *Conservation Biology*, 7(2):429–42.

Gibson, Clark C. and Stuart A. Marks. (1995). Transforming Rural Hunters into Conservationists: An Assessment of Community-Based Wildlife Management Programs. *World Development*, 23(6):941–957.

Gordon, Robert J. (1985). Conserving Bushmen to Extinction in Southern Africa. In *An End to Laughter? Tribal Peoples and Economic Development*, Marcus Colchester, editor, pp. 28–42. London: Survival International.

(1990). The Prospects for Anthropological Tourism in Bushmanland. *Cultural Survival Quarterly*, 14(1):6–8.

(1992). *The Bushman Myth: The Making of a Namibian Underclass*. Boulder, Colorado: Westview Press.

Hitchcock, Robert K. (1985). Foragers on the Move: San Survival Strategies in Botswana Parks and Reserves. *Cultural Survival Quarterly*, 9(1):31–36.

(1988). *Monitoring, Research, and Development in the Remote Areas of Botswana*. Gaborone, Botswana: Government Printer.

(1991). Tourism and Sustainable Development among Remote Area Populations in Botswana. In *Tourism in Botswana*, Linda Pfotenhauer (Ed.), pp. 161–172. Gaborone, Botswana: The Botswana Society.

(1992). *Communities and Consensus: An Evaluation of the Activities of the Nyae Nyae Farmers Cooperative and the Nyae Nyae Development Foundation in Northeastern Namibia*. New York, New York: Ford Foundation and Windhoek, Namibia: Nyae Nyae Development Foundation of Namibia.

(1993). Ecotourism and Sustainable Development in Africa. In *Proceedings of the Conference on Natural Resource Management in Africa: Issues in Conservation and Socioeconomic Development*, Denis Hynes (Ed.), pp. 68–86. New York, New York: African-American Institute.

(1996). *Kalahari Communities: Bushmen and the Politics of the Environment in Southern Africa*. Copenhagen, Denmark: International Work Group for Indigenous Affairs.

Hitchcock, Robert K. and Rodney L. Brandenburgh. (1990). Tourism, Conservation, and Culture in the Kalahari Desert, Botswana. *Cultural Survival Quarterly,* 14(2):20–24.

Hitchcock, Robert K. and John D. Holm. (1993). Bureaucratic Domination of African Hunter-Gatherer Societies: A Study of the San in Botswana. *Development and Change,* 24(1):1–35.

(1995). Grassroots Political Organizing among Kalahari Bushmen. *Indigenous Affairs,* No. 3/95:4–10.

Hitchcock, Robert K., Rosinah Rose B. Masilo, and Poppy Monyatse. (1995). *Subsistence Hunting and Resource Rights in Botswana: An Assessment of Special Game Licenses and Their Impacts on Remote Area Dwellers and Wildlife Populations.* Gaborone, Botswana: Natural Resources Management Project (NRMP) and Department of Wildlife and National Parks.

Hitchcock, Robert K. and Marshall W. Murphree. (1995). *Report of the Field Assessment Team, Phase III of the Mid- Term Assessment of the LIFE Project, USAID/Namibia Component (690–0251.73).* Windhoek, Namibia: LIFE Project and USAID/Namibia.

Hitchcock, Robert K. and Fanuel M. Nangati. (1992). *Zimbabwe Natural Resources Management Project Community-Based Resource Utilization Component: Interim Assessment.* Report to USAID/Zimbabwe, Harare, Zimbabwe. Harare: United States Agency for International Development.

International Union for the Conservation of Nature and Natural Resources. (1985). *United Nations List of National Parks and Protected Areas.* Gland, Switzerland: IUCN.

Jackson, Cecile. (1993). Doing What Comes Naturally? Women and Environment in Development. *World Development,* 21(12):1947–1963.

Jacobsohn, Margaret. (1991). The Crucial Link: Conservation and Development. In *Going Green: People, Politics, and the Environment in South Africa,* Jacklyn Cock and Eddie Koch (Eds.), pp. 210–222. Cape Town: Oxford University Press.

(1995). *Negotiating Meaning and Change in Space and Material Culture: An Ethno-archaeological Study among Semi-nomadic Himba and Herero Herders in Northwestern Namibia.* Ph.D. Dissertation, University of Cape Town, Cape Town, South Africa.

Johnson, P.G. (1976). Wildlife as a Basis for Future Tourism Development. In *Proceedings of the Symposium on the Okavango Delta and Its Future Utilization,* Botswana Society, (Ed.), pp. 235–243. Gaborone: Botswana Society.

Johnston, Barbara R., (Ed.). (1990). Breaking out of the Tourist Trap. *Cultural Survival Quarterly,* vol. 14, no. 1 and vol. 14, no. 2. Cambridge: Cultural Survival Inc.

Kalahari Conservation Society. (1988). *Sustainable Wildlife Utilisation: The Role of Wildlife Management Areas*. Gaborone, Botswana: Kalahari Conservation Society.

Kiss, Agnes (Ed.). (1990). *Living with Wildlife: Wildlife Resource Management with Local Participation in Africa*. World Bank Technical Paper Number 130. Washington, D.C.: The World Bank.

Lee, Richard B. (1979). *The !Kung San: Men, Women, and Work in a Foraging Society*. Cambridge: Cambridge University Press.

(1993). *The Dobe Ju/'hoansi*. Second Edition. New York: CBS College Publishing.

Lillywhite, Malcolm and Lynda Lillywhite. (1991). Low Impact Tourism—Sustaining Indigenous Natural Resource Management and Diversifying Economic Development in Botswana. In *Tourism in Botswana*, Linda Pfotenhauer (Ed.), pp. 267–293. Gaborone: The Botswana Society.

Marshall, John. (1984). Death Blow to the Bushmen. *Cultural Survival Quarterly* 8(3):13–16.

Marshall, John and Claire Ritchie. (1984). *Where Are the Ju/Wasi of Nyae Nyae? Changes in a Bushman Society: 1958–1981*. Communications No. 9, Center for African Area Studies, University of Cape Town. Cape Town: University of Cape Town.

Marshall, Lorna. (1976). *The !Kung of Nyae Nyae*. Cambridge: Harvard University Press.

Mehra, Rekha. (1993). *Gender in Community Development and Resource Management: An Overview*. Washington, D.C.: International Center for Research on Women and World Wildlife Fund.

Ministry of Environment and Tourism. (1994a). *Policy Document: Conservation of Biotic Diversity and Habitat Protection*. Windhoek, Namibia: Ministry of Environment and Tourism.

(1994b). *Policy Document: Land-Use Planning: Towards Sustainable Development*. Windhoek, Namibia: Ministry of Environment and Tourism.

(1995a). *Policy Document: Wildlife Management, Utilization, and Tourism in Communal Areas: Benefits to Communities and Improved Resource Management*. Windhoek, Namibia: Ministry of Environment and Tourism.

(1995b). *Policy Document: Promotion of Community-Based Tourism Development*. Windhoek, Namibia: Ministry of Environment and Tourism.

Ministry of Wildlife, Conservation, and Tourism. (1992a). Draft Policy on Wildlife Management and Utilization in Communal Areas. Windhoek, Namibia: Environmental Planning Unit, Ministry of Wildlife, Conservation, and Tourism (MWCT), Government of Namibia.

(1992b). *Namibia's Green Plan (Environment and Development.* Windhoek, Namibia: Republic of Namibia.

Ministry of Finance and Development Planning. (1991). *National Development Plan 1991–1997.* Gaborone, Botswana: Government Printer.

Mogwe, Alice. (1992). *Who Was (T)here First? An Assessment of the Human Rights Situation of Basarwa in Selected Communities in the Gantsi District.* Occasional Paper No. 10. Gaborone, Botswana: Botswana Christian Council.

Nurse, G. T., J. S. Weiner, and Trefor Jenkins. (1985). *The Peoples of Southern Africa and Their Affinities.* Oxford: Clarendon Press.

Owen-Smith, Garth and Margaret Jacobsohn. (1989). Involving a Local Community in Wildlife Conservation: A Pilot Project at Purros, Southwestern Kaokoland, SWA/Namibia. *Quagga,* 27:21–28.

Payne, Holly. (1992). Report on Bushmanland's Land Use Plan (April 1992–October 1992). Environmental Liaison Officer Report, Department of Wildlife, Conservation, and Tourism and Nyae Nyae Development Foundation, Windhoek, Namibia.

Pfotenhauer, Linda, (ed.), (1991). *Tourism in Botswana.* Gaborone, Botswana: The Botswana Society.

Pleumarom, Anita. (1994). The Political Economy of Tourism. *The Ecologist,* 24(4):142–148.

Republic of Botswana. (1975). *National Policy on Tribal Grazing Land.* Government Paper No. 1 of 1975. Gaborone, Botswana: Government Printer.

(1986). *Wildlife Conservation Policy.* Government Paper No. 1 of 1986. Gaborone, Botswana: Government Printer.

(1989). *Tourism Policy in Botswana. A Draft Paper Produced for Purposes of Consultation.* Gaborone, Botswana: Government Printer.

Savage, Melissa. (1993). Ecological Disturbance and Nature Tourism. *Geographical Review,* 83(3):290–300.

Scudder, Thayer. (1996). Resettlement. In *Handbook for Water Resources and Environment,* Asit K. Biswas (Ed.). New York: McGraw-Hill.

Silberbauer, George B. (1981). *Hunter and Habitat in the Central Kalahari Desert.* Cambridge: Cambridge University Press.

Smith, Valene L. (1989a). Introduction. In *Hosts and Guests: The Anthropology of Tourism,* Valene L. Smith (Ed.), pp. 1–14. Second Edition. Philadelphia: University of Pennsylvania Press.

Smith, Valene L., (Ed.). (1989b). *Hosts and Guests: The Anthropology of Tourism.* Second Edition. Philadelphia: University of Pennsylvania Press.

Smith, Valene L. and Willian R. Eadington (Eds.). (1992). *Tourism Alternatives: Potentials and Problems in the Development of Tourism.* Philadelphia: University of Pennsylvania Press.

Swain, Margaret Byrne. (1989). Cuna Women and Ethnic Tourism: A Way to Persist and an Avenue to Change. In *Hosts and Guests: The Anthropology of Tourism*, Valene L. Smith (Ed.), pp. 71–81. Second Edition. Philadelphia: University of Pennsylvania Press.

Thoma, Axel. (1993). Tourism and the Ju/'hoansi of Nyae Nyae, Otjozondjupa Region. Paper presented at the Workshop on Responsible Tourism, Windhoek, Namibia, August 13–15, 1993.

United States Agency for International Development. (1989). *Regional Natural Resources Management Project (690–0251).* Washington, D.C.: USAID, Department of State.

USAID/Namibia. (1992). *Living In a Finite Environment (LIFE) Project Paper.* Windhoek, Namibia: USAID/Namibia and Washington, D.C.: U. S. Agency for International Development.

Volkman, Toby Alice. (1990). Visions and Revisions: Toroja Culture and the Tourist Gaze. *American Ethnologist,* 17(1):91–110.

Wells, Michael and Katrina Brandon, with Lee Hannah. (1992). *People and Parks: Linking Protected Area Management with Local Communities.* Washington, D.C.: World Bank, World Wildlife Fund, and U.S. Agency for International Development.

Whelan, Tensie, (ed.). (1991). *Nature Tourism: Managing for the Environment.* Washington, D.C.: Island Press.

Wilkinson, P. F. (1978). The Global Distribution of National Parks and Equivalent Reserves. In *International Experience with National Parks and Related Reserves,* J. G. Nelson, R. D. Needham, and D. L. Mann (Ed.). pp. 603–624. Waterloo, Ontario, Canada: University of Waterloo.

Wilmsen, Edwin N. (1989). *Land Filled with Flies: A Political Economy of the Kalahari.* Chicago: University of Chicago Press.

Wu, C. T. (1982). Issues of Tourism and Socioeconomic Development. *Annals of Tourism Research,* 9(2):313–348.

7

Tourism with Race in Mind: Annapolis, Maryland Examines its African-American Past through Collaborative Research

GEORGE C. LOGAN
MARK P. LEONE

The next several chapters in this volume focus on ways in which anthropologists have become directly involved in tourism initiatives. Rather than limiting themselves to seeking a better understanding of the human consequences of tourism, these individuals have begun to serve as mediators in their own right. For example, the following chapter by George Logan and Mark Leone describes the roles played by archaeologists in the interpretation of an American city's past. In this case, heritage tourism provides both a rationale for interpretation and an opportunity to expose visitors and community members alike to the value of archaeological research. Working in Annapolis, Maryland's state capitol, Logan and Leone reflect upon the extent to which representations of the city's past have been shaped by local power relations as well as by assumptions concerning which moments in the city's history were likely to be of greatest interest to visitors. One result has been that Annapolis' African-American past has received little attention. In their attempts to rectify this situation, Logan and Leone felt it was important that members of the city's African-American community be directly involved in decisions related to research priorities and subsequent interpretations. Collaborative efforts of this scope are still rare in heritage tourism.

The Society for American Archaeology includes as one of its six ethical principles that "archaeologists shall reach out to the public . . . to explain archaeological interpretations of the past" (SAA Ethics in Archaeology Committee, 1995). Archaeology increasingly portrays itself as a discipline committed to the stewardship of fragile and nonrenewable resources, and so many American archaeologists agree that public education and outreach are among our most important professional responsibilities. As a result, a growing number of people are learning about archaeological research in their communities through educational outreach. For almost fifteen years Annapolis, Maryland has been hosting an ongoing program in historical archaeology that is committed to public education.

"Archaeology in Annapolis" began in 1981 after the Historic Annapolis Foundation (HAF) invited anthropologists at the University of Maryland, College Park to conduct jointly sponsored research. By excavating and analyzing a variety of residential and commercial sites in the Historic District, archaeologists planned to develop a better understanding of the commercial base of the port city, its property and wealth structure and the relationships among individuals and groups who lived there (Potter and Leone, 1986).

Since most field work would be conducted in the summer months at the height of Annapolis' tourism season, the co-sponsors knew that the archaeological digs would attract considerable public attention and curiosity. Parker Potter came to the project during that first season to work with Mark Leone in developing public programs. "Archaeology in Public," helped make these sites places where visitors could learn about archaeology and the related processes of creating historical interpretations. On-site programs, consisting of site tours given by archaeologists, site placards and informative brochures, have been offered to visitors during most summers since 1983. Crucial to these programs has been the idea of using on-site examples to explain archaeological methods and then to show how insights drawn from archaeological evidence are used to develop historical interpretations (Leone, 1983b).

In 1988, after seven years of excavation and public educational programs, we initiated a program focused specifically on examining the city's African-American past. Tours, exhibits, brochures, and public presentations have emphasized the need for residents and especially for African-American Annapolitans to help us identify relevant issues in examining the city's African-American past. Listening to suggestions and criticisms from the community has helped us address local interests more effectively and by drawing the interest of outside scholars, this research has contributed to professional debates on interpreting African-American history.

In this article, we will discuss reasons for initiating a program focused on historic African-American sites. We will highlight ways in which the research provided for a collaborative spirit to develop between the archaeology crew members, most of whom were white and non-local, and the museum professionals, residents and interested tourists, many of whom were African-Americans. Next, we will highlight ways in which this initiative has contributed new insights into Annapolis' African-American past. These interpretations are based on archaeological analysis, oral history interviews and documentary research.

One measure of the success of this community-based research is the extent to which it is being used by established historic preservation groups. Specifically, we will discuss two archaeological sites which are now being developed as historic house museums. They are the Maynard-Burgess House and a ground-story room of the east wing in the Charles Carroll House. Although historical and archaeological research provides unequivocal evidence that African-Americans were principal figures in the history of each place, the groups creating the interpretations have framed the messages in terms of white origins. These two projects will serve as examples for showing that no matter what the perspective, historical interpretation inevitably serves contemporary interests and reveals present day biases. Although such interests and biases are seldom explicitly discussed, in this case they send a clear message to visitors: Annapolis history is still about white history. If historical interpretation is to serve the community as a whole, it must be based on a multiplicity of voices that represent competing and opposing interests which were and are part of the community. This should be a fundamental goal of any true community-based history. We hope to build on the initial successes of this program, but we recognize that it will happen only through commitments to more sustained efforts in collaborative research from both historic preservation groups and other community leaders.

Separate Histories

Interpreting colonial history has been a favored past-time in Annapolis for many years. It is a town noted for its well-preserved townscape and a strong sense of its own historical importance. The influence of preservation groups, most notably HAF, and other advocates of tourism, have grown considerably over the last forty years. Historic Annapolis, Inc., now HAF, formed in the 1950s for the purpose of sponsoring restoration projects in the downtown area. What was once a little known state capital earlier this century has become a nationally recognized center of historic preservation and tourism. However, proclamations of Annapolis' historical importance date back to at least the late 1800s, when Elihu Riley wrote *The Ancient City* (Potter, 1989, 1994).

Even though historical interpretation has been an important part of Annapolis' twentieth century identity, most visitors over the last thirty or forty years have been exposed to only a fraction of the city's past. Potter observed that, like many early historical sketches, Riley's work focused on the city's colonial elite class and on its relatively short lived status during the period as a social and political center. Many historical accounts have since paid inordinate amounts of attention to the colonial period and its upper-class citizens (Potter, 1989, 1994). Even though a great many different people have been part of Annapolis' past, few of their experiences have made it into mainstream historical interpretations, and it is not just tourists who have been slighted. Annapolis residents, who are also consumers of these histories, have come away with incomplete and sometimes distorted views of their own community's past. The interests of residents who desire a better understanding of local cultural heritage have not been served by this preoccupation with the colonial period and on the social elite, a perspective created primarily to attract tourism.

This is one of the reasons why Archaeology in Annapolis is committed to the idea of "giving a community back its right to its past." This commitment is based on "an understanding that once people understand how history is composed, they will take responsibility for seeing why it changes and how it is an active ingredient in their identity as a people and a community," (Leone, 1983a: 44).

Another theme identified by Potter in his research of how Annapolis uses its past is one of fragmentation. "History as it is usually presented in Annapolis, and as it has been for one hundred years, is as fragmented as it could be" (Potter, 1989:185). This virtually eliminates any chances for visitors to make connections between the community's past and its present, or for residents to gain any sense of connection with the history of the community in which they live. After an exhaustive study of walking tour presentations, brochures, guidebooks, historical sketches and books devoted to Annapolis history, Potter recognized that one of the deepest divisions in presentations of Annapolis' past has been between black history and white history. Moreover, discussions of the city's African-American past have consistently been set in the nineteenth century, leaving the eighteenth century's "Golden Age" essentially the exclusive domain of whites. Since most presentations of the city's past offered to visitors focus on the eighteenth century, it is understandable that most visitors know very little about Annapolis' African-American history.

Partly because of the limited perspective that HAF and other local preservation groups have chosen for public programs, they do not have a very positive relationship with most African-American residents. During conversations with African-American community activists, we learned that at least for the last thirty years, a prevailing opinion in the local black community has been that there is little reason to visit historic sites downtown, because they are only about white history. For most, there has simply been no relationship with HAF, but for some the relationship is perceived as antagonistic.

Examples of fragmented histories have become even more apparent to us since beginning this initiative. We experienced one such example during the 1990 excavation season, when fifteen to twenty African-American high school graduates visited Annapolis during a summer program. They were that year's class of Meyerhoff Scholars, students awarded full scholarships to the University of Maryland for their proven aptitudes in science and math. We met at the Banneker-Douglass Museum, and after touring an African-American archaeological site, the group was given an HAF walking tour. The contrast between Archaeology in Annapolis research and the HAF tour could not have been more apparent. During the tour, the guide talked about famous African-Americans from Maryland such as Thurgood Marshall and Matthew Alexander Henson, "co-discoverer" of the North Pole with Admiral Perry and four Inuit guides. There was no mention of other, local African Americans, or of historic African-American neighborhoods in downtown Annapolis, even though the group walked through one such waterfront neighborhood on its way to the archaeology lab. Prior to the tour we had introduced the group to two historic African-American sites in the downtown area, but the message conveyed on the tour, though certainly unintentional, was that even though black history is important, it is not a significant part of downtown Annapolis.

We do not mean to leave the impression that Annapolis has no understanding or appreciation for its African-American heritage, but for the most part this appreciation has existed within the African-American community. There is a wealth of documentation about Annapolis' African-American past. One important example is a book recently written by Philip Brown entitled, *The Other Annapolis*. In its pages are countless nineteenth and twentieth century photographs of historic African-American homes and neighborhoods throughout downtown.

The author documents a prideful heritage, but his title is an intentional reminder of the realities of living with segregation and racial prejudice.

Examining a City's African American Past Through Archaeology

In 1988, we had presented ideas about starting a collaborative project to the staff of the Banneker-Douglass Museum, which is also the home of the state's Commission on Afro-American History and Culture. During these initial meetings, we did not present a formal research design. Instead, we explained that two sites, which had previously been African-American neighborhoods were targeted for development, and it was our responsibility to determine the historical and archaeological significance of both sites. We explained that we could do the archaeology, but we thought that the question of significance should more properly be put to Annapolis' African-American community for its consideration.

The museum's director and assistant director recognized the potential of these projects as community-wide endeavors and began working with us in the earliest stages to develop appropriate research questions and to encourage community support and participation. They identified three research questions of interest to community residents which might also be answered through archaeology: "Do African-Americans have archaeology?", "We're tired of hearing about slavery, tell us about freedom!", and "Is there anything left from Africa?" (Leone et al., 1995: 112). We also wanted to include the broader Annapolis community in this research, so public educational programs became an integral part of the initiative.

Two characteristics came to define interpretive programs as a result of these initial planning sessions: research questions should be based on community interest; and the general project research design, as well as more specific research questions, should be flexible enough to be refined, when necessary, to more effectively address both the community's and our own research interests.[1] We expected that as more people became aware of the project, new interests and questions would be raised. If interpretive programs generated public dialogue, then such discussions may lead to new ideas for research. Future opportunities to study additional sites may also call for different kinds of research questions. Flexibility has been an important part of this research initiative, but the three politically and historically charged questions that came out of those first meetings have continued to guide both the research and public programs (Leone et al., 1995).

We created educational programs with an understanding that we were there to teach visitors about archaeology, but just as importantly, we were also there to learn why residents thought their community's past was important. This sharing of knowledge went well beyond simply listening to visitors during site tours. Archaeology in Annapolis soon began offering a summer field school devoted entirely to teaching oral history research methods. Our openness to learn from residents helped us become involved in projects that are adding more voices to historical interpretations.

Many of our research questions could not be answered until after we had left the field and had completed extensive analysis of the excavated sites. Therefore, we used on-site public programs as opportunities to talk with visitors about problems with historical interpretations that have either ignored black history or separated it from discussions of white history. We also spent a considerable amount of time asking questions and listening to visitors' responses, because we wanted to know more about how they viewed our research: Did they agree with our basic premise?; Did they find our research questions interesting?; Would they suggest topics for future research projects or education programs?. Encouraging dialogue about archaeological research and historical interpretation is a basic component of Archaeology in Annapolis public programs.

Since 1990, we have taken part in several weekend events, and the first one, the 1990 Kunta Kinte Commemoration and High Heritage Festival, was the most successful of our on-site public programs. The site we were working on was more than a mile from the Festival grounds. A considerably shorter distance had prevented all but a trickle of downtown tourists from visiting earlier that summer, but during this late September festival weekend more the 350 people took site tours. Almost half of these visitors were African Americans who were from the greater Annapolis area or were visiting Annapolis specifically for the Festival. Tour logs indicated that approximately the same percentage of visitors throughout the three month project were also African Americans (Logan, in press).

During this event we offered questionnaires at the conclusion of tours, asking people to give us some feedback that would help us create better programs in the future. Demographic information obtained from these forms indicates that more than twenty-five percent of visitors were from Annapolis, which is a much higher rate of local visitation than the average of ten percent at previous on-site educational programs (Logan, in press). Forms included multiple choice questions and three questions that required written answers. Approximately one third of these questions were left blank. The selected responses below provide an example of the kind of support this research has had over the last six years.

Responses to the question "What connection do you see between this site and everyday life today?" included:

> What is found on this site will help to fill a large gap in our history. This new information will help us to better understand a long overshadowed segment of our society.

> *This* site could help build bridges among groups in the community, not just add to the lore of academia.

> That much of the Annapolis life during the 1800s (i.e., black/white relations) seemed to be setting the pattern for the relations between the races today.

> As an African American who has been miseducated in America, it has reinforced my understanding of the need to better educate people.

> It is difficult to understand the present & how its problems can be solved, and how prior ones were, without knowing how the present community came to be.

> As an Afro-American I am pleased to know that we can integrate the past with the future and present. What a wonderful way to introduce our children to their own cultural past.

> The present community becomes more historically richer and enriched.

> (Logan, 1991:54–55)

Some of the responses to this question expressed the frustrations that many people have with respect to race relations in our society. Other responses focused on the belief that historical interpretation can help to improve conditions through better understanding.

When asked, "What did you learn about the history of African-Americans in Annapolis?" there were three general kinds of responses. Many repeated statements from the tour, some implied racially biased views in their responses, and others admitted a lack of understanding about African-American history.

> We learned that 1/3 of the population of Annapolis was black in the 1800s and that this was a predominantly black neighborhood.

> They were once lower class but lived well in their area.

That there were more here than I thought.

I didn't know that this was a "black area" of the town.

Housing close to where I live. I walk by this site frequently and had no idea what was buried here.

The fact that there *were* African-Americans in Annapolis.

Never knew the population of African-Americans in Annapolis was as large in the past and as large in the present.

Learned about the role and participation of African-Americans in Annapolis life in the 1800s–1900s (early). According to most historical exhibits in this city, you wouldn't even know blacks even lived here or participated in life in anyway.

(Logan, 1991:56–57)

The final question asked, "What did you learn about archaeology that you did not know before you visited the site?" Answers ranged from information about methods, to discussions of the project's focus on black history, to addressing the general lack of African-Americans engaged in archaeological research.

How different layers of soil can indicate the period in history that artifacts found in it were used.

How each level in the ground could tell you about time frames.

I really didn't know anything about archaeology until today.

I learned that there are probably few African-Americans engaged in this field probably again due to miseducation and racism and a need to focus on survival.

That archaeologists are interested in historical America and black America in particular.

Its not what we learned, its the fact that some majority Americans are giving recognition to others.

(Logan, 1991:58)

Not surprisingly most people responded to the question "What would you like to see on future tours?" by saying they would like to see examples of artifacts from the site. Encouraged by visitor enthusiasm, the following spring we worked with the staff members of the Banneker Douglass Museum to mount a museum exhibit entitled, "The Maryland Black Experience As Understood Through Archaeology." At the suggestion of the museum's assistant director, we had begun conducting oral history interviews to help us better understand the sites and their histories. The exhibit designer used excerpts from those initial interviews as a primary component of the exhibit text. The residents, not the archaeologists, provided interpretations of artifacts and the roles they played in everyday life. We provided additional text on panels, linking the sites that were represented in the exhibit and offering explanations of how archaeological analysis could provide information about the sites' earlier histories, or about aspects of everyday life that may have been taken for granted. The exhibit design was very effective in expressing the stated theme that plural voices compose the past.

From 1989 through 1992, archaeological research included excavations on three historic African-American sites. The first site, known historically as Gott's Court, had been an early twentieth century single-street neighborhood in the interior of a downtown city block. The twenty-five connected, two-story frame structures that formed the court were rented by working class African-American households.

The second site became known simply as the Courthouse site, because the county government planned to construct a courthouse expansion on the site. African-American households had owned lots and homes there since the middle of the nineteenth century, and by 1874 construction of Mount Moriah African Methodist Episcopal Church had begun. On that site, the Church would serve a significant portion of Annapolis' African-American population for the next one hundred years. The Gott's Court and Courthouse sites were purchased by City and County governments earlier this century and both were asphalt covered parking lots when excavations began. The Mount Moriah congregation had moved to a new location, and the historic building had been placed on the National Register of Historic Places and now houses the Banneker-Douglass Museum.

The third site, the Maynard-Burgess House lot, is a single lot with a standing historic structure named after the two African-American households that owned the property from 1847 through 1980 (McWilliams, 1991). Together, the three sites represent a cross-section of African-American households living in Annapolis during the late nineteenth and early twentieth centuries.

The goal of this research is to create an archaeology of African-Americans that all contemporary residents may use as a body of knowledge for understanding the past, so that they may gain a better sense of how the community has come to be in its present form. We have found that this is a history characterized by negotiation that involved accommodating white society while maintaining distinct cultural identities defined from within African-American communities. It is not a history dominated by grotesque oppression and physically violent racism, but it is a history of people creating a stable community within a community in the face of somewhat more subtle forms of racism.

What was daily life like for African-Americans in Annapolis during this period? Evidence suggests that for many it did not look like abject poverty. Rather, it looked coherent and stable, but this does not mean that African-Americans were blind to the processes of oppression working against them.

Turn-of-the-century African-American literature is replete with discussions of the need to avoid white surveillance by appearing to assimilate, while maintaining distinctions that were recognized within African-American culture (Mullins, 1993). Wiley Bates, a highly successful Annapolis businessman of the period, made this point quite clearly in his autobiography. "The Negro . . . tries to make people believe what he is not, by the imitation of the shadow and not the real substance," (Bates, 1928:14, as cited in Mullins, 1993:6).

With the Victorian age came an exponential increase in the number of choices available to consumers, and just as for white households, African-American households began purchasing many of these new products. The degree to which households accepted certain dominant Victorian-era values can be examined through an analysis of their material consumption patterns. Unique to the African-American experience, however, were barriers of both race and class for which complex negotiating strategies were developed. Mark Warner and Paul Mullins, co-directors of the Maynard-Burgess research project, suggest that these strategies involved choosing between three basic options: to fully buy into the local market economy; to engage in selective consumerism; and to opt out of the local market economy altogether. Results of their analysis indicate that African-Americans used all three strategies in a fashion described as situational negotiation. Using faunal materials, glass bottled goods and ceramics as their primary archaeological evidence, Warner and Mullins have developed insightful interpretations of African-American consumer choice and consumer behavior during the Victorian period (Warner, 1995; Mullins, 1993).

Faunal analysis of the Maynard-Burgess assemblage shows that all three options were employed in acquiring meat (Warner, 1995). The presence of commercially cut bones shows that the Maynards and the Burgesses were selectively purchasing meat in the marketplace and that their processes of selection were relatively stable through time. Faunal remains also suggest that the Maynards and the Burgesses opted out of the market at times by supplementing their diets with locally caught seafood and possibly also with chickens raised in the yard (Warner, 1995). When we interviewed residents of the neighborhood that surrounded Mount Moriah AME Church, we learned that children often fished and crabbed. One resident also remembered that his grandfather and three neighbors raised chickens when he was a young boy. He remembered once walking into the post office and hearing the constant peeping of all the baby chicks that had arrived through mail order (Kaiser, n.d).

Based on analysis of identifiable bottles that were excavated from the Maynard-Burgess site and Gott's Court, Mullins suggests that the Maynards and at least some Gott's Court residents favored nationally advertised bottled goods over those of local manufacturers and pharmacists. Of the 87 bottles that were recovered from a small interior cellar, filled in during the late 1880s, none were locally produced, but 26 were nationally advertised brands. Likewise, at Gott's Court, none of the 54 identifiable glass bottles and table vessels that were recovered during preliminary excavations were from Annapolis bottlers or pharmacists. Mullins points out that in the market, African-Americans were more vulnerable to racist attitudes of local merchants when buying local products and bulk food than when buying nationally advertised packaged foods. With bulk food and local goods, African-Americans may have had to accept inferior quality and arbitrarily high prices. In contrast, when purchasing national brands, consumers were more likely to receive consistent levels of quality at more stable prices (Mullins, 1993).

For African-Americans, daily life was a struggle against racism and economic marginalization in the face of maintaining a shared cultural identity. Likewise, the consumption of material goods involved a complex array of strategies used on a situational basis to resist supporting the predominantly white, and therefore, biased marketplace on the one hand, and to select consumer goods that held status within African-American communities on the other. These selective strategies produced consumer behavior patterns that appeared on the surface to mirror behavior advocated by whites, but through archaeological analysis, documentary research and studies or oral history, important subtle differences may be identified.

Another measure of the program's success is the impact the work has had on other institutions. Three specific events related to historic preservation issues show that our research has helped change the criteria for determining which archaeological and architectural resources are deemed significant in Annapolis' Historic District. Since 1989, two major cultural resource management contracts on historic African-

American sites in the downtown area have been supported by state, county and city government funds. As a direct result of our preliminary excavations on both the Gott's Court and Courthouse sites and the success of collaboration with members of the black community winning proposals for full-scale excavations were required to include a focus on turn-of-the-century African-American heritage and to budget for public interpretation while the excavations were in progress. The third event was that the Maynard-Burgess House, now a city-owned property, was named a City Historic Site and the City Council is supporting efforts to open it as a museum focused on African-American history. It is clear that local support for these research initiatives has helped bring about public policy changes in the way Annapolis researches, preserves, and interprets its past.

Another site excavated during the 1991 season was the ground story of the Charles Carroll House. It is known as the home of one of Maryland's most famous political figures during the late eighteenth and early nineteenth centuries. The archaeological excavations were a preliminary step in the restoration of this historic structure, and for that reason the initial research design focused mainly on architectural issues such as room arrangements and changes in the use of space over time. We did not consider the Carroll House project to be relevant to African-American heritage. One long-held assumption about this property has been that slaves lived in work areas away from the mansion and formal garden. The sites of these work areas had long since been destroyed. Therefore, it was not expected that we would find material evidence of slave life in areas now within the three acre historic site.

During the excavations, however, we discovered a collection of objects associated directly with twelve individual quartz crystals that had been placed under the early-1800s floor in one of these ground story rooms. Subsequent research demonstrated that the objects related to a tradition that had its origins in West African divination systems (Logan, 1995; Logan et al., 1992; Jones, 1995). The discovery is important because it shows that at least some enslaved African-Americans in the Mid-Atlantic colonies managed not only to retain traditional cultural beliefs and values, but they also continued communicating those beliefs through expressions that involved material culture.

The discovery has invited us to look critically not only at certain historical interpretations, but also at ourselves as members of contemporary American communities. Having focused on landscape archaeology in the terraced garden during previous seasons, we approached excavations inside the ground story with related questions about formal design. Early on during 1991, we were focusing on the site's white history without fully considering alternative perspectives. In essence, our questions were influenced by the same biases that we were criticizing across town. The interpretation of this discovery provides a strong critique of traditional notions about African cultural heritage in the Mid-Atlantic. It is known that traditions associated with West African cultures were practiced among American slaves in certain areas, but prevailing views among scholars of the Mid-Atlantic colonies had been that such traditions did not survive to any significant degree. Second, and possibly more important, the context of this discovery brings us face to face with one of the most fundamental problems associated with historical fragmentation, and that is that the power it has to perpetuate distorted views of the past often goes unrecognized. During the Carroll House excavations, evidence of African-American cultural expression became tied inextricably with the "showpiece" home of one of Maryland's most prominent white citizens of the eighteenth and early nineteenth centuries. If this unique collection of objects had not been recovered from the Charles Carroll House before its renovation, African-American slaves would still probably be absent from interpretations of that site, even though Charles Carroll of Carrollton was among the state's largest slave owners. This project serves as an example for everyone, including archaeologists and historians, of how important it is to critically examine historical interpretations in an effort to identify and minimize the biases inherent in the messages they convey.

Historic Annapolis Foundation and the Charles Carroll House of Annapolis, Inc., are now in the process of deciding how to interpret the Maynard-Burgess House and the ground story room of the east wing in the Charles Carroll House. Both groups should be commended for working toward expanded interpretations of African-American heritage in Annapolis. Recent decisions concerning interpretations on both sites, however, are likely to alienate members of the African-American community, especially those who have been involved in this collaborative research initiative.

Architectural renovations are now complete in the Carroll House ground story. Aside from reconstructing a raised wooden floor in the east wing room based on archaeological evidence, no interpretation of the room as a slave dwelling has been installed. As a result of changes instituted by the Catholic Order of the Redemptorists, the property owners, site development has now shifted away from research toward publicity and more traditional forms of living history interpretation. It appears that, for the foreseeable future, the east wing room will remain silent about the fact that, during the early 1800s, it was occupied by enslaved African-Americans.

Renovations at the other property are only just beginning. Recently a large plaque was attached to the front porch identifying the site as, "The Maynard-Burgess House, Constructed ca. 1780–1870, An Historic African-American Site." The initial date for construction is based on an architectural analysis and applies only to portions of the structure's interior core, but that structure was not built on this site. The analysis asserts that the building was moved to the site in the mid-1800s, presumably by a white owner of the lot, but the original location and owner of the structure remain unknown. According to the analysis, the property was then sold to John Maynard, a free African-American, who initiated major changes between 1847 and 1860. It was about ten years later that he probably constructed a two-story addition onto the back of the house.

The troubling point about this interpretation is that Historic Annapolis Foundation has fixed a date to this house that creates vague origins vaguely in the eighteenth century with a white owner. This was done even though a trained architectural historian could identify only minor exterior details from that period. When interior renovations are complete, almost none of the early structural framing will be visible. By emphasizing architecture instead of people, this interpretation highlights the debate over the structure's colonial origins instead of its primary importance as a free African-American home during the mid 1800s.

Many people recognize that both Historic Annapolis Foundation and the Charles Carroll House of Annapolis, Inc., have vested interests in interpreting the city's colonial origins and the contributions of its leaders. One of the principal uses of establishing historical origins is to establish historical legitimacy and to "mark the territory." After establishing a date of construction that spans almost a century, HAF will undoubtedly spend a great deal of energy interpreting the building's origins which are not part of its status as an historic African-American site. The implicit message could be viewed as a metaphor reflecting long-standing, biased notions not only about Annapolis history, but also about the history of American society: At its core and its origins, the structure is White. All other characteristics, including African-American influences are secondary add-ons.[2]

Historic preservation organizations must always identify competing and sometimes opposing contemporary interests when interpreting the past and then they must choose which perspective or which voice should be the focus of interpretation. Results of Archaeology in Annapolis research clearly show that African-American contributions are the most significant and most clearly documented components of the two sites discussed here. African Americans should have the clear and dominant voice on each site not simply because it is "long overdue," to quote visitor responses, but because it is both appropriate and necessary. Despite the successes of this collaborative research initiative, historical interpretation will continue to serve divisive interests in Annapolis until the larger and longer-term benefits of creating more inclusive accounts of the past are more widely recognized and appreciated.

Conclusion

This initiative has significantly broadened our perspective of Annapolis' past to include African-Americans in interpretations of eighteenth, nineteenth and twentieth century life. While significant, however, our contributions are still limited. Our educational programs have emphasized that most historical interpretations of Annapolis underrepresent African-Americans. A principal goal of the public research has been to work toward eliminating these kinds of artificial divisions, because they serve to maintain separations in contemporary society.

Fragmentation is a deeply rooted characteristic not only of historical interpretation in Annapolis, it can be seen to a greater or lesser degree in community histories throughout the country. As a result of classroom treatments of American history, most Americans think of this country's past not as a series of developments to the present, but as many isolated events with little relation to one another and with no connection to contemporary life. Archaeology in Annapolis has worked to counter this trend in its research and public programs by exploring ways in which archaeological evidence can be used to examine modern social concerns. For example, learning about the histories of African-Americans in Annapolis was not the only reason we have been conducting this research. We also want to examine the history of racial segregation and prejudice through specific historical examples. By identifying mechanisms through which such oppressive social constructions have developed and operated in the past, we contend that people are more likely to recognize the various forms of these strategies at work in the present, and will then be more likely to challenge them in the future.

Notes

1. A more detailed discussion of the on-site educational programs that developed as part of this initiative is included in "Archaeologists, Residents, and Visitors: Creating a Community-Based Program in African-American

Archaeology," in *Annapolis Pasts: Historical Archaeology in Annapolis, Maryland*, edited by Paul Shackel, Paul Mullins, and Mark Warner, University of Tennessee Press, Knoxville, in press.

2. Historical interpretations often convey unspoken messages just as effectively as those which are explicitly stated. The authors are indebted to Cheryl Coursey, who recognized that the Maynard-Burgess House serves as a powerful metaphor for criticizing interpretations that focus on the Anglo-American origins of American society. Such a focus is counterproductive to any project working toward inclusivity, because it promotes exclusive claims.

References

Brown, Philip L. (1994). *The Other Annapolis, 1900-1950*. The Annapolis Publishing Company, Annapolis, Maryland.

Jones, Lynn D. (1995). "The Material Culture of Slavery From an Annapolis Household." Paper presented at the Annual Meeting of the Society for Historical Archaeology, January 4–8, Washington, D.C.

Kaiser, Hannah Jopling. (n.d). Unpublished oral history interviews on file, Department of Anthropology, University of Maryland, College Park, MD.

Leone, Mark P. (1983a). "The Role of Archaeology in Verifying American Identity: Giving a Tour Based on Archaeological Method." *Archaeological Review From Cambridge*, 2, no. 1, pp. 44–50.

(1983b). "Method as Message: Interpreting the Past with the Public," in *Museum News*, 62, no. 1, pp. 34–41.

Leone Mark P., Paul R. Mullins, Marian C. Creveling, Laurence Hurst, Barbara Jackson-Nash, Lynn D. Jones, Hannah Jobling Kaiser, George C. Logan, and Mark S. Warner. (1995). "Can an African-American historical archaeology be an alternative voice?" in *Interpreting Archaeology: Finding meaning in the past*, edited by Ian Hodder, Michael Shanks, Alexandra Alexandri, Victor Buchli, John Carman, Jonathan Last and Gavin Lucas, 110–124. London and New York: Routledge.

Logan, George C. (in press). "Archaeologists, Residents, and Visitors: Creating a Community-Based Program in African-American Archaeology," in *Annapolis Pasts: Historical Archaeology in Annapolis, Maryland*, edited by Paul Shackel, Paul Mullins, and Mark Warner, University of Tennessee Press, Knoxville.

(1995). "African Religion in America," in *Invisible America: Unearthing Our Hidden History*, Mark P. Leone and Neil Asher Silberman, Henry Holt and Company, Inc., New York.

(1991). "Historical Archaeology and African-American Heritage in Annapolis: A Program of Public Interpretation for the Community." Project Director Evaluation for the Maryland Humanities Council, on file, Department of Anthropology, University of Maryland, College Park, MD.

Logan, George C., Thomas W. Bodor, Lynn D. Jones and Marian C. Creveling. (1992). "1991 Archaeological Excavations at the Charles Carroll House in Annapolis, Maryland (18AP45)," site report on file, Department of Anthropology, University of Maryland, College Park, MD.

Logan, George C. and Parker B. Potter, Jr. (1990). "African-American Archaeology in Annapolis, Maryland." Brochure on file at Historic Annapolis Foundation, Annapolis, MD.

McWilliams, Jane W. (1991). *Historical Title Search and Documentation, 163 Duke of Gloucester Street.* Unpublished report prepared for Port of Annapolis, Inc., Annapolis, MD. February. On file at Historical Annapolis Foundation, Annapolis, Maryland.

Mullins, Paul R. (1993). "'A Bold and Gorgeous Front': The Contradictions of African-America and Consumer Culture, 1880–1930." Paper presented at the School of American Research Advanced Seminar, "The Historical Archaeology of Capitalism," October 3–7, Sante Fe, New Mexico.

Potter, Parker B., Jr. (1989). *Archaeology in Public in Annapolis: An Experiment in the Application of Critical Theory to Historical Archaeology.* Ann Arbor, Mich.: Univ. Microfilm International.

(1994) *Public Archaeology in Annapolis: A Critical Approach to History in Maryland's Ancient City.* Washington: Smithsonian Institution Press.

Potter, Parker B., Jr. and Mark P. Leone. (1986). "Liberation Not Replication: "Archaeology in Annapolis" Analyzed." *Journal of the Washington Academy of Sciences, 76,* no. 2, pp. 97–105.

Riley, Elihu. *The ancient city: a history of Annapolis, in Maryland. 1649–1887.* Annapolis: Record Printing Office.

SAA Ethics in Archaeology Committee (1995). "Principles of Archaeological Ethics," in *Ethics in American Archaeology: Challenges for the 1990s,* edited by Mark Lynott and Alison Wylie, Lawrence, Kansas: Allen Press.

Warner, Mark S. (1995). "From the Market and From the Water: An African-American Household's Changing Responses to a Commercial Marketplace." Paper presented at the Annual Meeting of the Society for Historical Archaeology, January 4–8, Washington, D.C.

8

Tourism in the Lower Mississippi Delta: Whose Field of
Dreams? The Struggle Among The Landed Aristocracy,
The Grass-Roots Indigenous and The Gaming Industry

STANLEY E. HYLAND

*As more regions begin to view tourism development as an important compo-
nent in their strategies for economic growth, they are faced with making critical decisions as to what kinds of tourism to encourage. In this chapter, Stanley
Hyland discusses his involvement as Director of Research for the Lower Mississippi Delta Development Corporation, a regional commission encompassing seven southern states. Hyland describes the process as one that was not
only meant to identify potential cultural and natural resources for tourism development, but also to encourage greater regional integration. The struggle to
achieve this end was complicated by the presence of competing images of the
region, each represented by powerful constituencies. The Commission's recommendations favored a view of regional heritage that emphasized cultural
and environmental diversity and sought to include groups and interests that
had not previously received much attention in the region's tourism promotion.
This "new" grassroots image was in contrast to a prevailing focus on the antebellum south, on civil war sites, and on urban centers that Hyland suggests
was favored by the region's landed aristocracy and by many local chambers of
commerce. This situation was further complicated in the early 1990s, when
gaming interests won approval for the operation of casinos in the region. Hyland contrasts the painstaking efforts made by the Commission to seek public
input into their decision-making with the strategies employed by the gaming
industry to win approval for casino gambling.*

Introduction

In this chapter Erve Chambers notes that "tourism can be considered not only as an activity, but also as an orientation to the modern world." Towards this end the U.S. south in general, and the Lower Mississippi Delta region in particular, is currently in an intense struggle to redefine its image and redirect its future. The three major sets of interests in this struggle can be grouped as the old landed aristocracy, the grassroots proponents of cultural and environmental heritage, and the large-scale gaming industry. Each interest actively seeks tourism through the cultivation of an image that enhances its access to resources associated with tourists and solidifies its social and political position within the region.

This chapter focuses on one major initiative of the grassroots proponents of cultural and environmental heritage to redirect private, federal, and state resources in a systematic way as the basis for the economic development of a seven state region that has been labeled by the U.S. Congress as the poorest in the nation. (Lower Mississippi Delta Development Commission, 1989). The examination of this effort is made in the context of both the larger, better capitalized interests of the landed aristocracy and the gaming industry. Particular attention is focused on the real and potential role of applied anthropologists and folklorists in influencing how tourism is manifest in the Lower Mississippi Delta region through the development of an on-going relationship with the proponents of cultural and environmental heritage.

The Region

Until the mid-1970s the South was largely portrayed by the media (Campbell, 1981; Chappell, 1978; Matthews, 1976; Smith, 1983; Time Magazine, 1976) as a homogeneous region characterized by an agriculturally dominated economy, lower wages, politically conservative, culturally isolated, a strong sense of place, and unequal in the treatment of African-Americans (McKinney and Bourque, 1971). Initially rural sociologists under Howard Odum (Brazil, 1989) at the University of North Carolina, Chapel Hill, conducted empirical studies to document localized traditions on the Coastal Plain. Subsequently, anthropologists Morland (1968) and Hill (1977) did much to discredit the image of a monolithic South. Most recently Wilson and Ferris' (1989) monumental work *Encyclopedia of Southern Culture* clearly defines the major cultural areas and documents the variation of localized folk traditions.

Pillsbury (1989) in a summary article on cultural landscapes notes, "The South is at once both the most visible and most ambiguous of all American cultural landscapes . . . The vision of a unified southern cultural landscape is thus more myth than reality." Even Pillsbury's six major cultural landscapes (regions) fails to capture the apparently more obvious sixteen ecological regions identified by the Corps of Engineers (Lower Mississippi Region Comprehensive Study Coordinating Committee, 1974) and plotted by Clay, Escott, Orr and Stuart (1989). Of these sixteen ecological regions some have seen tremendous industrial growth, others have remained primarily agricultural, while still others have remained undeveloped because of environmental constraints such as flooding.

Within the context of increasing poverty and decreasing resources, the U.S. Congress in 1988 designated two of these regions as "poorest in the United States" (Lower Mississippi Delta Development Commission, 1989) and called for a "comprehensive strategic plan for economic development for the year 2000." The region stretching from the confluence of the Ohio and Mississippi Rivers and extending south to New Orleans was called the Lower Mississippi Delta (LMD) and included a seven state, 219 county area immediately adjacent to the lower Mississippi River (see Figure 1).

The Image of the Mississippi Delta Region

Historically to counter the dominant image of poverty and backwardness the Southern elite, principally in the form of the landed aristocracy and later the local chambers of commerce, built upon three counter images. The images sought to blend the modern and the ancient. The first of these images is that of a warrior south as captured in its homage of the Civil War battleground such as Vicksburg. The Civil War battlegrounds remain the number one tourist attraction to the outsider. A second image is that of a highly civilized agrarian region as characterized in the antebellum homes of Natchez and the mansions between Baton Rogue and New Orleans. These homes reflect the refined, ordered, romantic, rustic way of life of the agricultural South. State Offices of Tourism and major media organizations are major proponents and continue to emphasize this image in its lure of tourists (Wright, 1991).

The third image that is nurtured by the local chambers of commerce and represented by the urban skylines of New Orleans, and Memphis is controlled urban development. Historians Brownell (1975) and Cobb

Figure 1. Lower Mississippi Delta Region. The Lower Mississippi Delta is comprised of portions of seven states bound together through their ties to the Mississippi River.

(1993) note that Southern boosterism sought to portray that industrialism in the Mississippi Delta occurred in a more controlled fashion than that of its counterparts in the North. Specifically, Southern Progressives argue that they have avoided management labor conflicts and high wage costs, as well as, have developed massive sport complexes and museums. Local chambers of commerce continue to sell the new South through these images.

The Counter Images in the Mississippi Delta

These major images have served to orient the outside world that the South is a unique blend of the best of an agrarian society that has embraced the best of industrialism. The image suggests a ruling elite that manages economic growth while displaying historic values attractive to tourists. The acceptance of these images, however, runs counter to the large numbers of citizens living in poverty and the empirical work of anthropologists and folklorists who have documented the diversity of local lifeways and customs in the lower Mississippi Delta (Wilson and Ferris, 1989; Owens, 1992; Hyland and Collins, 1991; Williams and Williams, 1984).

The Economic Development Initiative in the Delta and Tourism

Within this context Congress in 1988 created a federal commission to develop a comprehensive strategic plan for economic development in a seven state Lower Mississippi Delta region by the year 2000. The Congressional mandate explicitly required that the Commission hold public hearings in each of the seven states and solicit recommendations through the use of additional hearings and conferences on important subject areas.

The Grassroots Planning Process

In the third public Commission meeting held in the state of Tennessee, a group of citizens (including the Center for Southern Folklore) proposed a citizens' conference on cultural tourism. This conference was held in Greenville, Mississippi and called **"Preserving and Promoting Our Heritage."** Responding to this proposal the Lower Mississippi Delta Development Commission funded the two major regional organizations associated with a knowledge of local folk traditions—the Center for Southern Folklore in Memphis and the Center for the Study of Southern Culture at the University of Mississippi to convene a conference on tourism and economic development. In addition, the Director of Research for the Commission who was an anthropologist was assigned to coordinate the planning effort.

To insure an open, representative, broad-based participation in the conference, a questionnaire was sent to individuals, groups, county

officials, and chamber of commerce offices in each of the 219 counties of
the Lower Mississippi Delta to identify local tourism activities and
other tourist entities. In addition a Steering Committee was established
to insure a balance by geography, race and gender. A total of 253 people
participated in the conference. All told, 37 percent of the Lower Mississippi Delta Commission's 219 counties were represented. Most of the
participants were affiliated with community based groups and mom
and pop operations although all tourism interests were invited.

The Plan for Cultural Heritage in the Lower Mississippi Delta

The LMDDC sponsored conference stated goal was "to explore the
positive relationship between all types of preservation (architectural,
cultural, environmental, and historic) and tourism and to develop a set
of recommendations for consideration in the final report of the LMDDC
to Congress." Towards this goal the final report of the conference concluded "the conference achieved its **major goal**—bringing together representatives of all the LMDDC states, and getting them to begin
thinking of the Delta as a cultural and geographic region. Throughout
the conference, two themes—'seeing ourselves though new eyes'
and the value of **linking the subregions' similarities while cele-
brating their differences**—remained important points of reference."
(LMDDC Tourism Conference Final Report, page 3).

More specifically the conference participants produced some 18 ten
year goals and some 82 recommendations reflecting a wide range of images related to tourism. These goals were sent to all conference participants and interested parties (those who could not attend the conference
but expressed an interest as well as those that read the media coverage
of the conference). The steering committee then met, reviewed comments, synthesized the initial ten year goals and recommended a format
that was consistent with the Commission's final report. It should be
noted that all the initial ten year goals were retained.

List 1 shows the range of ten year goals.

List 1: ten year goals of the Lower Mississippi Delta Development
Commission

1. By the year 2001, a regional tourism organization will be formed to
   pursue tourism development and marketing.

2. Through marketing, the Delta will become a major travel destination in America by the year 2001. The year 2001 will be celebrated
   with a year-long Delta Odyssey of events.

3. By the year 2001, a major north-south travel system will be developed with three travel arteries: the Mississippi River, the Great River Road and a continuous non-motorized bike and hike trail.

4. By the year 2001, an inland rail and road travel system or "Delta Loop," connecting major gateway cities of St. Louis, Memphis, New Orleans, Little Rock, Jackson and Baton Rouge, will be developed.

5. Delta communities will produce professional tourism leadership, develop their most important amenities, and boast good lodging and other service facilities by the year 2001.

6. By the year 2001, all of the Delta's significant historic and prehistoric sites and wetlands will be protected from destruction.

7. By the year 2001, the Delta will become a region known for the quality of its environment.

8. The Delta will sponsor a broad thematic range of special projects and programs which build a network of communities and attract visitors of many interests by the year 2001.

Native American Heritage Route
Delta African American Heritage Trail
River Corridor Tourism
Rail and Adjacent Town Tourism
Delta Depots
Cultural Destination Tourism: Folklife
Artistic Destination Tourism: Music & Literature
Natural Resource Attractions
Farm Tours
Senior Citizen Tourism

Two themes underlie List 1 and have relevance to the anthropological literature on tourism (Zamora, 1978; V. Smith, 1992; Boniface, 1993). One theme is related to cultural heritage/tourist activities; the other is related to process and organization and regional integration.

A review of the recommended major cultural heritage/tourist activities shows that there is no mention of the dominant images used by the outside and the Southern landed aristocracy and local chambers of commerce. Notably absent are the antebellum homes, civil war battlegrounds, skyscrapers, stadiums, and poverty. While there is mention of historic sites it is put into the context of prehistoric sites and environmental havens such as wetlands.

The primary emphasis is clearly on rural heritage and diversity. The picture of the Lower Mississippi Delta that emerges is heterogenous, non-urban, non-mainstream groups consisting of small town train depots, African-American trails, Native American heritage routes, folklife programs, music and literature destination points, and small farm tours. This image of the Mississippi Delta is in sharp contrast to that held by the outsider and the old Southern landed aristocracy. However, the image is obviously consistent with the published research and anthropologists and folklorists.

The linkage of cultural diversity and heritage to tourism and economic development may be partly explainable by their economic and political marginality in a poor region where development favors the petrochemical industries and large corporate farms. Cultural diversity, heritage and tourism in the broadest sense becomes an economic and political justification for their continued residence in this region. Carole Hill (1977) noted that the non-mainstream people (marginal) of the South understand the symbols of the dominant (core) groups and actively work to manipulate them for their gain. Tourism, heritage, and economic development are three of those symbols.

The second theme is related to process issues and the future of any organizational structure of tourism in the Delta. Here the recommendations reflect a picture of the Mississippi Delta as geographically isolated and one lacking in the skills necessary to participate in the political and economic decision-making structures of their respective states. Their concern is twofold. First they call for a shift in the distribution of economic and educational resources notably through highway, river, rail, and bike leadership training, and information centers.

The second related concern is one of regional integration as expressed in the call for a regional tourism organization. This is particularly interesting in a region that has been historically characterized as highly individualistic (Cash, 1939; Hill, 1977). The answer for this contradiction may reside in the political reality that economic resources for tourism have been centralized in the state capitols that are located outside the Mississippi Delta. In turn, tourism resources and marketing efforts have not been distributed to Delta areas. Hence the participants realize that without an ongoing organizational entity there is little hope for sustained attention and resources from the States.

The Results of the LMDDC Initiative to Date

The final recommendations to Congress from the Lower Mississippi Delta Development Commission have led to a mass of individual and small group actions that are currently impossible to track. However, on a larger scale there is evidence of institutional commitments to carrying out the LMDDC's tourism recommendations. All of these initiatives have directly involved anthropologists and folklorists in the design or execution. Several examples that show a range of cultural heritage activities include the following. The Center for the Study of Southern Culture at the University of Mississippi sends out a national newsletter that includes the mailing list of the Commission. The newsletter informs individuals and groups of folk programs and activities throughout the Mississippi Delta. Coupled with its *Encyclopedia of Southern Culture*, the image of the diversity of local Delta heritage is intellectually rooted in scholarship. In addition the Center has initiated a number of educational outreach activities such as an annual Mississippi River tour and educational conference.

Similarly, the Center for Southern Folklore in Memphis continues to disseminate information about the heritage of local groups in the Delta, as well as, sponsor an annual Heritage Festival. A pan-Native American Association has been formed in the region and is actively pursuing a Native American trail and cultural resource center. This discussion involves coalitions with the Department of Anthropology at the University of Memphis and state politicians. Work in Louisiana builds upon the Louisiana Storytelling Program (Owens, 1992) that encourages local communities to present their local culture through their stories.

In the environmental area the Mid-South Peace and Justice Center has received funding from the McKnight Foundation to work with low to moderate income African-American associations on environmental issues. In terms of bringing in new resources through philanthropy the Community Foundation of Greater Memphis has received major grants respectively from the Ford, Mott and Pew Foundations to expand their outreach efforts on cultural diversity and grassroots community development.

At the national level a major piece of federal legislation has been passed pertaining to the tourism recommendations of the Lower Mississippi Delta Development Commission. Specifically the "California Desert Protection Act of 1994" targets federal resources to support "Delta Region Heritage Corridors and Heritage and Cultural Centers" (Sec. 906, Senate Bill 4207) including a Delta region Native American Heritage Corridor and Cultural Center, a Delta Region African-American Heritage Corridor and Heritage and Cultural Center, a Music Heritage Program with specific emphasis on the Mississippi Delta Blues, as well as, a section on establishing a Delta Antiquities Trail and stabilizing ancient archeological sites and structures. This piece of legislation drew upon the expertise of the initial advisory groups as well as the anthropologists on the LMDDC staff.

Challenges to the Old and New Images—River Boat Gambling

While there is social and political networking and coalition building to support grassroots initiatives in cultural heritage and environmental conservation, it is important to note that this has been a
relatively slow process. Not only is it politically slow, but more importantly it is difficult to secure private capital on a large scale to execute
the recommendations on a comprehensive scale.

In marked contrast, the gaming industry from Las Vegas has entered the Mississippi Delta with great speed and efficiency. Building
upon the poverty and the image of riverboat gambling the gaming industry opened its assault on the Mississippi Delta with full force in
1991—one year after the final LMDDC recommendations to Congress.
Ironically, there was no testimony during the eighteen months of public hearings to suggest gaming in the Lower Mississippi Delta. Yet three
months after the final report to Congress casino backers had resolutions
in two Mississippi Delta counties to operate casinos with five other
counties scheduled within the year (The Commercial Appeal, November 18, 1990).

The Riverboat Gambling Plan

The major focus of gaming interests became the county of Tunica,
Mississippi, the poorest county in the region and within twenty miles of
the city of Memphis. Parenthetically, Jesse Jackson had visited Sugar
Ditch in Tunica County in his presidential campaign in 1988 and labeled
it as "the third world" on the Mississippi. The Board of Supervisors in
Tunica County described their support of casino gambling as a way to
provide development, jobs, tourist dollars, and new constructions. It is
a way to come out of economic depression (The Commercial Appeal,
November 30, 1990).

By February of 1991 local officials began to work in earnest with
outside gaming interests and state politicians to revise the state of Mississippi's gambling law. Some attention was given to returning a certain
percentage of the money for roads and education. One year later Tunica
had its first license for a floating casino reflecting an estimated $16–20
million outside investment. The image of riverboat gambling was translated by the locals as a new orientation to the outside world. A local Tu-
nican expressed this orientation in the local paper, "This is going to
change the whole way Tunica County is. We need to progress from the
plantation mentality to the point where Tunica will be a good place

for all people to live, not just the selected few, and the money from the gambling is going to be a big help if it is used properly" (The Commercial Appeal, May 1992).

The first river boat casino opened in October 1992 and by the year's end had generated $120 million. It employed 450 people from farmers to small businessmen at minimum wage. Translated the gaming industry's road and school tax generated $1.2 million in revenue for the County.

The apparent success sparked an intense casino development race. By February of 1993, twelve riverboat casinos were proposed at five sites. Eleven were subsequently approved. Within a year four more were approved. By 1994 twelve casinos had been opened, of which three closed because of inadequate financing and competition.

River Boat Gambling—The Results

By November of 1993 The Commercial Appeal estimated that 1.7 million people visited Tunica and left $14 million behind. This influx of tourists generated $3 million for the state of Mississippi. On the local level the county's school system has received more than $2 million in revenues from casino fees and taxes (Memphis Business Journal, November 1994). There were also visible signs of secondary development with hotels, apartments and condominiums. The local unemployment rate dropped significantly from 19.1% in 1990 to 9.9% in 1992. Land values went from $250 an acre to $25,000 and 1,000 acres of prime cotton land were taken out of production for casino development. Conversely rents increased and farms lacked laborers.

The major costs have been articulated by environmentalists and ministers. Built on a flood plain, twelve casinos have put a tremendous stress on the public infrastructure of water, sewerage and roads in addition to local plant and animal life in this wetland area (The Commercial Appeal, May 1993). Ministers have articulated a series of social costs including increased crime, broken families and gambling addiction (The Commercial Appeal, November 1993). An additional cost was noted by a state politician who pointed out that no local person had any of the ownership of the casinos (The Commercial Appeal, September 1993). The President of the Memphis Convention & Visitors Bureau expanded this cost to the local tourism and entertainment industry, "Memphians have a finite amount of discretionary entertainment dollars to spend, and if they spend it at the casinos, they're not going to spend it here. I think it will dramatically affect our tourism and hospitality industry" (Commercial Appeal, November 29, 1993).

Summary

In summary no one can doubt that there is an intense struggle over images and tourist dollars in the Mississippi Delta. The traditional images of the Civil War battlefields, antebellum homes and skylines nurtured by the landed aristocracy, and local chambers of commerce are no longer dominant in the Mississippi Delta. The counter images of local cultural heritage and diversity, as well as riverboat gambling are both widespread and well embraced by well defined constituencies. Both clearly have demonstrated an ability to use political and institutional forces to secure their footing in the Delta. The LMDDC conference participants not only grabbed hold of a political mechanism that had federal and state status but were also able to sustain their efforts through institutional coalitions. Similarly the gaming industry was able to quickly and efficiently secure state and local support to initiate and expand their operations.

Second is the fact that both the proponents of cultural heritage and the gaming industry have developed images that can effectively connect to national and international audiences. Both have developed maketing mechanisms that actively pursue this con-nection. In a very real sense these images with their correspon-ding orentations are opeing up the old closed system of the Mississippi Delta.

It should be apparent that while there are similarities in the images in that they are challenging the Old South, there are striking differences in what they mean for the future of the Mississippi Delta. The differences in orientation can best be captured in the distinction between economic development and economic growth. The riverboat gambling clearly embraces the philosophy of outside capital stimulating growth and maximizing its profits for outside investors. Local development issues such as quality of local education, adequate housing and health care, and crime are secondary concerns. The diversity and local heritage orientation draws on local ownership, local capital, and integration to local community institutions.

Lessons Learned for Applied Anthropologists

It is evident that applied anthropologists and folklorists in the Lower Mississippi Delta had a major role in the articulation of the image of diversity and local heritage. Specifically, the activities included:

- creating a comprehensive data base of local heritage projects,

- designing an inclusive process (through the structure of the LMDDC) where individuals and groups could participate and advance recommendations to individual states as well as the U.S. Congress,

- assisting in the dissemination of ongoing information about past and future activities,

- collaborating in the development of legislation, and directing programs and training efforts.

In contrast, anthropologists and folklorists have had no role in the entry and proliferation of the gaming industry in the Mississippi Delta. It would be easy to infer that anthropologists and folklorists should stick to what they know best and attack what they perceive as a threat. If we take a dichotomized position we run the risk of losing our holistic perspective about the transformation of the Lower Mississippi Delta region through a dynamic analysis of contrasting imagery. In addition, anthropologists miss at least two productive areas for expansion of our expertise.

The first is an understanding of how private capital can propel economic growth, or in this instance, community economic development. Can the gaming industry's tax be expanded to support the heritage recommendations of the LMDDC? If so, in what ways?

The second is an understanding of the secondary effects of the gaming industry on the areas of education, housing, health care, and job training in the rural Mississippi Delta. Equally important is how this new money coming into education and job training can be steered into programs that would broaden the understanding of multiculturalism and community building skills. These skills could in turn lead to new accountability questions about the gaming industry.

In conclusion, as the world moves toward an era of regional specialization and interconnectedness through the development of images, the Lower Mississippi Delta becomes a fascinating experiment in coalition politics and community building. Applied anthropologists must position ourselves to frame the questions and construct a new way of doing business.

References

Boniface, Priscilla and Peter Fowler. (1993). *Heritage and Tourism in 'the global village'*. London: Routledge.

Brazil, Wayne D. (1989). "Howard W. Odum." In *Encyclopedia of Southern Culture*. C. Wilson and W. Ferris (Eds.). pp. 296–97. Chapel Hill: University of North Carolina Press.

Brownell, Blaine A. (1975). *The Urban Ethos in the South, 1920–1930*. Baton Rouge: Louisiana State University Press.

Campbell, Edward. (1981). *The Celluloid South: Hollywood and the Southern Myth*. Knoxville: The University of Tennessee Press.

Cash, W. J. (1941). *The Mind of the South*. New York: Vintage Books.

Chappell, Frederick. (1978). The Image of the South in Film. *Southern Humanities Review*, 12:303–311.

Clay, James, Paul Escott, Douglas Orr, and Alfred Stuart. (1989). *The Land of the South*. Birmingham, Alabama: Oxmoor House, Inc.

Cobb, James C. (1993). *The Selling of the South: The Southern Crusade for Industrial Development, 1936–1990*. Urbana, Illinois: University of Illinois Press.

The Commercial Appeal. (1990). "Casino Backers Appeal to Economic Upswing." November 18, p. A1.

"Floating Casino Possible in Tunica." November 30, p. A1.

(1992). "Upbeat Views in Tunica Greet Prospect of Riverboat Casino." May 29, p. B1.

(1993). "Casinos, Made Millions in 1992." January 17, p. B1.

(1993). "Splash Spawns Tidal Waves of Casino Plans." February 28, p. A1.

(1993). "Nine Tunica Casino Sites Win OK." May 25, p. B1.

(1993). "Casinos Have Not Aided Mississippi." September 12, p. A12.

(1993). "Big, Real Big—Casinos Transform Tunica." November, 28, p. A1.

(1993). "Tunica Landowners Taking in Big Rewards As Values Soar." November 29, p. A9.

(1993). "Casinos Helping Upgrade Tunica Infrastructure." November 30, p. A8.

Hill, Carole. (1977). Anthropological Studies in the American South. *Current Anthropology*, 18:309–326.

Hyland, Stanley and Thomas Collins. (1991). Applied Anthropology at Memphis State University. *Practicing Anthropology*, 13:6–8.

LMDDC (Lower Mississippi Delta Development Commission). (1989). Tourism Conference Final Report. Memphis, TN: Lower Mississippi Delta Development Commission.

(1989). Body of the Nation: Interim Report to Congress. Memphis, TN: Lower Mississippi Delta Development Commission.

(1990). The Delta Initiatives: Realizing the Dream ... Fulfulling the Potential. Memphis, TN: Lower Mississippi Delta Development Commission.

LMRCS (Lower Mississippi Region Comprehensive Study Coordinating Committee). (1974). Lower Mississippi Region Comprehensive Study: Main Report. Memphis, TN: Corps of Engineers Office.

Matthews, Thomas. (1976, July 19). "The Southern Mystique." *Newsweek*, pp. 30–33.

McKinney, John and Linda Bourque. (1971). "The Changing South: National Incorporation of a Region." *American Sociological Review, 36*:399–412.

Memphis Business Journal. (1994, November 14). "Gaming Revenues Begin to Pay Off for Tunica County." p. 22.

Morland, Kenneth. (1967). "Anthropology and the Study of Culture, Society, and Community in the South." In *Perspectives on the South: Agenda for Research.* Edited by Edgar T. Thompson. Durham, N.C.: Duke University Press.

Owens, Maida. (1992). "The Louisiana Storytelling Program." In *Anthropology and Tourism,* V. Smith (Ed.), p. 31–33.

Smith, Stephen. (1983). "The Old South Myth as a Contemporary Southern Commodity." *Journal of Popular Culture, 16*:22–29.

Smith, Valene. (Ed.). (1992) "Anthropology and Tourism." *Practicing Anthropology, 14*:3–38.

Thompson, Edgar T. (Ed.). (1967). *Perspectives on the South: Agenda for research.* Durham: Duke University Press.

Time Magazine (1976, September 27). The South Today: Special Section. *Time,* pp. 29–99.

Williams, Charles and Hilda Williams. (1984). Contemporary Voluntary Associations in the Urban Black Church: The Development and Growth of Mutual Aid Societies. *Journal of Voluntary Action Research: 13*:19–30.

Wilson, Charles and William Ferris. (Eds.). (1989). *Encyclopedia of Southern Culture.* Chapel Hill: University of North Carolina Press.

Wright, Carol von Pressentin. (1991, February 10). Plantation Mansions on the Mississippi. *The New York Times*, pp 14–16.

Zamora, Mario, Vinson Sutlive and Nathan Altshuler. (Eds.). (1978). *Tourism and Economic Change*. Williamsburg, Virginia: Department of Anthropology, College of William and Mary.

9

Dilemmas of the Crossover Experience: Tourism Work in Bethlehem, Pennsylvania

CATHERINE MARY CAMERON

Applied anthropologists are motivated by an interest in seeing their knowledge translated into action. This chapter by Catherine Cameron demonstrates how complex and daunting this seemingly simple motive can become. In her case, Cameron did not initially seek a role as an applied anthropologist. She was motivated instead by an interest in conducting "pure" research related to a tourist-oriented festival in Bethlehem, Pennsylvania. But her initial contacts with local tourism officials led to opportunities to do contract research for festival organizers, and, in fairly short order, to her appointment as a board member of the Bethlehem Tourism Authority. Cameron describes the dilemmas that accompanied her becoming an actor in the very events she was trying to understand as an objective researcher. It is likely that, as anthropologists become more involved in both tourism research and development, further discussion of such issues will be needed. Decisions that accompany tourism development are not, as we have seen throughout this volume, without serious human consequences. Neither are the results of our research always as conclusive or comprehensive as we would like. When does any anthropologist reach a stage of knowledge at which he or she feels properly equipped to move from the realms of inquiry and reflection to those of action?

Since about 1985, I have found myself increasingly drawn into the tourism activities in the city where I live. Bethlehem, a small community of 70,000 people in eastern Pennsylvania, has embarked on a studied course of economic development through tourism. I have chronicled this history in several academic papers and some of these have had local circulation. As a result of my research, I have been invited to be a participant in the city's activities. My original involvement as an observer of the development of tourism has gradually metamorphosed into other roles such as contracted researcher and member of a municipal board and committees. These are in addition to my "regular job" of teaching anthropology to college students.

My experience in these applied capacities has given me a unique view of the process of tourism development and sometimes has provided me with privileged access to information. This perspective has been very helpful to my ongoing scholarly research. However, participating in this way has also raised certain issues and dilemmas for me which have not been a central feature of my academic life. Among these are the use of research findings in political agendas and class issues that emerge from tourism debates. I also find myself pondering whether or not I understand the local tourism environment better or differently than the natives who are both volunteers and professionals in the field, as well as the journalists who cover this industry. In this chapter, I want to report on these and other experiences that are involved in "crossing over." Before getting to this, I will offer an overview of the city and its tourism history.

Bethlehem and its Tourism Program

To most outsiders, Bethlehem connotes an image of big steel production and gritty industrial history. Indeed, this image is not wrong because the city has been the home of the Bethlehem Steel Company, in its various transformations, for more than a hundred years. What is less well-known is that the city, unlike many heavy industry sites of the northeast, has a deeper past that extends to the colonial era. Bethlehem was founded in 1741 by a Protestant sect called the Moravians. These Moravians constituted a quasi-utopian group whose society was originally based on a communal economy, egalitarian social principles, and fervent religious devotion. For almost the first century of its existence, the town was a closed, corporate community.

While Bethlehem attempted to maintain distance from the outside world, it gradually found itself in greater social proximity with non-Moravians. In large part, this was the result of the industrial boom of mineral exploration, canal construction, heavy manufacture, and later, the railroads. The town became an important urban node between the fields of anthracite, zinc, slate, and other minerals to the north in the Pocono Mountains and the growing city of Philadelphia that lay about fifty miles to the south. The forty-three mile canal system that followed the Lehigh River also linked it to the Delaware and Morris Canals to the east. Outsiders began to take up residence in Bethlehem during the first half of the nineteenth century. Smaby (1989:46) points out that in 1844 there were a thousand people in the town and that 85% were Moravian. By 1859, there were three thousand, but only 50% were Moravian.

The industrial development of the nineteenth century created a new municipality that lay to the south of the original settlement and across the Lehigh River. The Borough of South Bethlehem, created in 1865, was a classic industrial work site of factories, rail tracks, and smoke stacks tended by an ever-growing population of diverse ethnic groups who came initially from southern and eastern Europe and, later, from Puerto Rico, the American southwest, and Mexico.

Although the two Bethlehems were connected by a bridge (today three), culturally, they were worlds apart. As reported elsewhere (Cameron, 1991a), the two sections of the city have long suggested rich differences of history, ethnicity, and social class. The north side with its genteel Moravian heritage literally looks down on its alter ego: it begins as a rise on the north side of the river and flattens out to become a plateau containing a small downtown and historic residential neighborhoods. By contrast, the south side is a narrow valley strip circumscribed by the Lehigh River on one side and a long ridge known as South Mountain on the other. Several miles of steel making facilities run directly along the river; these are flanked by worker housing, ethnic churches, and small businesses.

The duality of the two Bethlehems persists to the present, and the north-south side distinction is a salient one to residents. Although the two sections were politically consolidated in 1917, the class and ethnic cleavage has remained palpable—the north-siders see the south side with the exception of the pastoral oasis of Lehigh University as a blight, while the south-siders are resentful of this attribution, holding up their participation in steel making as a significant contribution to America's industrial might. However, in spite of the connectedness steel workers feel to their neighborhoods and work site, their upwardly mobile sons and daughters usually leave the south side after college to live in the northern suburbs.

Although it has never reached a point of crisis, the schism in the city is a continuing point of tension in community life. From time to time, it resurfaces as an issue. The most recent reoccurrence has been in the context of a debate about the design and direction of tourism. Essentially, the conflict plays out between those who champion a program that emphasizes the earliest period of Bethlehem's history associated with the Moravians and those who want to chronicle the story of heavy industry. It appears that nineteenth century history is winning more support because the state of Pennsylvania has begun to invest in a program of canal restoration. This came about in response to a proclamation by the U.S. Congress in 1988 that the nation's canals should be known as National Heritage Corridors. Federal funds became available to those states willing to reclaim their canals as historic and recreational resources. A local commission was formed to study ways to put the canal era into the script of public history and invent new uses for the water corridor. This development has helped convince heritage planners that the gritty industrial period is also worthy of attention. Now, there is general support for the saga of steel and worker history although some still grumble that the addition of this more recent era will blur the perception that Bethlehem is primarily a colonial site.

To date, the kind of cultural tourism characteristic of Bethlehem puts a heavy emphasis on history and the expressive arts. The program began modestly in 1937 when the head of the Chamber of Commerce dubbed Bethlehem "the Christmas City." The first attractions were an enormous 37-foot star atop South Mountain and an elaborate lighting project in the commercial and Moravian district of the north side. Over the years, the Christmas program with its emphasis on lighting, music, and religious ceremony has been the mainstay of tourism, attracting hundreds of bus tours, as well as local residents (see Cameron and Gatewood, 1994). To the delight of downtown merchants, visitors also mix their pilgrimage to the New World Bethlehem with a healthy dose of shopping at the many quaint boutiques in the north side's commercial district.

History has been a natural and logical product for the city to develop for tourism, and, so far, most of it has been culled from the north side. The Moravian district in and around the downtown constitutes the core of Bethlehem's historic sites. Over the centuries, the Moravians have been faithful reporters of their own past. They have also continuously maintained and used the old stone and wooden buildings that are used for religious worship, missionary administration, education, and communal residence and assembly. However, some of the structures associated with early commerce have gone to ruin. These began to receive attention in the 1960s and 1970s when the city and historic societies planned several major restoration projects. A group called Historic Bethlehem Inc. undertook the reconstruction of an eighteenth century industrial site that includes a waterworks, tannery, and grist mill. Another bit of early history was reprised when a preservation society restored a building that began as a colonial inn but ended up as a men's rooming house. The Sun Inn, as it is called, reopened in 1978 as a museum and fine restaurant for visitors. Around the same time, the city and private citizens worked on the streets and commercial buildings of the business district. Many of the Victorian and Federal style buildings were restored, the standard concrete sidewalks were replaced with brick pavers, and glass lanterns were installed along the main street. The total effect of all these projects was to give the downtown and adjacent areas a charming historic ambience. These are the areas that have become the primary locus of tourist events.

Despite these efforts, tourism was not seen by local residents as a serious industry that could or should be developed until around 1980. While Bethlehem, like other cities, had its own small-scale tourism agency, efforts to cultivate a large visitor trade were minimal. The downtown has an appeal not unlike Colonial Williamsburg, but most people could not imagine the city as a major tourist destination. However, in the fallout period after the trauma of Bethlehem Steel's worst financial year of 1978, public officials and developers began to contemplate the possibility that the city's biggest employer and taxpayer would not recover its former strength.

And, indeed, it has not. Since the record loss of $488 million in 1977 and the layoff of thousands of white- and blue-collar workers that year, the company has posted losses on a regular basis. In the years where there has not been a deficit, it has been because of cost-cutting measures and the sale of assets. Between 1975 and 1984, the national workforce of Bethlehem Steel was reduced by 60%, from 115,000 to about 46,000 (Strohmeyer, 1986:150–159). The local workforce once stable at about 18,000 is now only a few thousand. About half of the workers are found in the structural steel plant that produced the famous I-beams that built the Empire State Building and the Golden Gate Bridge. In January 1994, the company announced that it would not spend the $250 million it had pledged to modernize the plant and in 1995, it announced what the workers feared most: that Bethlehem Steel would cease production of structural steel altogether. Presently, the company has engaged consultants to recommend ways to dispose of the steel making property.

Through the 1980s, the collective response to industrial decline in Bethlehem (and the wider Lehigh Valley of which it is a part) has been to solicit replacement industries. The region has been luckier than most places in the sense that a variety of new businesses from the service and light industrial sector have taken up residence in the cities of Allentown, Bethlehem, and Easton. According to development officials, the appeal of the region is its low cost of business operation, skilled workforce, good transportation system, and proximity to major markets in the northeast.

In this general flurry of activity, tourism has taken on a more significant role than ever before. People have begun to recognize that culture and history are financial assets that can be parlayed to a visitor audience and that there are important economic payoffs to tourism. They have also come to realize that the development of cultural amenities may contribute to that amorphous entity known as "quality of life," something that is seen as being important in luring new business to the region. Tourism, thus, is now actively sought and planned for.

The earlier renovation and historic reconstruction have become the infrastructure on which newer programmatic initiatives have been based. Two major festivals appeared in the 1980s: a nine-day music festival called Musikfest debuted in 1984 and a four-day festival of music, crafts, and highland games known as Celticfest arrived three years later. Both events transpire in parts of the downtown and an urban park near that location. Both bring in thousands of out-of-towners. The Musikfest Association which keeps records on its annual crowd sizes has tabulated an audience that exceeded one million in 1995. In the report that John Gatewood and I do for the festival every year, we estimate that almost half the audience comes from outside the Lehigh Valley. In recent years, the revenue generated from audience spending hovers around $10 million (Cameron and Gatewood, 1995). With findings such as this, few people doubt the lucrativeness of tourism anymore.

At the present time, the major tourist events are the month long Christmas program in December, Musikfest in August, and Celticfest in late September. Efforts are being made to develop other programs and physical facilities. Proposals include such things as an indoor performing arts theater and an outdoor amphitheater, a new visitors' center, a minor league baseball franchise, riverfront development, craft fairs, and the like. Not all of these have or probably will materialize, but there is no shortage of new ideas.

The organizational face of tourism has also been transformed. While a regional convention and tourism bureau has been in place since 1984, Bethlehem instituted its own municipal authority in 1988 (the Bethlehem Tourism Authority) to oversee tourism development. The thinking behind this was the belief that the regional agency could not devote sufficient energy to sell Bethlehem. For the first few years of its life, the authority did little beyond marketing work and some fine tuning of the Christmas program. However, the past few years have been much more active largely due to the fact that the lawyer who founded Musikfest took a leave from his corporate job to take on the position of executive director of the Authority. Since he has been there, he has co-ordinated the drafting of a very ambitious strategic plan and begun some new tourism programs: for example, a German style craft fair during the Christmas season called Christkindlmarkt.

The strategic plan is worth special mention. The plan is a rather detailed document that has identified several new program initiatives and renovation projects, not the least of which is the complete restoration and rebuilding of nineteen buildings in the eighteenth century industrial park originally established by the Moravians. Other projects include the construction of a new visitor and interpretation center and a large multipurpose pavilion. The plan identifies public and private partners which would undertake the financing of these projects. Other sections of the document rough out ideas about improving tourism operations. These range from new advertising efforts to infrastructural issues such as additional parking areas and personal comfort needs of tourists.

The plan's obvious function is to guide and control tourism development in the city. Its latent function which has become increasingly manifest is that it is meant to impress legislators in the state capital who distribute funds for historic restoration. Local heritage planners are painfully aware that, to date, Scranton and Pittsburgh have received most of the state's largesse for public history projects, and they believe that Bethlehem's strategic plan is likely to bring funding their way.

One quite unintended outcome, however, has been the appearance of a new debate about the possibility that tourism might actually become too successful. People have begun to worry that the plan's promise of a million visitors a year will unduly tax the city's infrastructure, have bad environmental side effects, and detract from the otherwise pleasant living circumstances for those who live in the downtown historic district. This surfaced during public meetings to discuss the strategic plan after copies of the document had been distributed and some press stories on the main capital projects anticipated.

There was at one meeting of about two hundred attendees a vociferous group of residents from the affluent historic district. Several months prior to this event, the mayor, yielding to the pressure to do something about the crowds and traffic during the highly successful Musikfest, created the group to study the impact of the festival on downtown neighborhoods and work with the festival association to come up with solutions to whatever problems were identified. The ad hoc study group on tourism, as it was called, turned out in force at the public meeting to challenge the latest tourism initiative. They raised the spectre of unruly hordes descending on the little town of Bethlehem, choking the streets with cars and keeping the residents from enjoying the downtown amenities. Some warned that expanded tourism would be experienced as a Musikfest everyday of the year. These complaints were fodder for local reporters who made good use of the debate in print for several months.

Members of the Tourism Authority who had been working under the assumption that most people wanted more tourism, were taken aback by this attack and privately hurt that their hard work to turn out the ambitious plan was being criticized. To counter the charge that the plan had been written behind closed doors and without much consultation, the Authority asked about fifty community-minded citizens to serve on a tourism advisory committee. Several meetings were held to review components of the plan and solicit advice. To the surprise of Authority members, there was no rancor and very little debate about growing the tourism industry. The creation of a community advisory committee apparently had the effect of muting the voices raised against tourism, at least for awhile.

The developments and debates chronicled thus far illustrate that tourism means serious business to local people. No longer do planners and city officials see tourism as a pleasant sideline for Bethlehem. Rather, the economic benefits are clear and widely appreciated, although there is certainly concern about controlled growth. I don't think anybody believes that tourism will ever be the kind of employer and tax generator that the steel company once was. However, people do recognize that tourism development is essential for the health of the city, not only for the jobs and revenues that are created, but for making the city a more attractive place for relocating companies. In addition, as was noted by a resident at the public meeting about the strategic plan, the new amenities and activities developed for visitors also benefit the locals by making the city a more attractive place in which to live.

There is no doubt that tourism is very much on the minds of the people of Bethlehem. In the decade I have been observing the community, the subject of tourism development has become a hot issue and one that has grown quite emotional. This is the environment into which I have been drawn, and I now report on my involvement in this forum.

Crossing Over

I would characterize myself as an accidental tourist on the topic of tourism in Bethlehem. My interests and background up until I stumbled onto this topic were varied, but tended towards the subjects of culture and artistic change and the field of ethnomusicology. I had, however, always been interested in community studies and had done a field research project of a small Ontario town during one summer in graduate school. It remains endlessly fascinating to me now that the major employer in this Canadian town was the Bethlehem Steel Company. The company owned and operated an iron-ore pit mine which employed hundreds of local people. When I did that study in the mid-1970s, I had no idea that just a few years later I would be living in the headquarters of that company, doing another community study of sorts.

My interest in studying Bethlehem was initially piqued by the events leading up to the first staging of Musikfest in 1984. Months prior to the festival, there was a blitz of advertising and press releases that struck me as being unusually professional looking for a non-profit organization. This presentation adumbrated the success of the actual event; the nine-day festival was well organized, well presented, and unfolded with hardly a hitch. Having decided I wanted to study the festival, I visited the managing director after its debut. It was immediately apparent that the office was a chaos of activity, and I was amazed that such frenzy could ever have yielded an event that had gone so smoothly. I learned that in addition to the small staff of three people, there were a variety of volunteer committees that orchestrated different aspects of the festival and a practicing attorney who was the mastermind of the event.

I figured out quickly that the standard observational/interview strategy would not work in this busy setting and offered my services as a volunteer. The director who was interested in monitoring the event and who had some volunteers survey the first year's audience asked me if I would undertake a more thorough survey the following year. It seemed to me that this function would be useful in several ways, and I agreed to his request. I co-opted John Gatewood, my husband and fellow anthropologist, to help because his quantitative and computer skills were superior to mine. We have done the annual surveys every year since 1985.

The timetable of the survey generally involves a spring meeting with festival personnel to modify the design of the questionnaire to current needs, a training session with the interviewers in the summer shortly before the festival, trouble-shooting during the event, and, then in the fall, the tedious job of coding, running programs, doing the analysis, and finally producing the report. Initially, we provided our services free of charge, but when the work became too onerous, we requested a discounted fee for the report.

In the time following my first contact with Musikfest, I did an ethnographic and historical study of the city and the festival, as well as secondary source research on the economic impact of the arts, tourism, and economic revitalization. From these sources and some of the survey data, I began to write about Bethlehem and the Lehigh Valley region for an academic audience (Cameron, 1987, 1989). I reported on the transformation of history and the arts into commodities and the role of the arts in revitalizing aging industrial cities, using Bethlehem as the case to make the main points.

Subsequently, I did two other research projects on the local arts and tourist scene. In the first, I studied a sample of arts and historical organizations, looking at their structure, marketing techniques, and sources of support. Because the study was funded by the city of Allentown (adjacent to Bethlehem), I put more emphasis on the organizations based there. One of the main findings was the extent to which business ideas and techniques had permeated the arts environment, a development I regarded as recent and due to greater competition for funding (see Cameron, 1991b). The second project involved John Gatewood as a co-researcher and was Bethlehem based. We were interested in assessing the image of the city to outsiders in particular during the Christmas season and in ascertaining the kinds of experiences that tourists sought out when they visited Bethlehem. Our methodology relied on ethnography, content analysis of the popular print medium's representation of the Christmas program, and a questionnaire survey of visitors (see Cameron and Gatewood, 1994).

My involvement as a researcher for Musikfest is probably better known than my role as an academic researcher. In this capacity, I have been called on, from time to time, to speak to the press about the key findings of the survey. I often receive calls from local reporters before each year's festival asking for the most recent findings about what is new and interesting from the last report. The director also occasionally asks me to make presentations to local and visiting groups about the festival and its function in the city.

No doubt because my work with Musikfest has become known, I have been drafted into community service in the form of committee involvement. In this regard, my longest period of service has been as a board member of the Bethlehem Tourism Authority, a position I held between 1988 and 1995. The overall purpose of the organization is to coordinate tourism development in the city, help groups in their efforts to create new programs, and generally market the amenities of Bethlehem to outsiders. After a period of difficulty involving the sorting out of specific goals and some staff problems, the authority hit its stride.

I am not the only academic person serving on the board. There is a museum director with a doctorate in history who teaches as an adjunct at Lehigh University and a retired architectural planner who has studied history and writes it as an avocation. I am, however, the only member of the nine-member board who writes about tourism in the city. I believe that I was asked to get involved because I collect the information that people currently want to know about.

In sum, I wear possibly three hats: community volunteer, contracted survey researcher, and academic researcher. No role is completely separate from any other, and each gives me insights and information that are helpful in other capacities. In many ways, it is an ideal situation because each function gives me a better understanding of the rich, unfolding tourism scene. But, I have also felt binds and dilemmas of various sorts. These are the issues I address now.

Applied Dilemmas

1. The Mystique of the Method

As most of us know, the discipline of anthropology is often fuzzily perceived by the public. The most common perception is that we are excavators of ancient ruins seeking answers to the origins of humanity. In spite of the fact that the reports and views of cultural anthropologists routinely appear in the media, the field and its methods remain a bit of a mystery to most people.

In my experience, the other social sciences have more currency in the community than anthropology. People are familiar with the idea that historians are interested in communities and do time-depth analysis or reporting. Economists and sociologists seem to have a reputation as "number crunchers," masseurs of existing or collectors of new data. Psychologists are best known for their counseling role, in private practice or social service offices. But, the fact that anthropologists may produce historical accounts, write ethnographies, or do survey work is not widely appreciated. Where I operate, both interpretive texts and quantitative information are accorded value. However, it is usually the historian who is asked to produce the narrative or otherwise report on the community, and the sociologist who is seen as the expert on numbers. The contribution that can be made by the anthropologist seems to be less visible.

Much of credibility I have in the community comes from the festival survey work I have produced with my husband. The numbers, percentages, correlations, and the tabularized data have more authority than does interpretive ethnography. This information is real, scientific, and otherwise "hard." I recall helping a folk music club attempt to find out more about the programming preferences and leisure pursuits of its membership. When they asked me for help in designing a survey questionnaire, I agreed, but suggested that, instead, an equally valuable means of getting the same information might be to conduct a series of focus groups to talk about programming. However, they didn't feel this would yield adequate or valid information, and they opted for the survey.

What the survey says appears to be unassailable truth. The Musikfest executive director told me that he carries along copies of the audience survey when he visits potential sponsors of the festival. I had always thought the report was mainly for internal use at the festival office, but he said that the corporate and professional sponsors of the event like the statistics and particularly the "Trends" section that gives a longitudinal perspective on different parameters such as audience ratings or spending. The meta-message of the report seems to be that Musikfest is business-like in its approach to the arts and is, thus, worthy of financial investment on the part of corporations. It must work, for the festival has been very successful in getting public and private support. The operating budget, garnered from sponsorships, grants, and sales, stands at about $2.5 million.

While surveys produce so-called hard data, I discovered that they pale in relation to the methods used by economists. One year, the Musikfest organization decided it wanted a different kind of reporting on economic impact other than that from the visitors' survey, and the festival commissioned a study by self-employed local economist. His method involved the use of state sales tax figures, and he estimated that the festival had an impact of about $10 million in the community. (This was consonant with the survey findings derived from reports on audience spending.) While my co-researcher and I regarded his method as more indirect than ours, I recall that the director described the economist's report as the "hard data" on the economic impact of the festival, while the survey data was "the soft data." It was a humbling experience.

For better or for worse, quantitative methods are the preferred mode of discovery in my local pond and, elsewhere, it appears. Even a badly done survey or incomplete interpretation of quantitative information has credibility. While surveys are helpful in generating certain kinds of information, they are *not* appropriate for all problems. The best approach to a complex problem is often a combination of methods. To my dismay, I haven't convinced my community colleagues of this idea.

2. The Use of Academic Research

The worst charge made about academic research is that it is sometimes arcane and esoteric, without any general value or application. I think most academics are not very worried about this perception because they usually orient to a small field of fellow specialists. However, when writing for a non-academic audience, we are presented with a new set of challenges, as I have discovered from experience.

Over the years that we have produced the Musikfest report, my coauthor and I have gradually learned how to modify the presentation to best communicate the results. In our first reports, we were verbose, overly technical, and presumed statistical knowledge on the part of our readers. We slowly figured from the occasions when we would make a verbal presentation to festival committees that either people were not reading the text very well or they were missing the main points. We began to think about ways to revise the report. This thinking was helped along by some advice from an anthropologist friend who works for a private research firm; he said that his presentations to clients usually only contain key words and brief paragraphs of phrases. While we were not prepared to produce a report of sound bites, we did make some concessions, namely the addition of an "executive summary" of the major findings and a more direct and succinct rendering of the prose. Now we believe that these reports satisfy our explanatory urges and the festival's desire to access the information quickly.

In my dealings with civic officials, I once received an unusual request. This happened in connection with a proposal I had submitted for funding to the Department of Community Development in the city of Allentown. The research plan involved a survey of the financial health of local arts and cultural organizations and their methods of revenue building. After receiving the grant, I was asked by a member of the funding committee to include some practical recommendations about ways that these non-profits might be incorporated into the economic redevelopment plans of the city. I would be underestimating to say that I felt daunted by such a task. Nonetheless, I did make some recommendations and ended up enjoying the experience to some extent.

My reluctance in this regard affirms a point made by Chambers (1989:chapter 6) that anthropologists are generally more comfortable explaining things than making or guiding policy. This is, no doubt, largely due to the fact that academic training prepares us to present and interpret our findings rather than take any action based on them. I also think part of our reticence to apply our knowledge rests on the concern that we understand social systems imperfectly. There is a certain risk in applying what we know, felt more keenly because we don't trust that we've got it completely right. The irony is that this imperfect understanding doesn't trouble others in decision-making roles as much as academics.

In my recent research projects, I have often produced two versions of the research data: one is a basic report which summarizes my findings; the other is a scholarly rendering of the information cast within the framework of anthropological concepts and models. I generally distribute the basic reports in the community to anyone who expresses interest in the topic. In a couple of instances, information from these has been used in connection with the Christmas program. For instance, one study found that more visitors actually came to Bethlehem by car than by tour bus, correcting an assumption that buses were the preferred conveyance. This finding prompted the tourism director to give more attention to the touring interests of small groups who were, in most cases, families.

Part of the payback to the community is in the reports I distribute, and I am pleased that my research provides information that can be used in practical ways. I do not, however, send out my published academic papers as freely. The reason for this is not entirely clear to me, but I think it is based on my concern that these fuller interpretive accounts might lead to a measure of self-consciousness and self-monitoring among the natives I watch, and I do not want to change their everyday behaviors and views. In addition, locally, there is a limited cast of characters and organizations. They are not at any risk as a result of my writing, as might be the case in a political delicate setting, but they are identifiable. Reminding my local informants that I am writing about them as much as anonymous tourists gives greater emphasis to my observational role than to my participation role. To a great extent, successful observing requires that one's subjects forget they're being watched, and I want to maintain this state of affairs.

So far, I have had few problems concerning the possible sensitivity of the information I produce. For the most part, I research and write about the activities of middle-class whites who are from business or the professions and who are involved in economic redevelopment or tourism. They are hardly in need of advocacy. However, there have been a few times of concern. One such occasion was when a community development official asked me in my study of arts organizations to rate the effectiveness of their outreach to a potentially large audience. Aside from the fact I didn't have the skills to evaluate the merit of one marketing strategy over another, I realized both that this disclosure could be detrimental to the level of support given to various arts organizations and that it could ruin my relationship with arts administrators. It was an obvious request to refuse. Most of the administrators I have encountered are woefully underpaid and overworked, and they labor diligently for the little arts support they get. In a sense, one could call them disadvantaged. At any rate, in my final report, I presented aggregated figures on the budgets of the groups so that no particular one could be identified, and I gave some emphasis to the finding that these groups were well-run.

As noted earlier, social class has recently become an issue in Bethlehem's tourism development. On the whole, the anthropological literature tends to associate this kind of issue more with developing societies than with complex ones. As Nash and Smith (1991) point out, there are a number of studies in the anthropology of tourism that address the potential for cultural and economic exploitation that may arise from this form of development, and most of these pertain to non-Western contexts. Nonetheless, concerns about the inequality between the host and guest roles and environmental degradation are also relevant to complex societies. In this regard, Peck and Lepie (1989) offer a model that can assess and possibly predict the impact of tourism on a community. In their study of three North Carolina areas, they describe the differential rates of tourism development that are causally related to the source of regulatory power in a community, in particular whether that control emanates from an external or internal locus.

In Bethlehem, there has not been much indication that any group has been disadvantaged by tourism development. In the restoration of the north side Moravian and adjacent districts, those who have been involved as the agents of change have also been the consumers of this action. However, with the proposals to document industrial history and the working-class heritage of the south side, some new problems are looming. These pertain to who will produce this history and how it will be disseminated to visitors. Although no one is yet talking in these terms, I expect that the ownership of cultural capital will be the issue that surfaces after the city makes a serious commitment to nineteenth century preservation on the south side. There are already some signs of a middle-class co-optation of working-class heritage. For example, one of the prominent themes of the year long 250th birthday of Bethlehem in 1992 was the celebration of the "cultural and ethnic diversity" of the city. Most of the events and displays pertaining to this theme was carried out by people who are not, themselves, part of this diversity.

I suspect the move to reify working-class history and industrial work sites will also lead to their gentrification. The oral historian, folklorists, and photo-essayists will no doubt descend on the ethnic neighborhoods to document the past, as they have in other parts of the state. The tours of the ethnic churches and work sites will be arranged; block restoration will begin; and, eventually the tourists will come. This in it-self is not a bad thing, but my concern is that the process of transfor-mation will lead to the transfer of cultural ownership. Although there is an active south side historical association with very capable leadership, I wonder if south side groups can retain control of their past and be par-ticipants in its retelling.

3. Losing Social Distance

When anthropologists go to the field, they are generally optimistic about achieving a certain degree of intimacy with the natives. Indeed, the "being there" side of fieldwork is what makes anthropological re-search unique in the social sciences. After departing a research setting, physical distance generally leads to some degree of social distance from place and subjects, allowing the researcher to gain a new perspective on his or her experience. Without this cognitive transition, the writing up phase would be difficult.

Since I live in my field setting, I am sometimes hard pressed to see both sides of an issue. This emerged as a problem when the strategic tourism plan, described earlier, was launched. As a member of the Tourism Authority, I had participated in the initial discussions about the plan and was a contributor to the text. In its public unveiling at a press conference, I was also one of the presenters. In the aftermath of some criticism and negative press about the plan, I felt the stings as keenly as fellow members of the Authority, and it was difficult for me to listen to other points of view with equanimity. I was an unabashed defender of the document; I found it hard to understand why some of the down-town residents argued for less, not more, tourism development and cast doubt on the veracity of the numbers and figures in the plan. I found myself planning some moves with other members to diffuse the nega-tive perception of the piece.

This event brought another applied dilemma into very sharp relief. Now, I was no longer "pure" in my motives and distanced from the events I purported to study as I learned I should be as a student. I had clearly become more of a participant than an observer. In the tradition of anthropology, this shift in involvement is valid in certain circum-stances, in particular if it is done in the name of humanitarian advocacy for an disempowered group. However, the Tourism Authority is not that, and in truth, in this action I simply behaved as a political actor.

In the bigger picture, close and on-going involvement in one's study site must inevitably lead to dilemmas such as this. There is no one correct posture for all situations, and researchers must decide how enmeshed they want to become. In my own case, I was troubled about both the loss of perspective and shift in involvement and began to consider ways to reposition my researcher hat squarely on my head. I began taking steps to undo my personal involvement. Eventually, I resigned from the Tourism Authority.

4. Dealing with Smart Natives

My tribe is smart and well educated. For example, my colleagues on the board of the Tourism Authority, with scarcely an exception, hold baccalaureate degrees and some have advanced or professional degrees in law, accounting, education, and finance. All are seasoned veterans of community boards and associations; each one is astute about local politics. One is the author and driving force behind Musikfest, the most successful of the tourist events in the city. While all have certain biases and various degrees of expertise, they are exceedingly capable people who, among other things, know how to draft by-laws, produce financial statements, address legal issues, make significant administrative decisions, and be active in tourism programming. From a status point of view, I am clearly in a situation of studying across rather than down. The question that often occurs to me, is whether I understand the local tourism scene better or differently than the natives.

As a board member or community volunteer, there have been some things, independent of research, that have been easy for me to do and other things that have been difficult. I would put activities such as assembling and interpreting information, engaging in planning, writing, and the like in the first category. On the other hand, there are things that have caused me consternation. At the monthly meetings of the tourism board, we are required to review financial statements that pertain to present and projected expenses and revenue. I confess the esoteric logic of accounting never fails to stymie me as I stumble through pages of numbers. Nor am I much better at knowing about the specialized domain of municipal by-laws or how to carry out a proposed ordinance.

I also find that there are so many new developments in tourism— for example, plans for a minor league franchise and park, canal restoration and riverfront development, new hotels—that I am chronically playing a catch-up game with respect to keeping abreast of new information. Further, there are rather good newspaper series on the subject of tourism or economic development. In reading these accounts, which involve historical depth and overview, I often wonder what separates *good* journalism from *good* ethnography. Probably, not very much. In the end, the difference may be a matter of degree rather than one of kind.

However, cultural anthropology is more than good ethnography. Whether intended or not, any community study has implications for other cases. The discipline stresses that these comparisons be fleshed out and made explicit. Thus, while I think it is important to write full accounts of Bethlehem, it is also useful to compare this community in transition with other aging, industrial cities of the northeast, of North America, of the Western world. The concerns of local people to keep the economic infrastructure vital parallel like concerns elsewhere. The motivations of people to tour and vicariously experience the lives of others are also not unique. The desire of residents to construct or invent a past has rich cross-cultural and historical connotations. Deeply involved with the tribe or not, the anthropologist cannot help but see the particular case among many. The distance and implied comparison holds us to the goal of identifying the dynamics of cultural systems.

Conclusions

This piece is a confessional of sorts. My study of tourism in Bethlehem has, inadvertently, led me into the affairs of this community more deeply than I would have imagined. I continue to sort out my roles and responsibilities as I combine involvement with detachment. As I reflect on my activities, I now see more clearly that the application of anthropology means much more than the offer of specific skills. The perspective that the discipline teaches us, as intangible as it seems, remains as important outside the academy as inside.

References

Cameron, Catherine M. (1987). The Marketing of Tradition. *City and Society,* 1:162–174.

(1989). Cultural Tourism and Urban Revitalization. *Tourism Recreation Research,* 14:23–32.

(1991a). Competing Images of Ethnicity and History in Urban Tourism. Paper given at the ninetieth annual meeting of the American Anthropological Association, November 20–24, 1991, Chicago, Illinois.

(1991b). The New Arts Industry: Non-Profits in an Age of Competition. *Human Organization,* 50:225–234.

Cameron, Catherine M. and John B. Gatewood. (1994). The Authentic Interior: Questing Gemeinschaft in Post-Industrial Society. *Human Organization,* 53:21–32.

(1995). Musikfest 1995 Visitors' Survey. Report for Musikfest Association, Bethlehem, Pennsylvania.

Chambers, Erve. (1989). *Applied Anthropology: A Practical Guide.* Prospect Heights, Ill.: Waveland Press.

Nash, Dennison and Valene L. Smith. (1991). Anthropology and Tourism. *Annals of Tourism Research,* 18:12–25.

Peck, John G. and Alice S. Lepie. (1989). Tourism and Development in Three North Carolina Coastal Towns. In Valene Smith (Ed.), *Hosts and Guests: The Anthropology of Tourism,* pp. 203–222. Philadelphia: University of Pennsylvania Press.

Smaby, Beverly P. (1989). *The Transformation of Moravian Bethlehem.* Philadelphia: University of Pennsylvania Press.

Strohmeyer, John. (1986). *Crisis in Bethlehem: Big Steel's Struggle to Survive.* Bethesda, Md.: Adler and Adler.

10

Tourism as a Subject of Higher Education: Educating Thailand's Tourism Workforce

ERVE CHAMBERS

In this chapter, Erve Chambers describes his role as a consultant with several universities in Thailand. Like many other countries that have become dependent on tourism as a major strategy for economic growth, Thailand has experienced an increased demand for trained personnel to serve the industry at all levels—from hospitality workers to tourism planners. Chambers suggests that there is a need to provide tourism students with a greater understanding of the social and cultural consequences of tourism, and that universities could play a major role in encouraging the development of appropriate tourism strategies for their countries. He notes that ideals of sustainable tourism and attempts to involve local communities in decisions concerning tourism development have been applied largely to small-scale, experimental programs, while major tourism initiatives continue to be developed with little thought to their human or environmental consequences. In Chambers' view, part of the problem is that many governments tend to view tourism as only a short-term solution to pressing economic problems, to be replaced by more stable industries as a country develops. A greater appreciation of the likelihood of long-term dependence on tourism should lead to increased interest in the consequences of the industry.

The rapid, global development of tourism has given rise to increased employment opportunities in the field, and along with that increase to a need for better means of educating the industry's workforce.

Tourism research centers and training programs are being established at institutions of higher education in many countries, with a range of activities that include preparing students for research, planning, and development careers, as well as vocational programs designed to equip students for direct employment with hotels, travel agencies, and other "hospitality" businesses. For the most part, these programs have been dominated by economic models and by a vocational ethos that rarely encourages a critical assessment of the varied consequences of tourism. They have tended to follow national trends in tourism development, which often focus on attracting and accomodating "first class" tourism to established facilities. Much less attention has been paid to understanding the social and cultural consequences of tourism, or to conveying such understanding to students, many of whom will become the front-line representatives of the industry. Where social phenomena are considered, they are generally limited to elucidating those human resource factors that contribute to maintaining a stable work force (c.f., Baum, 1993; King, 1994). The potential role of anthropology in such programs has remained virtually unexplored.[1]

This article describes such a role on the basis of my own experience as a Fulbright appointee in Thailand. I argue here that anthropological involvement in tourism higher education, not only has the potential of instilling greater appreciation of the social and cultural consequences of tourism, but can also often contribute a critical dimension to understanding how cultural and institutional factors favor particular tourism development strategies at the expense of other, possibly more appropriate and sustainable, approaches. While tourism higher education training programs presently tend to replicate national tourism policies, there remains the potential for such programs to provide the institutional base for introducing more innovative approaches to regional tourism development.

In Thailand, as in many other countries, the advent of tourism higher education is closely related to the country's recent successes in tourism promotion, as well as to a growing recognition of the varied consequences of that success. After several years of highly successful international tourism promotion, Thailand's tourism authority announced in 1989 that, rather than focus the next year's development effort on a new marketing theme (e.g., the 1987 "Year of the Tourist" and the 1988 "Arts and Crafts Year"), the department would devote its attention to the environmental and infrastructural problems that had accompanied rapid growth in the tourism sector. In parts of the country, these problems had already become acute. Eroding and polluted seascapes, unregulated hotel and condominium construction, shortages of fresh water and electricity, and growing public dissatisfaction had become commonplace problems at some popular tourist destinations. The country's reputation as a major destination for sex tourism had become a matter of concern for many Thai citizens. International visitors to Thailand were also complaining in greater numbers, registering their concern over increases in crimes against tourists, poor management of some of the country's tourism facilities, and (especially in Bangkok) the effects of traffic congestion and air pollution.

While solutions to the problems accompanying Thailand's increased dependency upon international tourism require a variety of responses, one clearly felt deficiency has been the lack of trained personnel to work in nearly every aspect of the industry, from tourism planning to hotel housekeeping. Tourism has become one of the country's most expansive employment sectors, and there are simply not enough people qualified to fill the new positions available. In response to this problem, and in league with a growing number of universities and colleges, the Tourism Authority of Thailand (TAT) has begun to actively encourage the development of new programs and facilities to train young people, mostly college students, in various aspects of the tourism industry. For the most part, this training has centered on those "quality" segments of the tourist population that Thailand has been most interested in attracting—vacationing families, conventioners, and generally high-spending visitors. Most of the graduates of these programs are expected to find employment with major hotels and travel agencies.

In 1991 I was given an opportunity to work with several Thai universities and colleges on issues related to "appropriate tourism development."[2] While this assignment was to be devoted primarily to consultation and research, the link between my interests and curriculum development in the new tourism training programs soon became obvious. Where better to encourage new or alternative approaches to tourism development than among those who will, through their employment, encounter the industry's problems on a daily basis? Less obvious, however, was the relationship between such concepts as appropriate and sustainable tourism and the curricula of many of those new training programs. For the most part, experiments with appropriate tourism have focused on local and community-based alternatives to large-scale tourism development. The new training programs were, on the other hand, devoting the greatest part of their attention to the "upscale" and presumably most lucrative end of the tourist market. These programs tend to be highly centralized and to focus on employment opportunities with established tourist destinations and major hotels. There is a dearth of models by which to even begin to judge the sustainability and cultural appropriateness of such endeavors.

My recent experience in Thailand has left me with an appreciation of the major role the country's educational institutions could play in responding to the myraid of problems that have arisen as a result of increased economic dependence upon tourism. By the same token, I have also gained a better understanding of some of the obstacles to a more culturally and environmentally responsive approach to tourism, not only in Thailand, but wherever tourism plays an important role in plans for national and regional development. In my opinion, these obstacles are not simply the result of short-sighted development schemes. They are also to be found in the limited scope (and occasional ideological near-sightedness) of the "alternatives" that are most often suggested.

Thailand's Tourism Dilemma

In 1987, with the inauguration of Thailand's "Year of the Tourist," the number of international visitors to the country increased by more than twenty percent. Similar gains have been experienced in subsequent seasons, with the exception of 1990–91, when Thailand suffered a tourism decline associated with recession in Europe and the United States, war in the Persian Gulf region, and, a military coup in Thailand. But even with occasional dips in tourist visits, tourism has retained its new found status as the country's major source of foreign currency—its largest "export" industry.

In most Western and heavily industrialized countries, it is difficult to fully realize the appeal of tourism for countries like Thailand. Not only are the prospects for internal capital investment and land speculation considerable, but the industry provides significant new employment in the construction and services sectors of the economy. More jobs become available, and wages can be impressive by national standards. For example, many newly trained students who find employment with Thailand's major hotels quickly outdistance their teachers in their earnings. The current shortage of skilled personnel to work in Thailand's tourism industry is conveniently matched to underemployment of the country's college graduates. Most of Thailand's universities, along with many private and technical colleges, have begun to offer tourism training programs within the past decade, and the country's extensive state teachers' college system is in the process of developing additional programs. Degrees are offered at the associate, baccalaureate, and graduates levels, and many institutions have also begun to provide non-credit short courses in tourism and hotel services. Although the curricula for these programs are not standard, most have focused on the basic skills of the industry and on language instruction. Significantly, many of the new programs originated in departments of language and, while some business schools have begun tourism programs, most existing educational opportunities exist within the framework of a liberal arts tradition.

In most of the programs, relatively little attention is paid to the environmental, social, and cultural consequences of tourism development. We can at least speculate that the reason for not including such topics has to do with the heirarchical nature of tourism development and planning in Thailand. It is expected that graduates of these programs will have little control over the ways in which tourism is manifest in their country. Accordingly, while social and behavioral issues are taught, it is often within the framework of learning to accomodate tourists (as in courses on tourist behavior) or acquiring the knowledge to inform tourists (as in courses devoted to Thai history, society and culture). These emphases are not unique to Thailand, but are common curricula practice in the training programs of most countries. They are also consistent with a tourism development policy that is centered on attracting what is presumed to be the "quality" and most lucrative segment of the tourist market—a strategy shared by most developing countries and often encouraged by international advisory groups such as the World Travel Organization.

Thailand's success in attracting international tourists has contributed to its economy, expanded the employment opportunities of its citizens, and generally enhanced the country's reputation, particularly among its Southeast Asian neighbors. But the development of the industry has been uneven, with the greater rewards being enjoyed by those who have the capital and means to invest in new development and facilities. These have primarily been international corporations and Bangkok-based investors. But it is in the countryside, on the beaches, in some of the more "exotic" mountainous regions, and at some provinicial capitols, that the impacts of rapid tourist development has been most acutely felt. Regional impacts of tourism in Thailand have included environmental pollution and degradation, loss of historic properties and landmarks, inadequate land use planning, dislocation (sometimes forced) of local populations, shortages and increases in the costs of foods and rents, increases in crime, and health problems. Local commentators, such as Thai journalists and intellectuals, have also suggested that international tourism has contributed to a degradation of Thai values and customary behavior. While none of these impacts can be attributed solely to tourism, and most are more reasonably attributed to rapid development in several segments of the Thai economy, it does seem clear that tourism has helped exasperate many of the country's growth-related problems. And, because international tourism is such a visible phenomenon, practiced in multitudes of exchanges between people of different countries and distinct values, the emotional impact of the industry is particularly strong.

Many Thai appear to support tourism development as "good for the country" (i.e., for the Thai national economy), but as not necessarily good for themselves or for the localities in which they reside. Such a dilemma is common during periods of rapid and uneven change. To what extent must a people tolerate an erosion of their way of life, or the degradation of their environment, in order to sustain economic growth? Over the past decade, many Thai have become less tolerant and increasingly critical of tourism in their country. Dissatisfaction has occasionally resulted in public demonstrations against new tourism development projects, a relatively rare social phenomenon in Thailand. Widespread charges of corruption against the Chatichai government, which was overthrown in 1991 by a military coup, included charges of inappropriate complicity with investors in the tourism sector.

Although none of these consequences of tourism are unique to Thailand, there are aspects of Thai culture, and circumstances of the country's history, which contribute to a somewhat unique situation. A Buddhist country, and relatively open to outside influences since before the turn of the past century, Thailand's people have generally welcomed visitors and imposed relatively few barriers to their travel or restrictions on their behavior. In contrast to many neighboring countries, Thailand's leaders have proven to be receptive to Western models for development and capitalist endeavor. A highly centralized government bureaucracy, dominated by the capitol in Bangkok, has contributed to Thailand's success in promoting and marketing tourism to international visitors, but has proven less capable of solving those environmental and social problems that occur on the regional or local level. On the other hand, deeprooted traditions of village and provincial autonomy, although muted in modern times, have made it difficult to establish or enforce appropriate land use measures throughout the country. Minority and "tribal" people, often of interest to tourists seeking unique cultural experiences, have traditionally had few rights of self-determination, and many are presently "illegally" occupying territories that have been declared national forest preserves. As these people become recognized as significant tourist commodities, their value increases in the view of many ethnic Thai, but schemes for their "preservation" are often paternalistic and restrictive.

Thai Buddhism also contributes to particular relationships with the environment—instilling, on the one hand, a respect for the natural world, and on the other a degree of environmental "fatalism" that is unfamiliar to most Western observers. The development of incentives for protecting environmental resources needs to account for this important value difference. (Chambers, 1994).

Most of the Thai involved in their country's tourism development are aware of the need to address problems associated with the rapid growth of their industry, which threatens to destroy the very resources on which it depends. And many Thai would agree that effective solutions need to be based in Thai culture and practice, rather than sought solely from responses derived of Western technologies and values. For these reasons, the idea of a sustainable approach to tourism, derived from and appropriate to Thai culture and values, can be appealing. There is, however, a tendency, not only in Thailand but throughout the world, to regard "sustainable" tourism as antithetic to capitalistic growth and development, leading to a situation in which most of its advocates are excluded from or willfully stand outside the industry's major spheres of influence. This situation serves to exasperate the country's tourism dilemma, seeming to force an either/or choice between those values that support the goals of economic growth and development and those that call for the preservation of Thailand's human and natural resources.

Toward Sustainability

The ideal of sustainable tourism is to draw upon a region's resources to attract and accomodate tourists without jeopardizing those resources. In some instances, it might even be possible to enhance rather than simply protect a region's environmental and cultural resources in association with responsible tourism development. These ideals have their appeal in part because, as I have noted above, tourism is rarely the only agent of change in regions where it occurs. In the face of multiple development pressures upon usually limited resources, tourism can, at least in theory, provide a rationale for environmental preservation and cultural conservation. Part of this rationale is found in the setting aside of particular resources from other forms of development in order to preserve them as tourist attractions.

The means of sustainable tourism are not as clear as its ideals. In Thailand and elsewhere, several factors have served to limit the success of efforts to promote sustainability. First, as noted above, such efforts are often seen as incompatible with the further growth and development of the tourist industry. They are often attempted on a small scale, focus on a particular locality or tourist site, and tend to have little effect upon or relationship to larger national and regional development trends. Such efforts seldom have the full sanction of a national government, or many influential allies, and their approach is often based squarely upon Western ideals of ecological awareness and human relations. Where direct assistance to minority groups is involved, as it often is, the efforts are frequently hampered by a well-intended but paternalistic ideology that seeks to preserve traits of minority cultures without affording the minority people viable opportunities to advance themselves or to participate as freely as they might like in the national or regional economy. The goal of responsible tourism is further inhibited by a tendency for groups that might otherwise be sympathetic to principles of sustainability to reject tourism as a means. In Thailand, for example, non-governmental agencies that are dedicated to preserving rural Thai communities usually reject tourism as an alternative development strategy (Phongphat & Hewison, 1990).

During my recent stay in Thailand, I had the opportunity to visit a number of the tourism training programs I have described above. One result of that interaction was the development of a sample curriculum devoted to social and cultural aspects of tourism development (Chambers, 1991). The curriculum combined an overview of much of the literature devoted to the human consequences of tourism with observations based on my prior research in Thailand. In preparing this document, I took the position that an understanding of the human consequences and implications of tourism should be an important aspect of the education of all students who were anticipating careers in the tourism industry, regardless of the types of employment opportunities they might be pursuing. In several respects, the curriculum was (at least implicitly) critical of the tendency of most training programs to focus so heavily upon careers related to "quality tourism," and was also critical of a tendency for Thailand's tourism planning to discount the importance of regional and community participation in tourism development. I felt then, and continue to feel, that these two tendencies are closely related.

The curriculum was based both on existing literature related to the human consequences of tourism and on my research in Thailand. Examples of the former include the use of case study material from Central American and the southwestern United States. Recent attempts to develop ecologically sound nature tourism in Belize and other Central American nations were used to demonstrate both the economic and environmental benefits to be realized from such an approach. A discussion of the ways in which some Native American pueblos in the southwestern United States strictly regulate and police the activities of tourists was offered to encourage Thai students to consider the appropriateness of similar measures for their country, especially in light of the observation that such controls actually seemed to be viewed favorably by many tourists who viewed them as evidence of the pueblo's sincerity in preserving their traditions.

My research in Thailand contributed to the curriculum in several ways. For example, I was able to point out that, while tourist visitation was often seen as a threat to the preservation of tradition among Thailand's tribal people, in many respects tourism actually encouraged ethnic villages to maintain important aspects of their past. Although some aspects of tourism in Thailand did not figure prominently in the curriculum, they were nonetheless the subject of intense discussions with Thai faculty. Chief among these were sex tourism and the growing specter of AIDS in Thailand. While many of the faculty were aware of the lack of basic information regarding HIV transmission among workers in the sex trade, I was able to provide added information concerning myths and inaccuracies about transmission that were maintained by many Western tourists—signaling a need to educate tourists as well as sex workers.

At this point, I do not know what impact my project has had on any of the programs I visited. My curriculum was not offered as a solution to any aspect of Thailand's tourism dilemma—such solutions, if they come at all, will be uniquely Thai. I am certain that the greatest beneficiary of my work has been myself. The experience gave me an opportunity to interact with tourism faculty and planners and to view tourism in the country from a perspective that was new to me. Whatever its current limitations might be, the rapid development of tourism higher education training programs is bound to have a considerable influence on the future of tourism in Thailand. While educational practice often follows change and innovation, it does sometimes play a leading role in directing change. It seems clear to me that Thailand's increased attention to tourism training has the potential, not only to prepare students for the most obvious careers in that industry, but also to redirect and shape much of the country's present orientation to tourism development.

With considerable reservation, because my experience is limited and because I am not Thai, I will attempt here to describe this potential in terms of several general observations. The basis of these observations is threefold. First, the potential described here is made possible by the rapid expansion of tourism training programs, not only in Thailand's capital, but also in many of its provinces. Second, my observations are based on a clear bias toward "local" involvement and initiative in tourism planning and development, and for approaches to tourism that have cultural appropriateness and sustainability as major goals. Third, it is important to note that these observations are not solely of my own manufacture—they have precedence in many other attempts to reconcile the consequences of tourism, including a number of promising activities that have begun in Thailand.

Observation One. The importance of local involvement and control.

There is no rule more easily generalized from the existing research on the social and cultural consquences of tourism than the observation that local involvement and control contributes to successful (i.e., sustainable) tourism development. Without opportunities to participate in planning, to realize gain from touristic enterprises, and to contribute to the monitoring and control of tourism in their areas, people quickly become dissatisfied if not openly antagonistic to tourism development in their communities. During the early stages of Thailand's recent tourism boom, this was clearly a problem. Most planning and promotion, including the selection of areas for tourism development and types of tourism to be encouraged, was in the hands of central authorities. This proved to be an efficient and effective way to market a country's tourism potential. It was much less effective in responding to uneven and necessarily local consequences of successful promotion. Given its highly centralized government bureaucracy, encouraging local control and initiative is still a problem in Thailand, although recent government willingness to provide support for tourism development projects that are initiated at the provincial and community level is an indication of change. These initiatives are part of an ongoing debate in Thailand over the advantages and disadvantages of decentralizing government authority. The fate of this debate will have clear consequences for the shape of tourism in the future.

By the same token, decentralization at the national level does not necessarily ensure full local participation in tourism planning and development. In the United States, for example, control over tourism enterprises is generally left to state and local authorities. In many such cases local regulations serve to limit participation, often making it difficult or impossible for the least advantaged of a community's members to engage in entrepreneurial activities associated with tourism. Countries such as Thailand—with their greater tolerance of street vendors, low-capital investment bungalows and eating places, and unofficial guides—actually offer more generous opportunities in this regard. Attempts to emulate a Western model of tourism development for Thailand, with greater control and regulation of small-scale entrepreneurial activities, would jeopardize the relative freedom to participate in the industry that many low-income Thai now enjoy.

Observation Two. The goal of sustainability is appropriate to all types and stages of tourism development.

It is important to overcome the idea that sustainable tourism is simply an alternative to large-scale tourism development, or that it is appropriate only to certain conditions, such as protecting minority populations or especially vulnerable environments. Although the issues will vary, sustainability of tourism development should be as much a part of planning first-class tourism facilties as it might be of promoting arts and crafts production in "tribal" villages. Appropriate tourism will not work as an "alternative" to business-as-usual; its effectiveness rests with the hope that ideals of sustainability can become guiding principles of national as well as local tourism policy.

Although the language of sustainability has entered general tourism discourse, there remains a considerable gap between professed ideals and reality. The economics of large-scale tourism facilities have not favored such principles. For example, a common measure of the success of resort hotels is how quickly investment costs are returned. Considerable less attention is paid to the economic relationships between a new facility and its existing communities. The greater potential for encouraging a more expansive goal of sustainability might well rest with the education of tourists who, as they become more knowledgeable as to the relationships between their activities and host environments, will hopefully become more selective in their choice of facilities and activities.

Observation Three. The economic appeal of tourism development cannot be ignored, but neither should it be overvalued.

Despite "leakage" of some tourism profits out of the country, and disproportionate realization of profits within, tourism has clearly contributed to Thailand's economic development over the past decade. Although the relative importance of different industries, including tourism, are likely to vary over time, it is unrealistic to assume that tourism will ever become an unimportant feature of the country's economy—after all, tourism remains an important concern of even the most highly developed national economies. Similarly, tourism does contribute to local and community economies in Thailand, as well as offering new employment opportunities to an underemployed population and providing avenues for social mobility. But, just as Thailand's national economic health is judged by the growing diversity of its economy, so can no community afford to become overly dependent upon tourism revenues. Again, there is a preponderance of research indicating that those local tourism endeavors that prove to be the most sustainable are found in communities that enjoy a diversified economy and are not overly dependent upon tourism.

The tendency to rate tourism as primarily, if not exclusively, an economic activity encourages an attitude of planning for the short term rather than for the long term. Tourism planning officials in developing nations often view tourism as a necessary but somewhat undesirable means to increased investment and favorable foreign exchange. This encourages maximizing exploitation of the resource in the short term, with the assumption that greater wealth will provide opportunities to develop other industries to replace tourism. A more realistic approach would not only consider the likelihood of long term reliance on tourism, but would also take into account the non-economic effects of the industry, such as how tourism impacts upon cultural expression, the interplay of national and regional identities, and relationships between different segments of a country's population.

Observation Four. In countries such as Thailand, educational institutions might well serve as the most reasonable locus for nationwide efforts to promote sustainable tourism.

One of the most difficult problems in promoting sustainable approaches to tourism development is identifying an institutional base that is widespread and influential enough to have an influence on national policy. It is unlikely that the industry itself, with its primary focus on economic development, will provide such a base. Government tourism authorities, with their focus on the short term, are similarly handicapped. Thailand's educational institutions are excellent candidates for providing leadership in this regard, particularly in light of the considerable respect accorded to institutions of higher learning in the country. The recent growth and expansion of tourism programs and departments in the nations colleges and universities, initiated primarily to provide new employment opportunities and trained personnel for the industry, could equally well serve to promote sustainable approaches to tourism development. On several campuses, there is already clear movement in this direction. Further, it is important to recognize that greater understanding of the social and cultural consequences of tourism, and of approaches to sustainable and appropriate tourism, is relevant to the career training of a wide variety of tourism profession-als—which is to say that the goals of specific types of skills development and of sustainability are not incompatible. Here, Thailand and other countries with rather rigid social structures might be at a disadvantage. There has, for example, been little interest in introducing social and cul-tural material into the curricula designed for training hospitality work-ers. It seems likely that this resistance is associated with a sense that such workers simply perform routine industry-related tasks and need not (perhaps should not?) be encouraged to consider the wider dimen-sions of their role in tourism development. In this sense, there is a clear link between the objectives of tourism instruction and a country's com-mitment to increased democratization.

Observation Five. The goal of sustainability suggests encouraging diverse approaches to tourism.

While much of Thailand's current tourism policy follows guide-lines established by such international organizations as the World Travel Organization, and focuses upon attracting and accomodating "first class" tourists, a more localized approach to tourism suggests the need for greater diversification, including increased attention to the im-portance and consequences of domestic tourism and the advantages and disadvantages of new styles of tourism (such as "nature" or "eco" tourism). The rationale for emphasizing "first class" or "quality" tourism is that economic return can be maximized with relatively fewer visitors who spend more money per capita and tend to isolate them-selves in self-contained resorts where their impact on local populations is presumed to be minimal. These assumptions are certainly contestable from the view of encouraging a more sustainable approach to develop-ment. The facilities and activities required to attract "first class" tourists are generally those that result in the greatest leakage of profits. Such fa-cilities also serve, in their isolation, to dramatically reduce the opportu-nities for the local population to intitiate tourist-related enterprises. The goal of sustainability suggests a need for taking another look at varieties of tourism that are often discouraged by major investors and local elites. For example, more adventuresome and low-cost modes of tourism, with such folk labels as "backpacker" and "hippie" tourism, do not con-tribute as richly per capita to Thailand's national economy. Such tourists are also less easily contained or controlled in the their activities, partic-ularly in countries like Thailand where tourists are permitted to travel freely. On the other hand, economy tourists are also the most likely to contribute directly to local and small-scale economies, because they depend more heavily on locally owned accomodations and services.

Observation Six. There is a far greater potential for educational institutions to focus attention on tourism in their local areas.

New tourism training programs have been developed in colleges and universities throughout Thailand, including some of the country's most remote provinces. The model that informs most of these programs tends to replicate current national tourism policy—students are trained for employment for work in first class hotels or with major travel agencies that focus their attention on "quality" tourism. Most of the provincial training programs, for example, seek practicums for their students in Bangkok or at major beach resorts. At the same time, independently of the educational institutions in their midst, many of Thailand's provincial governments have begun efforts to develop their own tourism potential. A more appropriate and sustainable model would encourage colleges to direct their training in a proactive way, directing students to practicums in their local areas, expanding their programs to give more students the entrepreneurial skills needed to develop small tourist-related businesses in their communities, and encouraging far greater participation on the part of local ethnic minorities. It is worth noting that there is precedence for such an approach. Many of the provincial colleges that are now developing tourism programs, and directing their students to employment in Bangkok and other established tourism centers, were founded as state teachers and agricultural colleges (much in the same manner as land grant colleges were established in the United States). Their purpose has been largely to prepare local students for employment in their communities. That most of the new tourism programs in these institutions have not yet adopted a similar model is testimony to the encompassing power of current national policy regarding tourism development.

Conclusions

Thailand's current tourism dilemma, and its replication in the new tourism training programs that are being developed throughout the country, is in part a result of the phenomenal rate of growth for the industry. It also has some of its roots in Thai traditions and conventions— the highly centralized government, conventions of authority and responsibility, religious principles, attitudes toward ethnic minorities, and Thai nationalism. But another part of the dilemma seems nearly universial, and clearly transcends the experience of Thailand. Until recently, very little attention has been paid anywhere to the human consequences of tourism. In some respects, Thailand is much further along than many other countries in its struggle with its tourism dilemma. This is true, for example, of the extent to which tourism has become a legitimate subject of higher education. It will be interesting to see whether the maturation of tourism training in Thailand will provide adequate experience and focus to encourage institutions of higher education to begin to direct, rather than simply follow, future trends in tourism development.

Notes

1. Nelson Graburn (1980) has discussed his experiences teaching the anthropology of tourism at the University of California, Berkley. David Blanton (1992) has described a human relations model for tourism education that he used in Africa.

2. The work was supported by a Fulbright Award and my major assignment was with the Tourism Department at Kasertsart University, in Bangkok. Toward the end of my assignment I was also asked to consult with the Ministry of Education in reviewing the development of tourism training programs at several provincial state colleges.

References

Baum, Tom. (1993). *Human Resource Issues in International Tourism*. Butterworth-Heinemann: Oxford.

Blanton, David. (1992). Tourism Education in Developing Countries. *Practicing Anthropology*, Vol. 14, No. 2.

Chambers, Erve. (1991). Social and Cultural Aspects of Tourism in Thailand. Kasetsart University: Bangkok.

(1994). Thailand's Tourism Paradox. In M. Hufford (Ed.), *Conserving Culture*. University of Illinois Press: Urbana.

Graburn, Nelson H. (1980). Teaching the Anthropology of Tourism. *International Social Science Journal*, Vol. 32, No. 1.

King, Brain. (1994). Tourism Higher Education in Island Microstates. *Tourism Management*, Vol. 15, No. 4.

Phongphit, Seri and Kevin Hewison. (1990). *Thai Village Life*. Mooban Press: Bangkok.

11

Hegemony and Elite Capital: The Tools of Tourism

M. ESTELLIE SMITH

The chapters brought together in this volume point to the growing signifi-cance of tourism as a strategy for economic development and as a mode of cul-tural expression. Tourism has not only become one of the world's largest industries, it is also becoming one of the most consequential in terms of gov-erning relations between people and shaping the ways in which we are all en-couraged to experience both familiar and distant places. The focus of this volume has been upon unravelling some of these consequences to exploring their complexity. The contributions have been particularly focussed on the va-rieties of ways in which the industry has come to be mediated by persons and institutions who stand outside the more traditional host/guest relationship. Several of the articles point to recent attempts to devise strategies for tourism that are more sustainable, more equitable in their means, and more diverse in their representation of "host" communities. The concluding article by M. Estellie Smith serves as a cautionary tale. In reviewing a number of international tourism developments, Smith points to the extent to which the industry can, even in its more seemingly benign expressions, come to serve the economic and political ends of local elites. That this is possible should hardly be surprising at this point. Whether or not it is an inevitable conse-quence of tourism, and to what particular enduring effects, is still an open question.

In all global polities, through the entire range of first through fourth world locales, there is a growing orientation to the development of tourism. This chapter examines the role and rationales of the indigenous elite in utilizing their material and non-material capital to expand tourism. It argues that furthering this particular form of economic development serves such national elite by (a) stabilizing their dominant position through the creation or expansion of the popular affiliation to an historically 'real' national identity and (b) encouraging socioeconomically 'divergent' groups to adopt life-styles embedded in and geared to world system commoditization.

The thesis, then, is that the growth of tourism offers at least short-term, positive opportunities to the political economy of nation-states while simultaneously permitting national elite new avenues for hegemonic management *and* personal increment of both goods and Good—all in the highly desired milieu of a more duratively-grounded geopolitical context.

Since the 1960s, development in economically marginal regions or countries has been a major concern of most polities, whether donor or recipient. Most plans appear to differ from classic colonialism primarily in their claim to being designed with input from and with the altruistic aim of directing benefits to the locale targeted for capital investment.[1]

For obvious (and some not so obvious) reasons, tourism has been an important component of most projects but this form of development exhibits distinctive features due essentially to what Bond and Ladman have called the 'peculiar characteristics of tourism as an export product' (Bond and Ladman, 1980: 232). For example, instead of the process involving a small number of alien and quasi-residential personnel—e.g., technicians, civil servants, and military, medical, educational or religious professionals—its success depends on massive numbers of consumers, usually 'foreign' and essentially transients who visit the targeted area for periods of time ranging from a few hours to a few weeks. Tourism is '. . . a service-oriented operation that may entail a great deal of face-to-face contact . . .' (Pi-Sunyer, 1977: 151). It also relies on a full range of external decision-makers, small firm personnel in the leisure travel market—travel agents and writers, media personnel, family-run hoteliers, and the like. Most importantly, it brings indigenes into continual and large scale contact with outsiders whose choice of where to travel instills indigenes with 'pride of place,' a sense of strangeness in the banal—and new aspirations.

That tourism requires foreigners in both the production and consumption sectors has led to a great concern with the extent, degree, type, and effect of foreigners on the host population. First, and by no means an insignificant factor, is both the desire of those involved to disassociate themselves with any suggestion of discredited colonialism—within a context that makes it difficult to avoid charges of neo-colonialism. Secondly, because of the obvious necessity to involve massive numbers of foreigners as initial service producers as well as ultimate consumers, 'Tourism is not a sector in which an autarkic approach is feasible' (Green, 1979: 88). This leads to the third reason why studies of tourism are concerned with the extent of foreign involvement—i.e., the dramatic effects of what has been labeled 'the demonstrator effect.' Here, primary concern is with the extent to which the paradoxical needs of providing tourists with an exotic milieu while at the same time making sure they have 'all the comforts of home,' encourages local populations to set as a goal (for many, frustratingly elusive in attainment) emulation of the affluent lifestyle of the visitors—no matter that such affluence is often spurious and that the locals may know it.

Not a little of the research and subsequent analyses that has directed tourist development has focused on avoiding the imposition on 'the folk' of LDCs the multinational world market system homogeneity and hegemony. However, one of the great difficulties in development work is the extent to which, with the best will and regardless of training which is supposed to sensitize one to the subtleties and potential pervasiveness of both the commoditization and hegemonic processes, one can become a hegemonic agent for the processes as well as the indigenous national decision-makers who seek to direct and benefit from integrating such processes in the local and national socioculture.

It is the last point that this paper addresses since, despite a plethora of data[2] on the role played by internal elite, this aspect of development—when not totally ignored—is often trivialized in analyzing the effects of development.[3]

As a poignant example of how one can serve as a hegemonic agent despite intents to the contrary, let me draw from the description of a West African project in which the Canadian ethnologist[4]—stresses his desire to avoid the kind of development that would deny tourists opportunities 'to discover what lies beyond the beach and come into contact with the real Africa' (Saglio, 1979: 321). At least by the time he wrote the paper, he was serving as Technical Advisor to the Senegal Department of Tourism and, he stresses, was sensitive to the kind of development that lends itself to the host population being subject to 'feelings of alienation' resulting from an 'abandonment of certain traditional values . . .' (p. 322).

He designed a program for what he identifies as 'discovery tourism,' a crucial component of which was encouraging visitors to travel to and reside in remote Senegalese bush villages whose inhabitants still followed a subsistence mode of production. It was deemed essential to the success of the program that, relative to the housing of the permanent population, the visitors' residences be organically integrated dwellings that would be architecturally consonant with the existing ambience of the people and providing an authentic context for visitor and host. Yet, my own reading of the description of attempts to engage the villagers in the process, leads to the conclusion that the operation was more likely to have educated them in the basics of the commoditization process and the market system. He tells us, for example, that:

> One purpose of the project was to restore the value of the traditional Diola dwelling by reproducing it as faithfully as possible. *Construction of these houses required a collective effort of a type that until then had never involved a monetary transaction and no standard existed for estimated costs. Many* meetings were held with the villagers to take account of such elements as the price of palm slats, the rate for cutting and clearing, the price of roof straw, and average village income [to be derived from tourism] [emphasis added].

In short, those who once deemed the cooperative creation of a dwelling as an act of social exchange—whether in obtaining the materials or through the act of construction itself—were laboriously educated in the monetized calculus of market exchange, taught how to commoditize the production, exchange, and consumption of the everyday stuff of their environment and, more importantly, transformed the social relations in which such behavior was grounded. It is not difficult to see how those who manage or influence the broad vectors of integration of the national socioculture into the international system, would find such villagers easier to guide into the commoditized world system.[5]

This chapter suggests that: first, since the literature on development tourism is rife with such examples, we may accept that the dynamics involved are common; and, secondly, being common, the commoditization process is, at the least, not antithetical to the aims of the internal elite—or, more likely, is a deliberate part of their programmatic goals for the national economy. For the remainder of the paper, I will briefly present the various ways in which the internal national elite benefit both in terms of goods, i.e., greater material affluence and in Good, i.e., increased non-material prestige, power and/authority.

1. Land-lords control the initial resource, land.

My own work in the Western Mediterranean has indicated that internal elite—local or national—are critically involved in, especially, the initiatory or pre-development stages, i.e., that period when, for example, transnational financing negotiations take place, locales for development are decided, primary contacts with external agents are made, and the critical decisions about necessary infrastructural foundations are set in motion. For example, prior to the development of tourism on Cyprus (pre-1960), 'land . . . was either for agricultural use or composed of sand dunes' (Andronicou, 1979: 261). By 1973, the market value of about 1/3 of an acre of seaside land in what was to become the tourist center of Famagusta jumped from US$4000 to US$375,000—though the price of dry-farming agricultural land only increased from roughly US$250 to US$400 per acre.[6] Similarly, Louis Pérez notes (1980: 252) that in the West Indies, 'soaring land values limit ownership of land to all but national elite and foreigners.'[7]

2. The elite have a greater capacity to 'manage' the production of laws that enhance their potential for greater profit at less risk.

It is not only in the control of land that the elite profit. The flight of elite capital abroad can be redirected to internal investment when they perceive more profitable and/less risky opportunities available at home. Clearly, when the obverse is true, capital flow can also reverse.[8] In his research on tourist development in the Philippines during the Marcos regime, Robert Britton tells us that:

> Elite self-interest has been amply documented elsewhere; in tourism, too, it is undoubtedly a powerful force. An extreme example comes from Manila, where fourteen international hotels with a total capacity of about 13,000 rooms were built to meet a predicted shortage during the 1976 World Bank conference. Construction firms with ties to the Marcos family harvested large profits, and other friends and relatives of Marcos own the properties. Financing came from various state sources and it was reported (NY Times) that 12% of the Philippines Development Banks funds were committed to the projects (1980:243).

In this scheme, the selling or, better, leasing of land for high returns is only the first step and is usually implemented at low risk by the passage of laws (e.g., zoning or environmental rulings) that direct developers to specific areas and exclude ('protect') others. Laws mandating a majority investment by nationals of the host country allows for the creation of or investment in, say, national firms where profit is derived not only from construction per se (including overcharging for shoddy materials and labor) but from opportunities for graft and bribery that comes with controlling the allocation of contracts to foreign firms as well as the distribution of sub-contracts and other employment locally.

Bonds used to finance the development pay high interest because of the
weak credit rating of many of the issuing units, but risk to the capital of
the national elite is actually relatively low because of loans from international development agencies and a judicious allocation of high risk
development to foreign investors.[9]

**3. Tourism development not only enhances the ability of the elite to
control dissident voices but encourages the development of
hegemonic consensus that makes control cheaper and capital
investment more profitable.**

Green (1979: 97) notes that, ' . . . from 1965 to 1980 on the order of
US$150 million has been or will be spent on tourist-oriented airport con-
struction or extension at Nairobi, Kilimanjaro, Mombasa, Kisimu, Kilimanjaro, Dar es Salaam, Entebbe, and Gulu.' The large sums expended
on infrastructure—notably jumbo jet airports—often seem to be in ex-
cess of the needs of the existing or any probable expanded tourism sector. Green goes on to note that,

> at a 10% opportunity cost of capital plus operating deficits, this repre-
> sents a US$20 million to US$25 million a year subsectoral drain from
> public revenue to tourism or US$20 to US$25 per tourist even if the
> number of visitors were to rise to a million a year. . . . It is doubtful
> whether government revenue from tourism exceeds US$20 million to-
> day (1979:97) .

It may be noted, however, that in addition to the profitable avenues just
outlined, such seemingly irrational investment of national capital has
two ancillary effects: First, such monumental architecture has, for mil-
lennia, enhanced the prestige of the elite and serves as visible representations of progress, prosperity and power. These may be hollow
symbols for some, but there is abundant evidence that significant numbers do see them as markers of, at least, better times to come. Secondly,
and, more pragmatically, they aid, if you will, in crowd control. Airports
with supersized runways allow major troop and arms movements; and
immense sports stadia may also serve to house political detainees
rounded up in massive sweep operations. Lastly, tourism is often ori-
ented to economically marginal areas hitherto neglected in the upper
echelons of the governing elite because of the lack of investment potential. Prior to development, the bad news is the low priority given the
needs of the generally impoverished population by the central authorities; the good news is that this same neglect gives a fair degree of autonomy to the population. The mechanisms of the State as well as the

elite have little effect on the daily round of life in such regions. The negligence, incompetence or an insufficiency of means of national and even regional governing elite, fosters both the necessity for and ability to formulate local patterns of self-sufficiency. That can, however, establish the basis for unrest and challenges to the State. The development of tourism brings, for better or for worse, the intrusion of the State. Not infrequently, civil unrest escalates either because of, say, rising expectations or rejection of features of State management. Since this 'discourages tourism,' the response may legitimate repression and even add to the ruling regime's legitimacy in the international arena where it will be congratulated for 'restoring order' and 'protecting the safety and property' of both transients and residents in the area. Britton notes that, during the last days of the Marcos regime, 'a prominent U.S. travel trade paper . . . wrote that Manila's streets were safe, "thanks to martial law."'[10] An additional spin can be divisiveness among the ranks of national devolutionists because some resist activities that bring a post-development decline in tourist revenues (cf., the course of events among the Corsican and Spanish Basque nationalist movement membership).

One example[11] serves to incorporate several of the points just made. In a study of tourism development in the state of Guerrero, Mexico, the population lived along a thin margin of the coast where the chief sources of income were derived from the harvesting of copra and sesame seeds, fishing, and some livestock production. The region, however, overwhelmingly consists of a 'totally unworked' mountain range.[12] Indeed, the inequities and frailties of the economy were such that the 1960s were marked by the emergence of 'guerrilla disturbances' (p. 112).[13] In the late 1960s, plans were lain to develop tourism in the region though the project did not actually begin until September, 1972 (p. 115). Now, 'just as work was getting under way in Zihuatanejo, construction was also begun on [an internally financed] iron and steel complex in Lazara Cardenas, only 120 kilometers from the project site.' This latter was so massive a project that analysts have maintained 'it had a clear-cut effect on the entire national economy . . .' (p. 116).

The two projects produced a profitable synergy: (1) Support for the guerillas shrunk and the threat of the guerillas to the national polity was considerably reduced because (2) the general populace perceived that the State was responding to their needs. Further, (3) the tourist project in particular (which had an announced aim of 'densifying' populations in the specific loci under development) created a more easily controllable population should unrest again emerge.[14] Finally, (4) the densification process assured a readily available worker population for *both* projects[15]—especially since (a) people were required to seek wage labor both to pay taxes or rents for the improved properties to which the State directed them, and (b) to buy food in the market since the zoning rules of their house plots forbade the production of vegetables or livestock (Reynoso y Valle and De Regt, 1979: 130).[16]

What is worthy of special note is that the juxtaposition of industrial park and tourist development is not uncommon; Nancy Evans (1979) reports the same linkages in her study of development in the Mexican state of Jalisco—including the strenuous efforts to move the populace into newly constructed housing with the same kinds of zoning restrictions.[17] The advantages to the national elite (not to mention their capital investment opportunities) in synchronizing the development of an infrastructure that will service what is generally perceived as the environmentally 'cleaner tourist industry (supported with international funding), along with that of a more socially and environmentally hazardous industrial development (internally financed) are obvious.

4. The successful exercise of power furthers success in the future.

Commonly, decisions are made about development at the national level with little if any input from the local population—who, usually, are only minimally apprised of the programs only after the operation makes its appearance in the local context, months and many stages along in the actual process. E. de Kadt (1979:24) notes that, 'Rather fewer will interfere when nationally powerful groups bend such regulations to their own advantage,' behavior so regularly occurring that it does much to 'reinforce existing inequalities' and, for example, in Puerto Vallarta, local authorities proved 'impotent in the face of the activities of economically powerful groups from Mexico's large cities.' This lack of control is an example of what Pablo González Casanova identifies as 'internal neocolonialism.' In this case, even though there were local representatives of a local planning authority, the role they were given to play was minimal, some maintaining that they were 'too intimidated by the power, status, and presumed expertise of outside officials to be forceful in presenting their views' (de Kadt, 1979:24).

The process by which the elite cultivate (in every sense of the word!) current resources for enhanced future returns[18] may be extremely subtle, and the explicitly stated ideologies of those involved may bear little relation to what is actually done. Laws may be passed that, on the face of it, work to the public good but, in reality, are of greater benefit (perhaps even primarily) to those who control wealth, power, and or authority. For example, as reported by Boissevain and Inglott (1979: 265–284) for Malta, the political shift in 1971 from the right-of-center National Party to the left-of-center Malta Labor Party appears to have only minimally affected the course of tourist development. To be sure, the Labor government—which rode to election victory on the crest of a wave of agitation about the inacessibility of housing for, especially, young couples—established an excellent record in building new housing (but, it might be asked, who owned the firms that got the contracts for the new housing and who gained power in the labor unions?); introduced measures to curb land speculation (though the measures were too late to curb the traditional elite, including the Church, from extraordinary profit-taking—and skirted the issue that much of the land used in development was transferred leasehold rather than freehold);[19] and even established watchdog agencies and minimum levels of employment for Maltese nationals in foreign-owned enterprises (which gave new avenues for traditional patronage networks). Further, there was a sharp increase in the price of fresh water (which benefited those who owned the firms from whom the government purchased the water), and a classification of hotels (that worked to the detriment of small and medium hotels but benefited the large hotels in which wealthy Maltese were invested in a variety of ways). There was, however, only a token response from the government to calls for reinforcing 'existing measures to control building and clean up beaches and other public recreation areas' (p. 279). In addition to all this, 'The wealthiest classes are . . . [still] favored by the income tax laws, for the maximum tax of sixty percent is applied annually to all incomes over £M2500 [about US$7000]!' However, 'Since prominent members of the two major political parties as well as the politically important General Workers Union are heavily involved in tourist-related activities,' Boissevain and Inglott (ironically?) conclude that, 'it is not likely that tourism will ferment class-based political conflict in the foreseeable future' (p. 276).

All this indicates (and recent evidence from Eastern Europe and China bears out) that one would be naive to expect political rhetoric to be related to actual behavioral variation among the governing elite.[20] Rather, one should focus on the crucial question *cui bono*—and how? I have tried to show that, in the commoditization of leisure and all of the other forms of commoditization which it, in turn, engenders, the internal elite play a major role and, in not a few cases, appear to be the major beneficiaries, not the least because of the role they play in establishing a hegemonic context within which the old, new and would be elite—whoever they are—derive benefits from the consensual ideology that informs and guides behavior as well as articulates itself in a coherent and systematic fashion and, as well, determines the plot, designs the stage setting, and even fixes the price of admission for the drama of profit, prestige, and power.

Notes

1. It might be argued that modern development differs by relying on and channeling funds either directly through agencies of the donor states or indirectly through contribution of such states to international lending agencies. A close examination, however, seems to indicate that private capital is as critical in the process as previously, the new twist being that a substantial amount of the start-up risks previously borne by the private sector is now diverted to the public sector.

2. So that the texts themselves as well as additional data would be readily available to readers I have deliberately placed my chief reliance on just two publications of collected papers. Both have been adjudged substantive contributions to tourism research and are readily accessible through most academic libraries. They are: *Tourism: Passport to Development? Perspectives on the Social and Cultural Effects of Tourism in Developing Countries*, Emanuel de Kadt (Ed.), 1979; and *Dialectics of Third World Development*, I. Vogeler and A. de Souza (Eds.), 1980. Despite that these were written some fifteen years ago, the major differences are that the problematics of the issues they (and I) raise, have intensified and become increasingly exacerbated.

3. One issue that must be considered is the problem of methodology. We are well aware of the difficulties of what Laura Nader has labeled 'studying up.' However, though well-insulated, the elite are not impervious to investigation though it requires a very different kind of field work from that in the standard ethnographies. It is not easy to wend one's way through the Byzantine pathways to penetrate to the core of the complex structure constructed to attain and or maintain the goods and Good which mark the elite. That structure has taken years, even generations to build and, in most cases, one should not expect to be able to 'deconstruct' it in in a few weeks or even months. However, it would seem that of all social scientists, anthropologists are the best suited to attempt the task since our investigatory procedures essentially depend on the slow, patient establishment of in-depth knowledge of an ethnographic context. But it can be done(see, e.g., G. E. Marcus, 1983 and Higley, Field and Grøholt, 1976). Unlike many other investigators, our training encourages us to *make* the time to follow multiple strands of the sociocultural web, accumulating and attempting to interpret bits and scraps of information that over time begin to fit together and give us a sense of networks, obligations, and reciprocal exchanges that sometimes take the genuine elite (as opposed to the *nouveau riche*) a generation or more to construct—the rise and fall of family wealth; marriages; debts, gifts and rewards; and, especially, the twists and turns of human

activity that seem inconsequential or even irrational until some seemingly stray bit of conversation or gossip makes them fall into place (and, curiously, at least some anthropologists seem to show less concern for various ethnical issues—e.g., protecting individual identities or limning out illegal activities—than when studying, say, the urban poor or rural peasantry).

4. Saglio, a Canadian national, worked under the auspices of the Canadian University Service Overseas (CUSO) which provided a supplementary salary, an all-terrain vehicle, and travel expenses.

5. Drawing on her own work experience, a student with whom I discussed this example (Mrs. Susan McBrearty) grimaced, and commented, 'And the poor "natives" can't even look forward to the end of their shift when they can escape from having to smile and be nice because "the customer is always right" !'

6. Andronicou admits that some speculators got wealthy but argues that others recognized the potential value and sold for handsome profits sooner or later. He does not, however, note what portion of the land was exchanged freehold versus leasehold. When the latter, it is the landlord who derives enormous benefits, though it may take some years—during which the land will probably continue to appreciate considerably.

7. Pérez notes that soaring land values, moreover, have made ownership of land on many islands prohibitive for all but small numbers of national elites and foreigners (see also, note 9).

8. As Marx ([1894] 1962: 251) pointed out, 'If capital is sent abroad, this is not done because it absolutely could not be applied at home, but because it can be employed at a higher rate of profit in a foreign country.'

9. Further, the employment brings prosperity and this helps stabilize the positions of those who control the government and, additionally, offers them opportunities to increase their power by the patronage exercised over sub-contracting opportunities and opportunities for employment ranging from the lowest unskilled day laborer to prestigious positions in the expanded bureaucratic structure that development requires. Government changes—even revolutions—do not necessarily alter the process; the new regime is sometimes little more than a change of the palace guard. In the Philippines, e.g., the same charges of nepotism and corruption were continually filed against members of the government of President Aquino (though the claims were said to be practiced in lesser magnitude—or at least more subtly) as occurred under the Marcos regime—and the Aquino family as well as its most powerful political rival are old and leading aristocratic lineages in the national elite system.

10. R. Britton, Shortcomings of Third World Tourism, in Vogeler and de Souza, pp. 241–248, 1980, pp. 244–245.

11. A. Reynoso y Valle and J. P. de Regt, 1979: 111–134.

12. However, in a discussion of the nature of the work force that aggregated during the period of intense construction development, we are told that ' . . . the majority of [construction] workers . . . seem to have come . . . primarily from the mountains' (p. 128). One is led to wonder how these people existed if the mountains were 'totally unworked.'

13. One item of particular note here is that the official stance maintained that development in these marginal areas was designed to create employment opportunities that would deter the stream of migrants to the major cities—yet no one has done a cost/benefit analysis to determine if the same amount of funds directed to urban problems would not be of greater benefit and deal more effectively with more issues of greater urgency.

14. Reynoso y Valle and de Regt note (p. 123) that, since development and the strict codes for land use, 'Poorer families are now moving into the hills, beyond the reach of utilities they cannot afford, where they can keep goats and grow subsistence crops to eke out a living.' If nothing else, these hills may prove fertile ground for social unrest, even growing guerilla activity.

15. Reynoso y Valle and de Regt (p. 127) note that at times, during the initial period of intense new construction, ' . . . there were as many as 35 construction companies on site with at least 4000 unskilled laborersand perhaps 1000 skilled workers and professionals.'

16. The authors emphasize that the new zoning regulations combined with existing (but now enforced) rules of land ownership. Among other changes, the villagers found that they were required (many for the first time) to pay taxes on their properties—taxes which included the costs of electricity, water, sewage systems, etc. 'Women, especially in the lower-class, were pushed to look for work outside the home. . . . the single mother [was] hit the hardest.' Given that most construction workers were 'single' males, forces conspired to expand both prostitution and impoverished single mothers with growing numbers of offspring. Thus, in addition to the commoditization process per se (e.g., food must be purchased in markets instead of grown for self-consumption), there was added pressure for villagers to become dependent on a wage economy. Finally, citing a study by J. Kennedy, A Russin and A. Martinez (1977), Reynoso y Valle and de Regt note (1979: 116) that, 'Opportunities . . . increased in the informal labor market for . . . washing clothes, renting rooms . . . selling food, and petty vending.' It is clear that the 'penny capitalism' of the informal economy was imposed by external factors (for discussions of the various dynamics of the informal economy, see Smith, 1989: 292–317 and Smith, 1990). One must wonder if the women prefered it to the household production they formerly practiced. That the populace was not blind to the long term consequences of the unfolding scenario is indicated by Reynoso y Valle and de Regt remarking (p. 116) that many villagers labeled those of their neighbors who favored development as 'harmful persons' who were 'selling out.'

17. Evans (p. 316) notes that the 4% interest rate on mortgages attracts buyers despite 'long and complicated paperwork that discourages anyone with little education from applying.' A minimum wage employee who is entitled to pay $6400 for a three bedroom house, has a mandatory 18% (about $20.66) deducted from an average monthly pay check of $114.75 (based on a twenty-five day month at the minimum daily wage of $4.59). It is perhaps overly cynical to question who ultimately profits from the construction and funding that underwrites such housing—and who pays the most. One may note, however, that in the context of remarks relative to problems created by '"internal neocolonialism"—an urban form of paternalism,' Evans (p. 309) reports that, according to a (1974) government brochure, 75% (28,364) of the Puerto Vallarta project investors were Mexican nationals—though we are not told how the dollar amount was spread (a) relative to national vs. foreign investors or (b) the distribution of investment holdings.

18. This is in line with my definition of 'capital' as 'resource-producing resources' (Smith, 1991: 51), a definition designed to make it especially possible for anthropologists to examine the role of capital in non-capitalist societies—i.e., in societies that pre-date the introduction of (or possess dual economic systems, one of which employs capital but is not embedded in) the modern market system, 'capitalism.'

19. Boissevain and Inglott (1979: 273) note that a pilot project in the development of Maltese tourism was initiated in 1963 by the privately owned Malta Developments which leasehold purchased a thousand acres of church-owned farmland for an annual ground rent of £N5000. The Santa Maria Project was developed into a 'first-class garden estate with chalets and villas' which, by 1970, was bringing the developers an annual ground rent of £M30,000. Ground rent increases were equally spectacular in other parts of the island: 'A plot of land with an original ground rent in 1962 of 250, in 1967 yielded 6500 a year. . . .' (p. 274). 'Private fortunes skyrocketed—to £M30 million in the extreme case of the Pace family Bical Enterprise' (p. 276). Though in some cases those who sold land leaseholds saw the ground rents jump spectacularly. One should be reminded that such 'sales' are temporary in that, at the end of the specified lease period, the land and any buildings (with their improvements) revert back to those who made the original leasehold sale. Freeholders, on the other hand, have borne no expenses (for improvements or taxes). At the expiration of the leasehold, the property returns to those who hold the freehold, at which time they are free to leasehold again—and again, and again—or sell freehold. It might also be added that a colleague who is knowledgeable about Malta tells me that, although the Bical Enterprise ultimately went into liquidation, indications are that the Pace family seems to enjoy continued affluence and, apparently, was careful to divert large sums of money out of it before this process began. Boissevain and Inglott (p. 276) remark that the economic potential in this process are considerable: ' . . . the building boom did create in the space of a few years a truly wealthy class.'

20. Indeed, Boissevain and Inglott stress (p. 279) that there has been a marked lack of success

> ... in influencing government policy (or its enforcement). .... There are no organized protest groups—potential members fear victimization if they criticize government. In a small country run by a powerful government there is basis for such fear. Protest is thus neither open nor sustained ... [and most] is limited to private grumbling and anonymous letters to the editors of the major newspapers.

There is a host of other areas in which a close investigation reveals the extent to which the elite benefit both directly (by accruing additional goods and Good) and indirectly (by incorporating those segments of the populations still imperfectly—if at all—incorporated into the hegemonic context of the market mentality.

References

Andronicou, A. (1979). Tourism in Cyprus. In *Tourism: Passport to Development? Perspectives on the Social and Cultural Effects of Tourism in Developing Countries*. A joint World Bank-UNESCO study, Emanuel de Kadt, ed. New York: Oxford University Press, pp. 237–65.

Boissevain, J. and P. Serracino. (1979). Tourism in Malta. In *Tourism: Passport to Development? Perspectives on the Social and Cultural Effects of Tourism in Developing Countries*. A joint World Bank-UNESCO study, Emanuel de Kadt, ed. New York: Oxford University Press, pp. 265–84.

Bond, M. E. and J. R. Ladman. (1980). International Tourism: An Instrument for Third World Development. In *Dialectics of Third World Development*, I. Vogeler and A. de Souza, eds. Montclair, NJ: Allanheld, Osmun, pp. 231–40; originally published in *The Nebraska Journal of Economics and Business* 11(1), 1972, pp. 37–52.

Britton, R. (1980). Shortcomings of Third World Tourism. In *Dialectics of Third World Development* , I. Vogeler and A. de Souza, eds. Montclair, NJ: Allanheld, Osmun, pp. 241–47.

Casanova, Pablo González. (1965). Internal Colonialism and National Development. *Studies in Comparative International Development*, 1(4),1965 [as cited in de Kadt 1979: 24].

Evans, N. (1979). The dynamics of tourism development in Puerto Vallarta. In *Tourism: Passport to Development? Perspectives on the Social and Cultural Effects of Tourism in Developing Countries*. A joint World Bank-UNESCO study, Emanuel de Kadt, ed. New York: Oxford University Press, pp. 305–20.

Green, R. H. (1979). Toward Planning Tourism in African Countries. In *Tourism: Passport to Development? Perspectives on the social and cultural effects of tourism in developing countries*. A joint World Bank-UNESCO study, Emanuel de Kadt, ed. New York: Oxford University Press, pp. 79–100.

Higley, J. and G. L. Field, K. Grøholt. (1976). *Elite Structure and Idology: A Theory with Applications to Norway*. New York: Columbia University Press (Oslo: Universitetsforlaget).

de Kadt, Emanuel, ed. (1979). *Tourism: Passport to Development? Perspectives on the Social and Cultural Effects of Tourism in Developing Countries*. A World Bank-UNESCO Study. New York: Oxford University Press.

Kennedy, J., A. Russin and A. Martinez. (1977). The impact of tourism development on women: A case study of Ixtapa-Zihuatanejo, Mexico. A restricted circulation report to the World Bank, July.

Marcus, G. E. (1983). The Feduciary Role in American Family Dynasties and Their Institutional Legacy: From the Law of Trusts to Trust in the Establishment. In *Elites: Ethnographic Issues*, G. E. Marcus, ed. Albuquerque: University of New Mexico Press (A School of American Research Book), pp. 221–56.

Marx, K. (1962). *Capital* III (edited by F. Engels, 1894). Moscow: Foreign Languages Publishing House.

Pérez, L. A., Jr. (1980). Aspects of Underdevelopment: Tourism in the West Indies. In *Dialectics of Third World Development*, I. Vogeler and A. de Souza, eds. Montclair, NJ: Allanheld, Osmun, pp. 249–55; originally published in *Science and Society*, 4:473–80, 1973/4.

Pi-Sunyer, Oriol. (1977). Tourists and Tourism in a Catalan Maritime Community. In *Hosts and guests: The anthropology of tourism*, V. L. Smith, ed. Philadelphia: University of Pennsylvania Press, pp. 149–56.

Reynoso y Valle, A. and J. P. de Regt. (1979). Growing pains: Planned tourism development in Ixtapa-Zihuatanejo. In *Dialectics of Third World Development*, I. Vogeler and A. de Souza, eds. Montclair, NJ: Allanheld, Osmun, pp. 111–34.

Saglio, C. (1979). Tourism for Discovery: A Project in Lower Casamance, Senegal. In E. de Kadt, *Tourism: Passport to Development? Perspectives on the social and cultural effects of tourism in developing countries*. A World Bank-UNESCO Study. New York: Oxford University Press, pp. 321–35.

Smith, M. Estellie. (1991). The ABCs of Political Economy. In *Early State Economics*, H. J. M. Claessen and P. van de Velde, eds. New Brunswick, CT and London: Transaction Publisher (Political and Legal Anthropology Series), pp. 31–74.

———. (1989). The Informal Economy. In *Economic Anthropology*, S. Plattner, ed. Stanford: Stanford University Press, pp. 292–317.

Smith, M. Estellie, ed. (1990). *Perspectives on the Informal Economy.* Lanham, MD: University Press of America, Society for Economic Anthropology Monographs in Economic Anthropology No. 8.

Smith, V. L., ed. (1977). *Hosts and Guests: The Anthropology of Tourism.* Philadelphia: University of Pennsylvania Press.

Vogeler, I. and A. de Souza, eds. (1980). *Dialectics of Third World Development.* Montclair, NJ: Allanheld, Osmun.

Contributors

A. Lynn Bolles is Professor of Womens Studies and Affiliate Professor of Anthropology, African American Studies, and Comparative Literature at the University of Maryland, College Park. Her research focus is on the political economy of women of the African Diaspora. Recently published books include *Sister Jamaica* (University Press of America) and *We Paid Our Dues* (Howard University Press).

Catherine Mary Cameron is Associate Professor of Anthropology at Cedar Crest College in Allentown, Pennsylvania. She has been studying tourism initiatives and the construction of heritage in Bethlehem since 1985 and has recently begun research on the arts and tourism in Grenada.

Erve Chambers is Professor of Anthropology at the University of Maryland, College Park. He has done research on tourism in Thailand as well as in Baltimore, Maryland. Chambers is author of *Applied Anthropology: A Practical Guide* (Waveland Press) and past president of the Society for Applied Anthropology.

Betty J. Duggan received her Ph.D. in Anthropology from the University of Tennessee, Knoxville. She has worked in public humanities and museum programming, taught university and college courses, and managed archaeological projects. Fieldwork among the Eastern Cherokees and in several southern Appalachian communities led to her research interests and publications in such areas as tourism and cultural conservation.

Robert K. Hitchcock is Associate Professor of Anthropology and Coordinator of African Studies at the University of Nebraska, Lincoln.

215

His research on tourism has been done among Ju/'hoansi Bushmen in Namibia and Botswana. Currently he is involved in designing and monitoring natural resource management projects in Africa and among Native Americans in the northern Great Plains.

Stanley E. Hyland is Associate Professor of Anthropology at the University of Memphis. While collecting data for the article in this volume he was Director of Research for the Lower Mississippi Delta Development Commission. He continues to be involved in inner city community development, cultural heritage, and environmental issues in the Mid-South region.

Mark P. Leone is Professor of Anthropology at the University of Maryland, College Park. He has published widely in historical archaeology and has worked in Annapolis, Maryland's capital city, since 1981. He helped found Archaeology in Annapolis, a program of excavation and interpretation based on the city's historic remains. Using critical theory as defined first by Georg Lukacs, and then by Jurgen Habermas, he created Archaeology in Public for the visiting tourists and residents of the city.

George C. Logan is Assistant Project Archaeologist with Woodward-Clyde Consultants. During 1989–92 he served as Supervisor of Public Programs for Archaeology in Annapolis, directing on-site educational programs and helping create museum exhibits. Since that time he has served as an archaeologist with other public sites in the Mid-Atlantic region.

R. Timothy Sieber is Associate Professor of Anthropology at the University of Massachusetts at Boston. He has done research on tourism and urban development in Boston, and is currently completing a book on waterfront revitalization in Boston Harbor.

M. Estellie Smith is Research Professor of Anthropology at Union College, Schenectady, New York. She is currently working on the changing role of city, region, and state in the European Union, with a focus on transnational fishery management and tourism in the EU and North America. She is a Fellow of the AAAS and past president of the Society for Urban Anthropology and the Society for Economic Anthropology.

Elvi Whittaker is Professor of Anthropology at the University of British Columbia, Vancouver, Canada. She has done research on tourism and migration in Hawaii, and is currently studying indigenous tourism in the Northern Territory and the Western Kimberleys of Australia and tourism initiatives in the Baltic.

Index